Windows® 8.1

Paul McFedries

Visual

A Wiley Brand

Teach Yourself Visually™ Windows® 8.1

Published by
John Wiley & Sons, Inc.
10475 Crosspoint Boulevard
Indianapolis, IN 46256

www.wiley.com

Published simultaneously in Canada

Library of Congress Control Number: 2013949527

ISBN: 978-1-118-82623-2

Manufactured in the United States of America

10 9 8 7 6 5 4 3 2 1

Trademark Acknowledgments

Contact Us

For general information on our other products and services please contact our Customer Care Department within the U.S. at 877-762-2974, outside the U.S. at 317-572-3993 or fax 317-572-4002.

For technical support please visit www.wiley.com/techsupport.

Sales | Contact Wiley at (877) 762-2974 or fax (317) 572-4002.

Credits

Acquisitions Editor
Aaron Black

Project Editor
Jade L. Williams

Technical Editor
Vince Averello

Copy Editor
Marylouise Wiack

Director, Content Development & Assembly
Robyn Siesky

Vice President and Executive Group Publisher
Richard Swadley

About the Author

Paul McFedries is a full-time technical writer. He has been authoring computer books since 1991 and has more than 85 books to his credit, including *Windows 8 Visual Quick Tips, Excel Data Analysis Visual Blueprint, Teach Yourself VISUALLY Excel 2013, Teach Yourself VISUALLY OS X Mavericks, The Facebook Guide for People Over 50, iPhone 5s and 5c Portable Genius,* and *iPad 5th Generation and iPad mini 2 Portable Genius,* all available from Wiley. Paul's books have sold more than 4 million copies worldwide. Paul is also the proprietor of Word Spy (http://www.wordspy.com), a website that tracks new words and phrases as they enter the English language. Paul invites you to drop by his personal website at www.mcfedries.com, or you can follow him on Twitter @paulmcf and @wordspy.

Author's Acknowledgments

It goes without saying that writers focus on text and I certainly enjoyed focusing on the text that you will read in this book. However, this book is more than just the usual collection of words and phrases designed to educate and stimulate the mind. A quick thumb through the pages will show you that this book is also chock full of treats for the eye, including copious screen shots, meticulous layouts, and sharp fonts. Those sure make for a beautiful book and that beauty comes from a lot of hard work by Wiley's immensely talented group of designers and layout artists.

They are all listed in the Credits section on the previous page, and I thank them for creating another gem. Of course, what you read in this book must also be accurate, logically presented, and free of errors. Ensuring all of this was an excellent group of editors that I got to work with directly, including project editor Jade Williams, copy editor Marylouise Wiack, and technical editor Vince Averello. Thanks to all of you for your exceptional competence and hard work. Thanks, as well, to Wiley Acquisitions Editor Aaron Black for asking me to write this book.

How to Use This Book

Who This Book Is For

This book is for the reader who has never used this particular technology or software application. It is also for readers who want to expand their knowledge.

The Conventions in This Book

❶ Steps

This book uses a step-by-step format to guide you easily through each task. Numbered steps are actions you must do; bulleted steps clarify a point, step, or optional feature; and indented steps give you the result.

❷ Notes

Notes give additional information — special conditions that may occur during an operation, a situation that you want to avoid, or a cross reference to a related area of the book.

❸ Icons and Buttons

Icons and buttons show you exactly what you need to click to perform a step.

❹ Tips

Tips offer additional information, including warnings and shortcuts.

❺ Bold

Bold type shows command names, options, and text or numbers you must type.

❻ Italics

Italic type introduces and defines a new term.

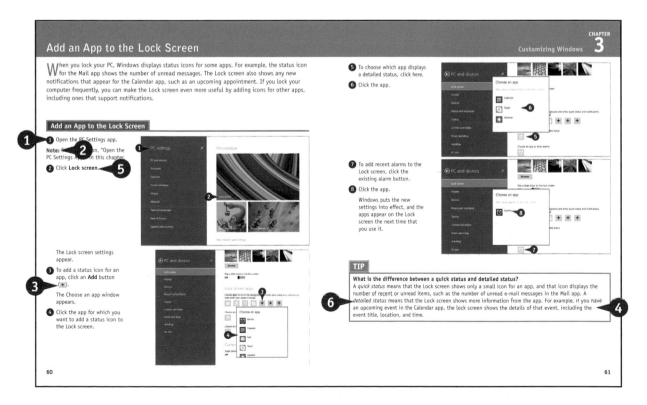

Table of Contents

Chapter 1   Getting Started with Windows

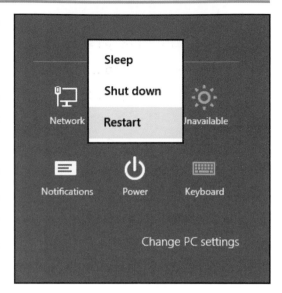

Chapter 2   Launching and Working with Apps

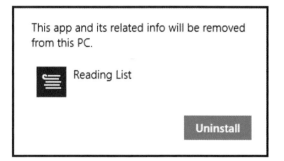

Chapter 3 · Customizing Windows

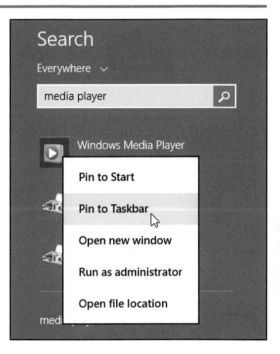

Chapter 4 · Surfing the World Wide Web

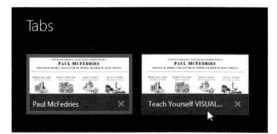

Table of Contents

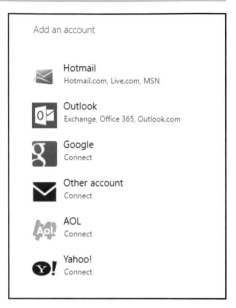

Chapter 7   Performing Day-to-Day Tasks

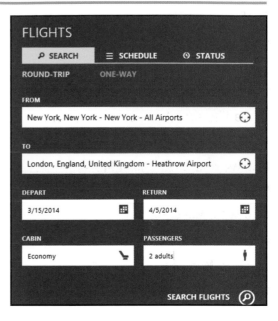

Chapter 8   Working with Images

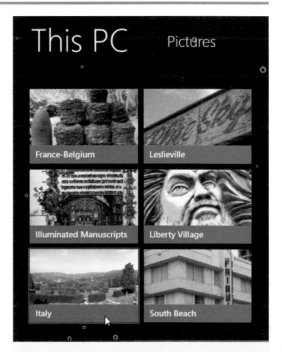

Table of Contents

Chapter 9   Working with Multimedia

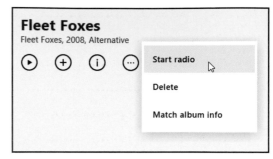

Chapter 10   Editing Documents

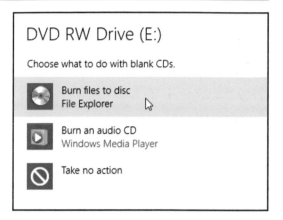

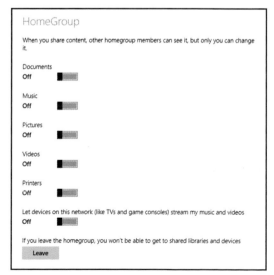

Table of Contents

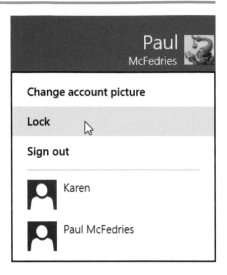

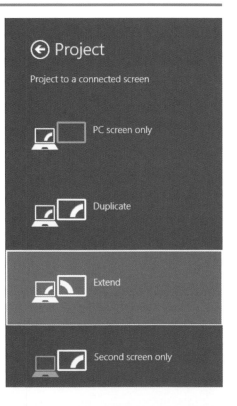

Chapter 15   Maintaining Windows

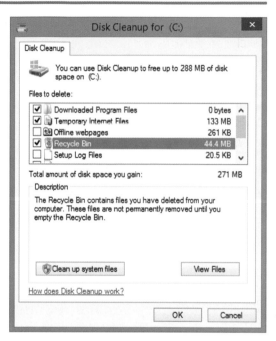

CHAPTER 1

Getting Started with Windows

Are you ready to discover Windows? In this chapter, you tour the Start screen, learn about the mouse, connect to your network, and more.

Start Windows

When you turn on your computer, Windows starts automatically, but you may have to navigate the sign-on screen along the way. To prevent other people from using your computer without your authorization, Windows requires you to set up a username and password. You supply this information the very first time you start your computer, when Windows takes you through a series of configuration steps. Each time you start your computer, Windows presents the sign-on screen, and you must enter your username and password to continue.

Start Windows

1 Turn on your computer.

A After a few seconds, the Windows Lock screen appears.

Note: If you do not see the Lock screen, you can skip the rest of the steps in this section.

2 Press `Enter`

If you are using a tablet, place a finger or a stylus on the screen, slide up an inch or two, and then release the screen.

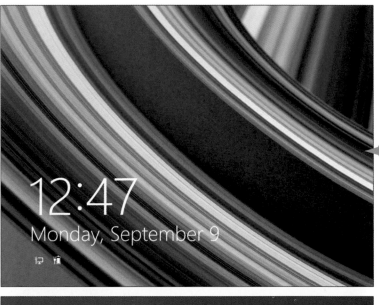

The Windows sign-on screen appears.

3 Click inside the **Password** box.

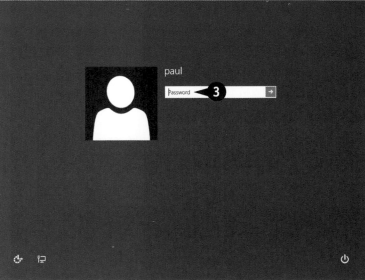

④ Type your password.

⑤ Click the **Submit** arrow (➡)
or press `Enter`

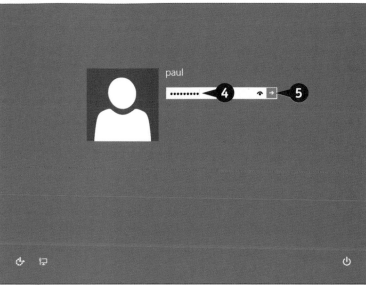

The Windows Start screen
appears.

TIPS

How can I be sure that I am typing the correct password characters?

If you know there is no danger of someone reading your password, click and hold the **Display Password Characters** icon (👁). This changes the dots to the actual characters. When you release the icon, the characters return to dots.

On my tablet, Windows lights up each key as I tap it, so is it possible for someone to determine my password by following these taps?

In theory, yes, if you think that someone might see your password clicks. Click **Hide keypress**, which is the key to the left of the spacebar. This prevents Windows from lighting up each key as you click it.

Explore the Windows Start Screen

Before getting to the specifics of working with Windows, take a few seconds to familiarize yourself with the basic elements of the Start screen. These elements include the Start screen's app tiles, live tiles, your user tile, and the Desktop tile.

Understanding where these elements appear on the Start screen and what they are used for will help you work through the rest of this book and will help you navigate Windows and its applications on your own.

Ⓐ Tile

Each of these rectangles represents an app or a Windows feature. Most of the programs that you install will add their own tiles to the Start screen.

Ⓑ User Tile

Use this tile to access features related to your Windows user account.

Ⓒ Live Tile

Some tiles are *live* in the sense that they display frequently updated information, such as the current weather shown by the Weather tile and the stock data shown by the Finance tile.

Display the Charms Menu

Y ou can access many of the Windows options, settings, and features by displaying the Charms menu. One of the design goals of Windows was to keep the screen simple and uncluttered. Therefore, the Start screen displays no menus, toolbars, or other elements that are normally associated with computer programs. Instead, you access these extra elements using gestures. One of the most useful of these extra elements is the Charms menu.

Display the Charms Menu

1 Position the mouse pointer (◊) in the upper-right or the lower-right corner of the screen.

If you are using a tablet, place your finger or your tablet stylus on the right edge of the screen and then swipe your finger or the stylus along the screen to the left for an inch or two.

Windows displays the Charms menu.

A Click **Search** to locate apps, settings, or files on your computer.

B Click **Share** to send data from your computer to other people.

C Click **Start** to return to the Start screen when you are using an app.

D Click **Devices** to see a list of device-related actions you can perform.

E Click **Settings** to adjust the Windows options.

Get to Know the Windows Apps

You can get up to speed quickly with Windows by understanding what each of the default Start screen tiles represents and its function. Most of the Start screen tiles are *apps,* short for *applications,* which are programs that you use to work, play, and get things done with Windows.

A Mail

Use this app to send and receive e-mail messages.

B Calendar

Use this app to schedule appointments, meetings, and other events.

C Finance

Use this app to track stocks, get financial news, and more.

D Weather

Use this app to get the latest weather and forecasts for one or more cities.

E Desktop

This app represents the Windows desktop.

F Reading List

Use this app to store articles from other apps for later reading.

G SkyDrive

Use this app to send files to your SkyDrive, which is an online storage area associated with your Microsoft account.

H Skype

Use this app to place Internet-based phone calls.

I People

Use this app to connect with the people in your life; you can store contact data, connect with your Facebook and Twitter accounts, and more.

Ⓐ Photos

Use this app to view the photos and other pictures that you have on your computer.

Ⓑ Video

Use this app to watch the videos and movies stored on your computer, as well as to buy or rent movies and TV shows.

Ⓒ Music

Use this app to play the music files on your computer, as well as purchase music.

Ⓓ Games

Use this app to download games that you can play on either your computer or your Xbox gaming console.

Ⓔ Camera

Use this app to connect with your computer's camera to take a picture or video.

Ⓕ Store

Use this app to install more apps from the Windows Store.

Ⓖ Food & Drink

Use this app to read articles about food, cooking, and wine, locate and save recipes, create a

shopping list, and more.

Ⓗ Health & Fitness

Use this app to read health articles and to track your diet, workouts, and health.

Ⓘ Maps

Use this app to find locations on a map and get directions.

Ⓙ News

Use this app to read the latest news in categories such as politics, technology, and entertainment.

Ⓚ Sports

Use this app to get the latest sports schedules and scores, follow your favorite teams, view standings and statistics, and more.

Ⓛ Internet Explorer

Use this app to navigate sites on the World Wide Web (WWW).

Ⓜ Help + Tips

Use this app to find tips and articles about how to use Windows.

Using a Mouse with Windows

If you are using Windows on a desktop or notebook computer, it pays to learn the basic mouse techniques early on because you will use them for as long as you use Windows. If you have never used a mouse before, remember to keep all your movements slow and deliberate, and practice the techniques in this section as much as you can.

Using a Mouse with Windows

Click the Mouse

1 Position the mouse pointer (🔖) over the object you want to work with.

2 Click the left mouse button.

Windows usually performs some operation in response to the click, such as displaying the desktop.

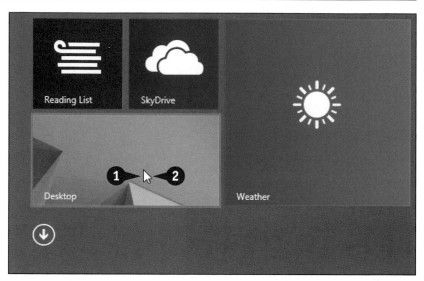

Double-Click the Mouse

1 Position the mouse pointer (🔖) over the object you want to work with.

2 Click the left mouse button twice in quick succession.

A Windows usually performs some operation in response to the double-click action, such as displaying the Recycle Bin window.

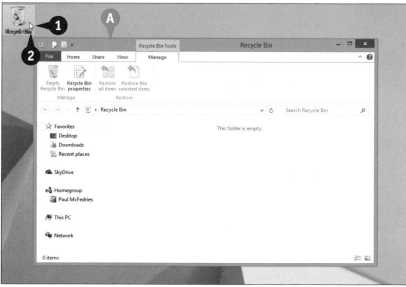

Right-Click the Mouse

1. Position the mouse pointer (↖) over the object you want to work with.
2. Click the right mouse button.

B Windows displays a shortcut menu when you right-click something.

Note: The contents of the shortcut menu depend on the object you right-click.

Click and Drag the Mouse

1. Position the mouse pointer (↖) over the object you want to work with.
2. Click and hold the left mouse button.
3. Move the mouse to drag the selected object.

C In most cases, the object moves along with the mouse pointer (↖).

4. Release the mouse button when the selected object is repositioned.

TIPS

Why does Windows sometimes not recognize my double-clicks?

Try double-clicking as quickly as you can, and do not move the mouse between clicks. If you continue to have trouble, use the Start screen to type **double**, and then click **Mouse** to open the Mouse Properties dialog box. Click the **Buttons** tab. In the Double-Click Speed group, click and drag the slider to the left (toward Slow).

How can I set up my mouse for a left-hander?

Set up the right mouse button as the primary button for clicking. On the Start screen, type **button**, and then click **Change the buttons on your mouse** to open the Mouse settings screen. Click the **Select your primary button** ☑ and then click **Right**.

Connect to a Wireless Network

If you have a wireless access point and your computer has built-in wireless networking capabilities, you can connect to the wireless access point to access your network. If your wireless access point is connected to the Internet, then connecting to the wireless network gives your computer Internet access, as well. Most wireless networks are protected with a security key, which is a kind of password. You need to know the key before attempting to connect. However, after you have connected to the network once, Windows remembers the password and connects again automatically whenever the network comes within range.

Connect to a Wireless Network

1 Position the mouse pointer () in the upper-right or the lower-right corner of the screen to display the Charms menu and then click **Settings**.

The Settings pane appears.

2 Click the **Network** icon (▦).

Ⓐ Windows displays a list of wireless networks in your area.

3 Click your network.

4 To have Windows connect to your network automatically in the future, click to activate the **Connect automatically** check box (☐ changes to ☑).

5 Click **Connect**.

If the network is protected by a security key, Windows prompts you to enter it.

6 Type the security key.

B If you want to be certain that you typed the security key correctly, temporarily click and hold the **Display Password Characters** icon (🔒).

7 Click **Next**.

Windows connects to the network.

8 Display the Charms menu and then click **Settings**.

C The network icon changes from Disconnected (📶) to Connected (📶) to indicate that you now have a wireless network connection.

 TIP

How do I disconnect from my wireless network?
To disconnect from the network, follow these steps:

1 Display the Charms menu and then click **Settings**.

2 Click **Connected** (📶).

3 Click your network.

4 Click **Disconnect**. Windows disconnects from the wireless network.

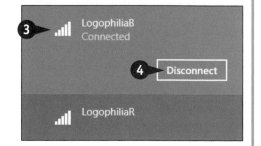

Create a Microsoft Account

You can get much more out of Windows by using a Microsoft account. When you connect a Microsoft account to your Windows user account, many previously inaccessible Windows features become immediately available. For example, you can use the Mail app to access your e-mail and the SkyDrive app to store documents online. You can also download apps from the Windows Store, access your photos and documents anywhere online, and even synchronize your settings with other PCs for which you use the same account.

Create a Microsoft Account

Start a Microsoft Account

1 From the Start screen, type **account**.

Windows displays the "account" search results.

2 Click **Manage your account**.

Windows displays the PC Settings window with the Accounts page selected.

3 Click **Connect to a Microsoft account**.

Windows asks you to verify your current account password.

④ Type your password.

⑤ Click **Next**.

Configure an Existing Microsoft Account

If you want to create a new Microsoft account, click **Sign up for a Microsoft account** and then skip to the next subsection.

① Type your e-mail address.

② Type your password.

③ Click **Next**.

Windows asks how you want to receive your security code to verify your account.

④ Select a method.

⑤ Click **Next**.

Switch to a Microsoft account on this PC

First, confirm your current password.

paul

Current password ●●●●●●●● ④

⑤ Next   Cancel

Connect this PC to your Microsoft account

Use one account to sign in to Windows and other Microsoft devices and services. Sync settings online to make your PCs look and feel the same — for example, browser favorites and history.

Email address   win8books@live.com ①

Password   ●●●●●●●● ②

Sign up for a Microsoft account

③ Next   Cancel

Help us protect your account

You need to use a security code to verify your account.

How would you like to receive your code?   Text (416) 898-8100 ④

I already have a code

Skip this for now

⑤ Next   Cancel

TIPS

How do I create a new account using either Outlook.com or Windows Live?

When you type the e-mail address, type the username that you prefer to use, followed by either **outlook.com** or **live.com**. If the username has not been taken, Windows recognizes that this is a new address, and it creates the new account automatically.

Can I use a non-Microsoft e-mail address?

Yes, you can. Windows does not require that you use an Outlook.com, Windows Live, or Hotmail e-mail address from Microsoft. If you have an e-mail address that you use regularly, you are free to use that with your Windows account.

continued ▶

Create a Microsoft Account (continued)

How you proceed after you type your e-mail address depends on whether you are creating a new Microsoft account or using an existing account. Using a Microsoft account with Windows can help if you forget your account password and cannot log in.

You can provide Microsoft with your mobile phone number, so if you ever forget your password, Microsoft will send you a text message to help you reset your password. You can also give Microsoft an alternative e-mail address, or you can provide the answer to a secret question.

Create a Microsoft Account (continued)

Windows sends the security code and then prompts you to enter it.

6 Type the security code.

7 Click **Next**.

8 Skip to the "Complete the Account" subsection on the facing page.

Help us protect your account

Before you can continue, you need to enter the security code we sent to (416) 898-8100.

| Security code | 1234567 ◄ **6** | ✕ |

Use a different verification option

Skip this for now

7 ► Next ‖ Cancel

Configure a New Microsoft Account

The account information page appears.

1 Type the e-mail address you want to use.

2 Type your password in both text boxes.

3 Fill in the rest of the boxes with your personal information.

4 Click **Next**.

Sign up for a new email address

You can use your Microsoft account to sign in to Xbox LIVE, Windows Phone, and other Microsoft services.

Email address	win8books	@	live.com ⌄ ◄ **1**
New password	•••••••• ◄ **2**
Reenter password	•••••••• ◄ **2**
First name	Paul
Last name	McFedries
Country/region	United States ⌄
ZIP code	46290	✕

4 ► Next ‖ Cancel

The Add Security Info page appears.

 5 Type your birth date.

6 Type your mobile phone number.

7 Type an alternate e-mail address.

8 Choose a secret question and then type the answer to the question.

9 Click **Next**.

10 Click **Next** (not shown).

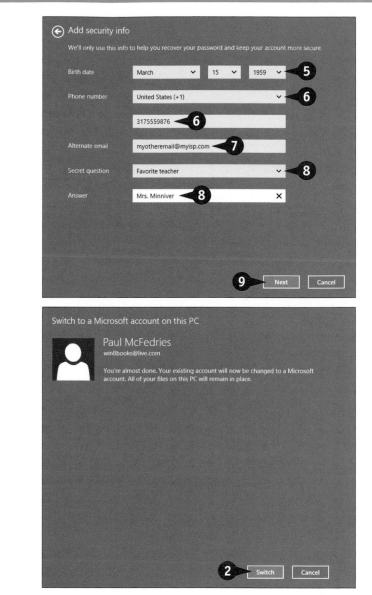

Complete the Account

Windows displays some information about SkyDrive.

1 Click **Next** (not shown).

2 Click **Switch**.

Windows connects the Microsoft account to your user account.

The next time you start Windows, you can use your Microsoft account e-mail address and password to sign in.

TIP

If I no longer want to use a Microsoft account with Windows, can I remove it?
Yes, you can revert to using your original user account at any time. Note, however, that you will no longer see any personal data on the Start screen, you will not be able to access your files online, and your settings will no longer sync between PCs. To remove the Microsoft account, switch to the Start screen, type **account**, and click **Manage your account**. In the Accounts page, click **Disconnect**. Type your Microsoft account password, click **Next**, type your local account password (twice) and a password hint, and click **Next**. Click **Sign out and finish** to complete the removal.

Work with Notifications

To keep you informed of events and information related to your computer, Windows displays notifications, so you need to understand what they are and how to handle them. As you work with your computer, certain events and conditions will display a notification on the screen. For example, you might add an appointment to the Calendar app and ask the app to remind you about it. Similarly, someone might send you a text message, or you might insert a USB flash drive, and Windows will question what you want to do with its contents.

Work with Notifications

Ⓐ When an event occurs on your computer, Windows displays a notification, such as when you insert a USB flash drive.

① Click the notification.

Ⓑ If you do not want to do anything with the notification at this time, click **Close** (☒).

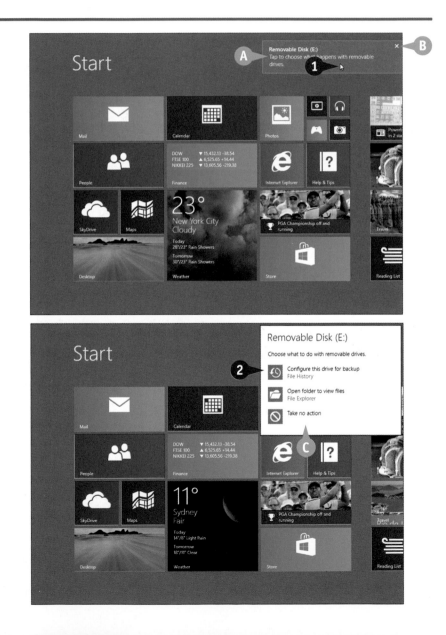

Ⓒ Windows displays options related to the notification.

② Click the option that you want to use.

Windows carries out the task.

Put Windows to Sleep

You can make your computer more energy efficient by putting Windows into sleep mode when you are not using the computer. *Sleep mode* means that your computer is in a temporary low-power mode. This saves electricity when your computer is plugged in, and it saves battery power when your computer is unplugged. In sleep mode, Windows keeps your apps open. This is handy because it means that when you return from sleep mode, after you sign in to Windows again, you can immediately get back to what you were doing.

Put Windows to Sleep

① Position the mouse pointer (⬉) in the upper-right or the lower-right corner of the screen to display the Charms menu and then click **Settings**.

The Settings pane appears.

② Click the **Power** button (⏻).

③ Click **Sleep.**

Windows activates sleep mode.

Note: To return from sleep mode, press your computer's Power button.

Restart Windows

You can restart Windows, which means that it shuts down and starts up again immediately. This is useful if your computer is running slowly or acting funny. Sometimes a restart solves the problem.

Knowing how to restart Windows also comes in handy when you install a program or device that requires a restart to function properly. If you are busy at the time, you can always opt to restart your computer manually later, when it is more convenient.

Restart Windows

1 Shut down all your running programs.

Note: Be sure to save your work as you close your programs.

2 Position the mouse pointer (⬉) in the upper-right or the lower-right corner of the screen to display the Charms menu and then click **Settings**.

The Settings pane appears.

3 Click the **Power** button (⏻).

4 Click **Restart**.

Windows shuts down, and your computer restarts.

Shut Down Windows

When you complete your work, you should shut down Windows. However, you do not want to just shut off your computer's power. Instead, you should follow the proper steps to avoid damaging files on your system. Shutting off the computer's power without properly exiting Windows can cause two problems. First, you may lose unsaved changes in open documents. Second, you could damage one or more Windows system files, which could make your system unstable.

Shut Down Windows

1 Shut down all your running programs.

Note: Be sure to save your work as you close your programs.

2 Position the mouse pointer () in the upper-right or the lower-right corner of the screen to display the Charms menu and then click **Settings**.

The Settings pane appears.

3 Click the **Power** button (⏻).

4 Click **Shut down**.

Windows shuts down and turns off your computer.

CHAPTER 2

Launching and Working with Apps

To do something useful with your computer, you need to work with an app, one that comes with Windows 8 or one that you install manually.

App updates 10 updates available

Windows Reading List Productivity	**Bing Food & Drink** Food & Dining
Windows Sound Recorder Tools	**Maps** Tools
Windows Calculator Tools	**Video** Music & Video
Windows Alarms Tools	**Windows Scan** Tools
Music Music & Video	**Games** Games

Select all   Clear   Install

Explore the Windows Store

You can use the Windows Store to research and install new applications (apps) on your computer. The traditional methods for locating and installing new apps are to purchase an app from a retail store or to download an app from the Internet. The retail-store method is inconvenient and time-consuming, and the Internet method is potentially unsafe.

A better solution is to use the Windows Store, which is directly accessible from the Start screen. It is fast and efficient, and you always know that you are getting safe apps.

Explore the Windows Store

1. On the Start screen, click **Store**.

The Windows Store appears.

2. Right-click the screen.

A. The Windows Store displays its category names.

3. Click the category that you want to view.

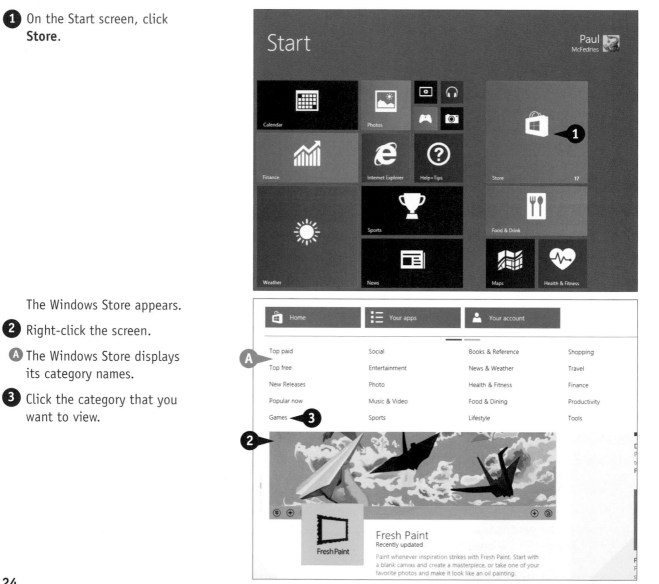

The Windows Store displays the main categories in the category that you selected.

B Click **Top paid** to see a list of the most popular paid apps in the category.

C Click **Top free** to see a list of the most popular free apps in the category.

D Tap any tile to go directly to its app.

4 Click **See all**.

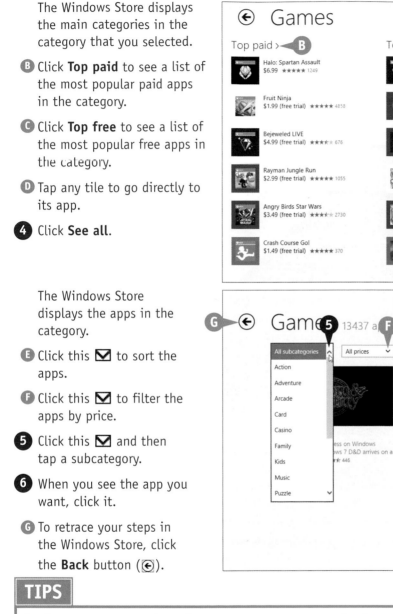

The Windows Store displays the apps in the category.

E Click this ☑ to sort the apps.

F Click this ☑ to filter the apps by price.

5 Click this ☑ and then tap a subcategory.

6 When you see the app you want, click it.

G To retrace your steps in the Windows Store, click the **Back** button (◉).

TIPS

Is there a way to see just the most recent apps added to the Windows Store?
Yes. In the Windows Store, scroll right to the **New Releases** category on the main screen. Examine the features of the new releases or click **New Releases** to display a list of the apps that have most recently been added.

Is there a quick way to locate an app?
Use the Search for apps box in the upper-right corner of the Windows Store screen. Click inside the box and start typing the name of the app. As you type, the Windows Store displays a list of matching apps. When the app you want appears, click it.

Install an App

If Windows 8 does not come with an app that you need, you can obtain the app and then install it on your computer. How you start the installation process depends on whether you obtained the app from the new Windows Store that comes with Windows 8.1 or you downloaded the app from the Internet. If you purchased the app from a retail store and received a physical copy of the software, you install the app using the CD or DVD disc that comes in the package.

Install an App

Install from the Windows Store

1 On the Start screen, click **Store**.

Note: You need a Microsoft account to install from the Windows Store. See Chapter 1.

The Windows Store appears.

2 Tap the app you want to install.

Note: See the section, "Explore the Windows Store," to learn how to navigate the Windows Store.

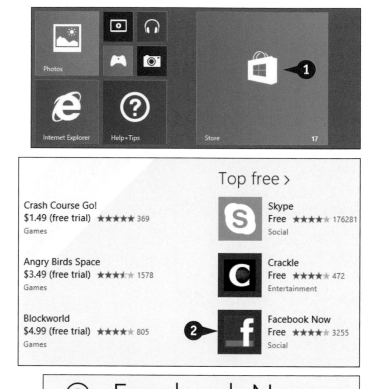

3 Tap **Install**.

If the app is not free, tap **Buy**, instead, and then tap **Confirm**.

Windows 8.1 installs the app.

Install a File Downloaded from the Internet

1 On the Start screen, type **downloads**.

2 Click **Downloads**.

Note: If you saved the downloaded file in a folder other than Downloads, use File Explorer to find the downloaded file. To view a file with File Explorer, see Chapter 10.

The Downloads folder appears.

3 Double-click the file.

The software's installation app begins.

Note: For compressed files, extract the files, and then double-click the setup file. See Chapter 10 for more information.

4 Follow the installation instructions the app provides.

How do I install software from a CD or DVD?
Insert the disc and, when the AutoPlay dialog box appears, click **Run** *file*, where *file* is the name of the installation app (usually SETUP. EXE). Then follow the installation instructions the app provides (these installation steps vary from app to app).

How do I find my software's product key or serial number?
Look for a sticker attached to the back or inside of the CD case. Also, look on the registration card, on the CD, or on the back of the box. If you downloaded the app, the number should appear on the download screen and on the e-mail receipt that you receive.

Start an App

To perform tasks of any kind in Windows 8.1, you can use one of the apps installed on your computer. The application you use depends on the task you want to perform. For example, if you want to surf the World Wide Web, you use a web browser application, such as the Internet Explorer app that comes with Windows 8.1.

Before you can use an application, however, you must first tell Windows which application you want to run. In Windows 8.1, you can run selected apps using either the Start screen or the Apps screen.

Start an App

Using the Start Screen

1 Click the tile for the app you want to launch.

Note: If you have more apps installed than can fit on the main Start screen, scroll to the right and then click the app tile.

The app runs.

A If you launched a Windows 8 app, it takes over the entire screen.

To close a Windows 8 app, press **Alt** + **F4** .

Using the Apps Screen

1 Position the mouse pointer (⌖) anywhere on the Start screen.

2 Click **All apps** (⊙).

The Apps screen appears.

3 Click the app you want to run.

Windows 8 launches the app.

Is there an easier way to locate an app?

Yes, perform an Apps search to locate it. Press ⊞+Q to open the Search pane. Begin typing the name of the app. As you type, Windows displays a list of apps that match the characters. When you see the app that you want, click it to run the program.

How can I start an app that does not appear on the Start screen, the Apps screen, or in the Apps search results?

For many tools and utilities, Windows recognizes these programs based only on their filenames, not their program names. Therefore, use the Search pane to run a search on the filename, if you know it.

Understanding Windows 8 App Windows

Windows 8 supports two very different types of apps: Windows 8 and Desktop. A Windows 8 app is a new type of program that is designed to work specifically with Windows 8. Windows 8 apps take up the entire screen when they are running, and they hide their program features until you need them.

By contrast, a Desktop app runs on the Windows 8 desktop and runs inside a window. This section focuses on Windows 8 apps; the next section covers Desktop apps.

Ⓐ Toolbar

The toolbar offers buttons, lists, and other items that offer easy access to common app commands and features. Some buttons are commands and some have lists from which you can make a choice. Note that not all Windows 8 apps come with a toolbar. Right-click the screen or press ⊞+Z to display the toolbar. If you are using a tablet, swipe down from the top edge of the screen to display the toolbar.

Ⓑ Application Bar

The application bar contains icons that give you access to various app features and commands. Note that in some apps, the application bar appears at the top of the screen rather than at the bottom. You use the same techniques to display the application bar as you do for the toolbar.

Ⓒ Settings

The app settings are commands that you can select to configure and customize the app. To display the settings, press ⊞+I and then click a command, such as Settings. On a tablet, swipe in from the right edge of the screen to display the Charms menu, tap **Settings**, and then tap a command.

Understanding Desktop App Windows

When you start a Desktop application, it appears on the Windows 8 desktop in its own window. Each application has a unique window layout, but almost all application windows have a few features in common. Note that in Windows 8, some Desktop apps come with a ribbon and some come with a menu bar and toolbar. Both types are shown in this section.

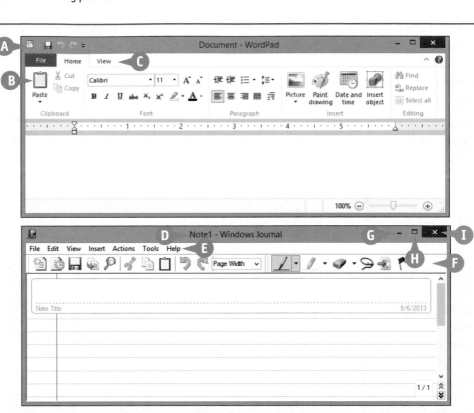

Ⓐ Quick Access Toolbar

In a ribbon-style app, this part of the window gives you one-click access to a few commands.

Ⓑ Ribbon

This appears only in ribbon-style apps, and it offers buttons that give you access to an app's features. Some buttons are commands and some are lists.

Ⓒ Ribbon Tabs

Clicking a tab displays a different selection of related ribbon buttons.

Ⓓ Title Bar

The title bar displays the name of the app. In some apps, the title bar also displays the name of the open document. You can also use the title bar to move the window.

Ⓔ Menu Bar

The menu bar contains the pull-down menus for the Desktop app. In some apps, you must press Alt to see the menu bar.

Ⓕ Toolbar

Buttons that offer easy access to common app commands and features appear in the toolbar. Some buttons are commands, and some have lists.

Ⓖ Minimize Button

Click the **Minimize** button (🗕) to remove the window from the desktop and display only the window's taskbar button.

Ⓗ Maximize Button

To enlarge the window either from the taskbar or so that it takes up the entire desktop, click the **Maximize** button (🗖).

Ⓘ Close Button

When you click the **Close** button (❌), the app shuts down.

Using a Ribbon

M any of the Windows 8 Desktop apps come with a ribbon, so you need to know how to use the ribbon to properly operate and control the app. The ribbon is the strip that lies just below the title bar. The ribbon gives you access to all or most of the app's features and options. These items are organized into various tabs, such as File and Home. Windows 8 apps that come with a ribbon include File Explorer, the desktop version of WordPad, and Paint.

Using a Ribbon

Execute Commands

1 Click the ribbon button that represents the command or list.

Note: If the ribbon button remains pressed after you click it, the button toggles a feature on and off, and the feature is now on. To turn the feature off, click the button to unpress it.

Ⓐ The app executes the command or, as shown here, drops down the list.

2 If a list appears, click the list item that represents the command.

The app runs the command.

Select a Tab

1 Click the tab name.

Ⓑ The app displays the new set of buttons represented by the tab.

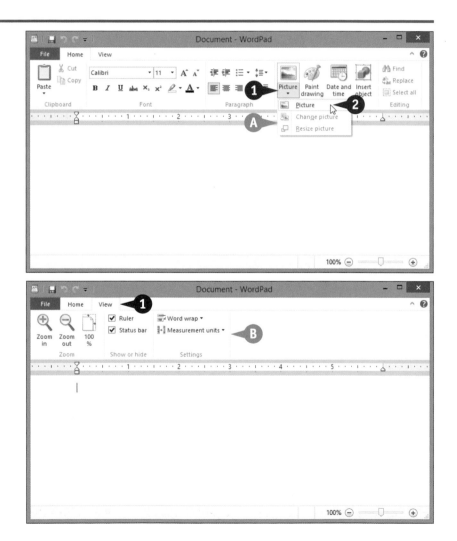

32

Access File-Related Commands

1 Click the **File** tab.

C The app displays a menu of file-related commands.

2 Click the command you want to run.

Hide and Display the Ribbon

1 Click **Minimize the Ribbon** (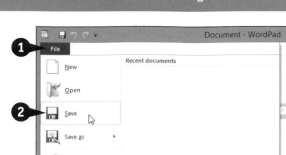).

The app hides the ribbon and changes ▲ to ▼.

To display the ribbon, click ▼.

TIPS

Can I add other commands to the Quick Access toolbar?

Yes, you can add as many commands as can fit on the Quick Access toolbar. To add a command to the Quick Access toolbar, locate the command on the ribbon, right-click it, and then click **Add to Quick Access Toolbar**.

My Quick Access toolbar is full. How can I get more of my preferred commands on the Quick Access toolbar?

The easiest way to do this is to move the Quick Access toolbar under the ribbon to get more room. Right-click the ribbon and then click **Show Quick Access Toolbar below the Ribbon**.

Using a Pull-Down Menu

When you are ready to work with an app, use the pull-down menus to access the app's commands and features. Each item in the menu bar represents a *pull-down menu*, a collection of commands usually related to each other in some way. For example, the File menu commands usually deal with file-related tasks such as opening and closing documents. The items in a pull-down menu are either commands that execute some action in the app, or features that you turn on and off. If you do not see any menus, you can often display them by pressing the Alt button.

Using a Pull-Down Menu

Run Commands

1 Click the name of the menu you want to display.

Ⓐ The app displays the menu.

You can also display a menu by pressing and holding **Alt** and pressing the underlined letter in the menu name.

2 Click the command you want to run.

The app runs the command.

Ⓑ If your command is in a submenu, click the submenu and then click the desired command.

Turn Features On and Off

1 Click the name of the menu you want to display.

Ⓒ The app displays the menu.

2 Click the menu item.

Click a submenu if your command is not on the main menu.

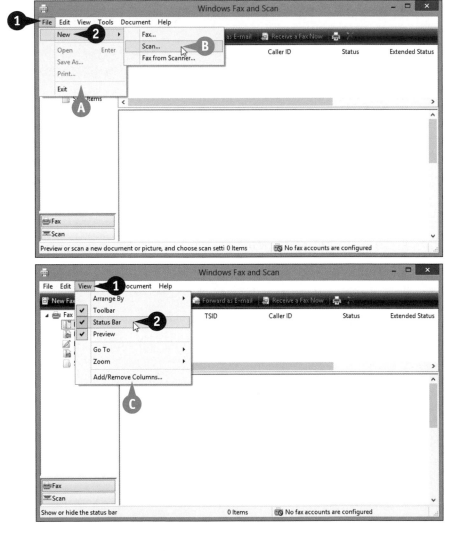

34

Using a Toolbar

You can access many app commands faster by using the toolbar. Many apps come with a toolbar, which is a collection of buttons, lists, and other controls displayed in a strip, usually across the top of the app window, just below the menu bar.

Because the toolbar is always visible, you can always use it to select commands, which means that the toolbar often gives you one-click access to the app's most common features. This is faster than using the menu bar method, which often takes several clicks, depending on the command.

Using a Toolbar

Execute Commands

1 Click the toolbar button that represents the command or list.

A The app executes the command or, as shown here, drops down the list.

2 If a list appears, click the list item that represents the command.

The app runs the command.

Display and Hide the Toolbar

1 Click **View**.

2 Click **Toolbars**.

3 Click a toolbar.

B If the toolbar is currently displayed (indicated by ☑ in the View menu), the app hides the toolbar.

If the toolbar is currently hidden, the app displays the toolbar (indicated by ☑ in the View menu).

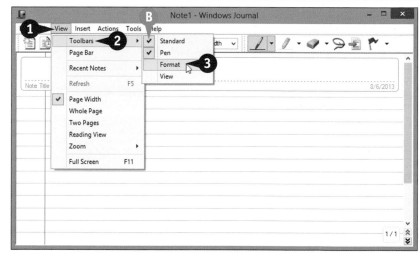

Understanding Dialog Box Controls

You often interact with an app by selecting options or typing text using a dialog box, which is a small window that appears when an app has information for you, or needs you to provide information. For example, when you select the Print command to print a document, you use the Print dialog box to specify the number of copies that you want to print.

You provide that and other information by accessing various types of dialog controls. To provide information to an app quickly and accurately, you need to know what these dialog controls look like and how they work.

A Option Button

Clicking an option button turns on an app feature. When you click an option button, it changes from ○ to ●.

B Check Box

Clicking a check box toggles an app feature on and off. If you are turning a feature on, the check box changes from ☐ to ☑; if you are turning the feature off, the check box changes from ☑ to ☐.

C Command Button

Clicking a command button executes the command that appears on the button face, such as OK, Apply, or Cancel.

D Tab

The various tabs in a dialog box display different sets of controls. You can choose from these settings in a dialog box to achieve a variety of results.

E Spin Button

The spin button (⬍) enables you to choose a numeric value.

⑥ List Box

A list box displays a relatively large number of choices, and you click the item you want. If you do not see the item you want, you can use the scroll bar to locate the item.

⑥ Text Box

A text box enables you to enter typed text.

⑥ Combo Box

The combo box combines both a text box and a list box. Either you can type the value you want into the text box, or you can use the list to click the value you want.

① Drop-Down List Box

A drop-down list box displays only the selected item from a list. You can open the list to select a different item.

① Slider

A slider enables you to choose from a range of values. Use your mouse to drag the slider bar ([▭]) down or to the left to choose lower values, or up or to the right to choose higher values.

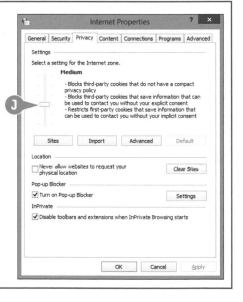

Using Dialog Boxes

You need to know how to use each of the various dialog box controls to get the most out of any app. Many dialog box controls are straightforward. For example, you click an option button to select it; you click a check box to toggle it on and off; you click a tab to view its controls; and you click a command button to execute the command that appears on its face. Other dialog box controls are not so simple, and in this section, you learn how to use text boxes, spin buttons, list boxes, and combo boxes.

Using Dialog Boxes

Using a Text Box

1 Click inside the text box.

A A blinking, vertical bar (called a *cursor* or an *insertion point*) appears inside the text box.

2 Use **Backspace** or **Delete** to delete any existing characters.

3 Type your text.

Enter a Value with a Spin Button

1 Click the top arrow on the spin button (⟳) to increase the value.

2 Click the bottom arrow on the spin button (⟳) to decrease the value.

B You can also type the value in the text box.

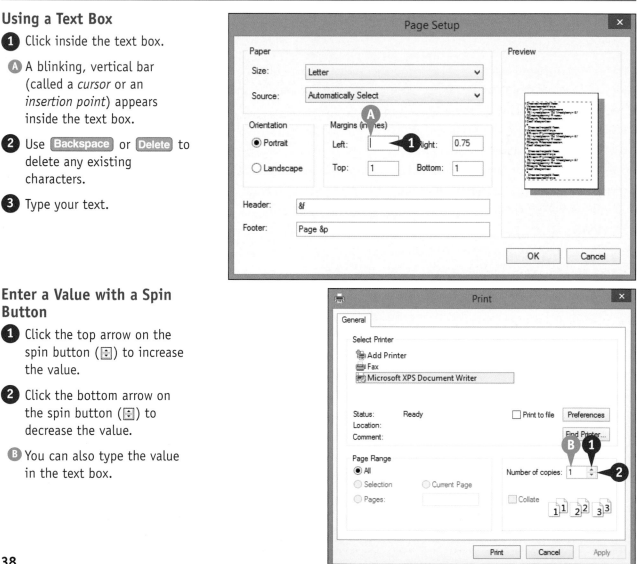

Select a List Box Item

1 If necessary, click the down arrow () to scroll down the list and bring the item you want to select into view.

Note: See the "Using Scroll Bars" section to learn how to use scroll bars.

2 Click the item.

C You can click the up arrow () to scroll back up through the list.

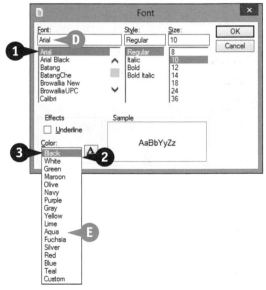

Select an Item Using a Combo Box

1 Click the item in the list box to select it.

D You can also type the item name in the text box.

Select an Item from a Drop-Down List Box

2 Click the drop-down arrow ().

E The list appears.

3 Click the item in the list that you want to select.

TIP

What are some keyboard shortcuts that I can use when working with dialog boxes?

Enter	Selects the default command button	Tab	Moves forward through the dialog box controls
Esc	Cancels the dialog box	↑ and ↓	Moves up and down within the current option button group
Alt +*letter*	Selects the control that has the *letter* underlined	Alt +↓	Drops down the selected combo box or drop-down list box

Using Scroll Bars

If the entire content of a document does not fit inside a window, you can see the rest of the document by using the window's scroll bars to move the contents into view. If the content is too long to fit inside the window, use the window's vertical scroll bar to move the content down or up as required. If the content is too wide to fit inside the window, use the horizontal scroll bar to move the content right or left as needed. Scroll bars also appear in many list boxes, so knowing how to work with scroll bars also helps you use dialog boxes.

Using Scroll Bars

Scroll Up or Down in a Window

1 Click and drag the vertical scroll box down or up to scroll through a window.

You can also click the up arrow (⬆) or down arrow (⬇).

A The content scrolls down or up.

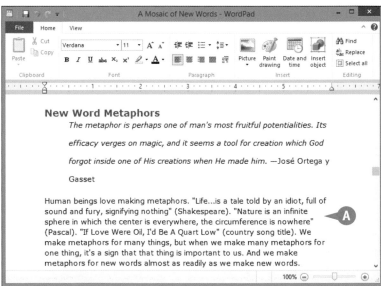

Scroll Right or Left in a Window

1 Click and drag the horizontal scroll box.

You can also click the right arrow (▶) or the left arrow (◀).

B The content scrolls left or right.

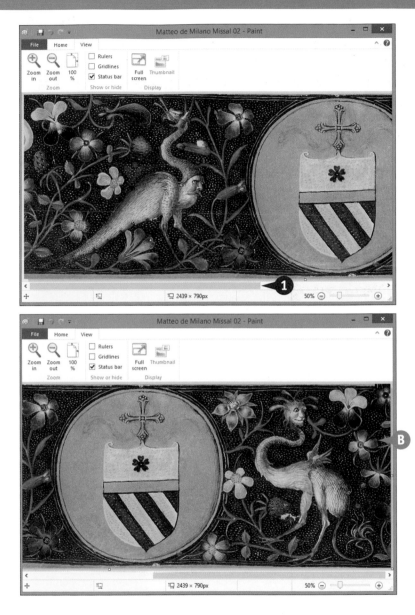

Switch Between Running Apps

If you plan to run multiple applications at the same time, you need to know how to switch from one application to another with ease. In Windows 8, after you start one application, you do not need to close that application before you open another one. Windows 8 supports a feature called *multitasking*, which means running two or more applications at once. This is handy if you need to use several applications throughout the day. For example, you might keep your word processing application, your web browser, and your e-mail application open all day.

Switch Between Running Apps

Switch Windows 8 apps Using the Mouse

1 Move the mouse pointer (⇖) to the top-left corner of the screen.

Ⓐ Windows 8 displays the most recent app you used.

2 Move the mouse pointer (⇖) down the left edge of the screen.

Ⓑ Windows 8 displays a list of your running Windows 8 apps.

3 Click the app you want to use.

Switch All Apps Using the Keyboard

1 Press and hold **Alt** and press **Tab**.

Ⓒ Windows 8 displays thumbnail versions of the open apps.

2 Press **Tab** until the window in which you want to work is selected.

3 Release **Alt**.

Switch Desktop Apps Using the Taskbar

1 Click the taskbar button of the app to which you want to switch.

Note: You can also switch to another window by clicking the window, even if it is the background.

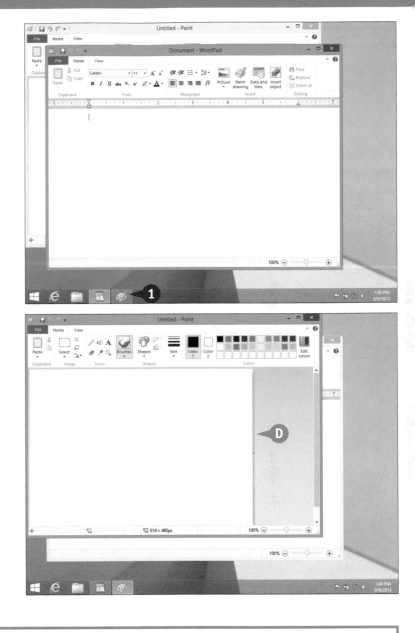

Switch Desktop Apps Using the Keyboard

1 Press and hold **Alt** and press **Esc**.

D Windows 8 brings the next Desktop app to the front.

2 Press **Esc** until you see the app you want to use.

3 Release **Alt**.

TIP

How can I switch between apps using a tablet?
Windows gives you two options. To cycle through your running apps, use a finger or stylus to swipe in from the left edge of the screen. As you swipe, your finger or stylus drags in the next app window. When you see the window you want, release your finger or stylus to switch to that app. To switch to an app, swipe in from the left edge of the screen. When you see the next app window, drag it back to the left edge of the screen. Windows displays a list of running apps, so you can now tap the one you want to use.

Update an App

You can ensure that you are using the latest version of an app by using the Windows Store to install an available update. After a software company releases an app, its programmers continue to work on it. They add new features, improve existing features, fix problems, and close security holes.

After fully testing these improvements and fixes, they place the new version of the app in the Windows Store, which alerts you that there is an update. You can then install the new version.

Update an App

1 Switch to the Start screen.

A If you have updated apps available, you see the number of updates here.

2 Click **Store**.

The Windows Store app appears.

3 Click **Updates**.

The Windows Store displays a list of the available updates.

Ⓑ If you want to update only some of the apps, click **Clear**.

Ⓒ If you prefer to update all of the apps at once, click **Select all** and skip to step **5**.

④ Hold down and click each update that you want to install.

⑤ Click **Install**.

Windows 8 installs the app updates.

TIP

How do I update Windows 8?

By default, Windows 8 is configured to automatically check for updated system files each day. If any updates are available, Windows 8 downloads and installs them automatically. If you know of an important update, you can check for it manually if you would rather not wait for the automatic check. Press ⊞+C (or swipe left from the right edge of the screen) to display the Charms menu, click **Settings**, and then click **Change PC settings** to open the PC Settings app. Click **Update & Recovery** and then click **Check now.**

Uninstall an App

If you have an app that you no longer use, you can free up some disk space and reduce clutter on the Start screen by uninstalling that app. When you install an app, the program stores its files on your computer's hard drive, and although most programs are quite small, many require hundreds of megabytes of disk space. Uninstalling an app you do not need frees up the disk space it uses and removes its tile (or tiles) from the Start screen (if it has any there) and the Apps screen.

Uninstall an App

Uninstall a Windows 8 app

1 Use the Start screen or the Apps screen to locate the Windows 8 app you want to uninstall.

Note: To display the Apps screen, right-click an empty section of the Start screen and then click **All apps**.

2 Right-click the app.

Ⓐ Windows 8 displays the application bar.

3 Click **Uninstall**.

Windows 8 asks you to confirm.

4 Click **Uninstall**.

Windows 8 removes the app.

Uninstall a Desktop App

 On the Start screen, type **uninstall**.

2 Click **Programs and Features**.

The Programs and Features window appears.

3 Click the app you want to uninstall.

4 Click **Uninstall** (or **Uninstall/Change**).

In most cases, the app asks you to confirm that you want to uninstall it.

5 Click **Yes**.

The app's uninstall begins.

6 Follow the instructions on the screen.

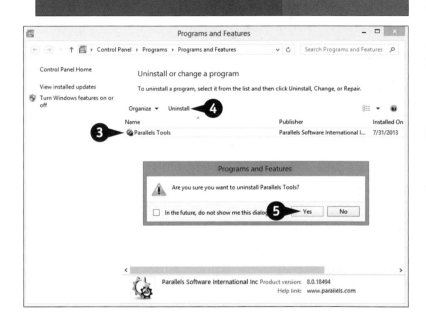

TIPS

How can I uninstall the app that is taking up the most space?

Press ⊞+C to display the Charms menu, click **Settings**, and then click **Change PC settings**. Click **Search & apps** and then click **App sizes** to see a list of apps sorted by size. To remove an app, click it, click **Uninstall**, and then click **Uninstall** again.

What is the difference between an Automatic and a Custom uninstall?

The Automatic uninstall requires no input from you. It is the easiest, safest choice and therefore the one you should choose. The Custom uninstall gives you more control, but it is more complex and suitable only for experienced users.

CHAPTER 3

Customizing Windows

Windows comes with a number of features that enable you to personalize your computer. Not only can you change the appearance of Windows to suit your taste, but you can also change the way Windows works to make it easier to use and more efficient.

Configure the Start Screen

You can personalize how the Start screen looks and operates to suit your style and the way you work. For example, you can rearrange the Start screen tiles so that the apps you use most often appear together on the screen.

You can also make your Start screen more useful and more efficient by resizing some of the app screen tiles. For most apps, the Start screen supports three tile sizes: Small, Medium, and Wide. Some apps also support a Large size, which is the same width as Wide, but twice as tall.

Configure the Start Screen

Move a Tile

1 On the Windows Start screen, click and hold the app tile that you want to move.

2 Drag the tile to the position that you prefer.

A Windows reduces the tile sizes slightly and adds extra space between the tiles.

3 Release the tile.

B Windows moves the tile to the new position.

Change a Tile Size

C This is an example of the Small size.

D This is an example of the Medium size.

E This is an example of the Wide size.

F This is an example of the Large size.

1 Right-click the app tile that you want to resize.

G Windows displays the application bar.

2 Click **Resize**.

3 Click the size you want.

H Windows resizes the tile.

TIPS

Can I combine similar apps into a single group of tiles?

Yes. Drag the first app tile all the way to the left edge of the screen until you see a vertical bar, and then release the tile. Windows creates a new group for the app tile. To add other tiles to the new group, drag and drop the tiles within the group.

Can I name an app group?

Yes. This is a good idea because it makes the Start screen even easier to use and navigate. Right-click an empty section of the Start screen and then click **Customize**. Click **Name group** above the group you want to name, type the group name, and then press **Enter**.

Pin an App to the Start Screen

You can customize the Start screen to gain quick access to the programs that you use most often. If you have an app that does not appear on the Start menu, you usually open the app by swiping up from the bottom edge of the screen to reveal the application bar and then clicking All Apps. For the apps you use most often, you can avoid this extra work by *pinning* their icons permanently to the main Start screen. After you have pinned an app to your Start screen, you can launch it by scrolling right and clicking the app.

Pin an App to the Start Screen

1 Move the mouse pointer (⟨) anywhere on the Start screen.

2 Click **All apps** (⊙).

The Apps screen appears.

3 Locate the app that you want to pin to the Start screen.

4 Right-click the app tile.

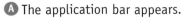 The application bar appears.

5 Click **Pin to Start**.

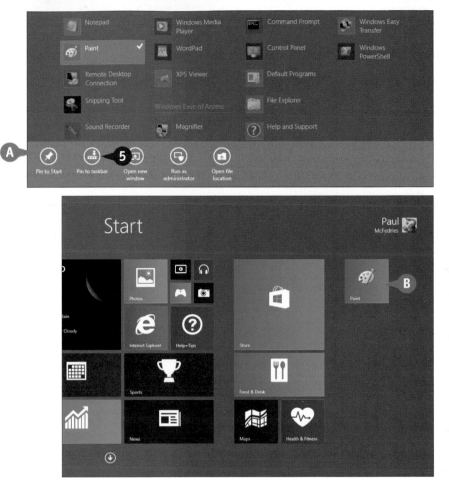

Windows returns to the Start screen.

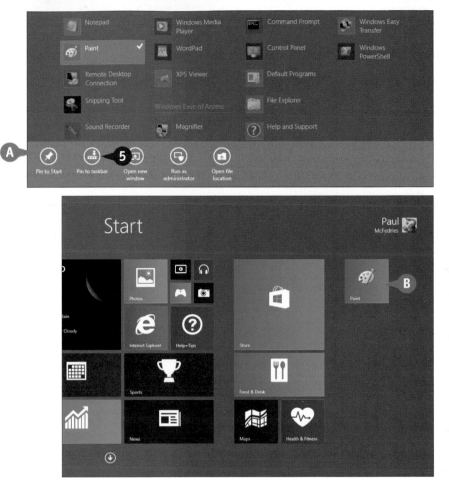 A tile for the pinned app appears on the Start screen.

TIPS

Can I remove an app from the Start screen?

Yes, you can remove any app tile from the Start screen, even the default apps that come with Windows. To do so, right-click the app tile to open the application bar and then click **Unpin from Start**.

What happens if the app I want to pin does not appear in the Apps screen?

You can still pin the app to the Start screen by searching for it. Switch to the Start screen and begin typing the name of the app that you want to pin. Windows displays a list of apps with matching names. When you see the app, right-click it and then click **Pin to Start**.

Open the PC Settings App

You can configure and customize many aspects of your Windows system using the PC Settings app. PC Settings is the Windows app that you use for customizing and tweaking your PC. Many of the tasks that follow in this chapter, including changing the Start and Lock screen backgrounds and adding an app to the Lock screen, are performed using the PC Settings app. PC Settings also offers a wealth of other options that you can use to customize your PC.

Open the PC Settings App

1 Move the mouse **pointer** (⍾) to the top-right or bottom-right corner of the screen.

The Charms menu appears.

2 Click **Settings**.

The Settings pane appears.

3 Click **Change PC settings**.

The PC Settings app appears.

A Use the tabs on the left side of the screen to navigate the PC Settings app.

TIP

If I know which tab of the PC Settings app I want to use, is there a quick way to display it?

Yes, you can use the Settings Search pane, which enables you to quickly search for the setting that you want to work with. Display the Charms menu and click **Search** to open the Search pane. Use the **Search** list to click **Settings**, and then begin typing the name of the tab or setting you want.

For example, if you want to go directly to the Accounts tab, type **accounts** and then click **Add, delete, and manage other user accounts** in the search results. Note that PC Settings items appear in the search results with the PC Settings icon ().

Change the Start Screen Background

To give Windows a different look, you can change the default Start screen background. The Start screen background is the area that appears "behind" the tiles. By default, it consists of an abstract pattern formatted with a green color scheme. If you find yourself using the Start screen frequently, the default background might become tiresome. If so, you can liven things up a bit by changing both the background pattern and the background color.

Change the Start Screen Background

1 Move the mouse pointer (⬚) to the top-right corner of the screen.

The Charms menu appears.

2 Click **Settings**.

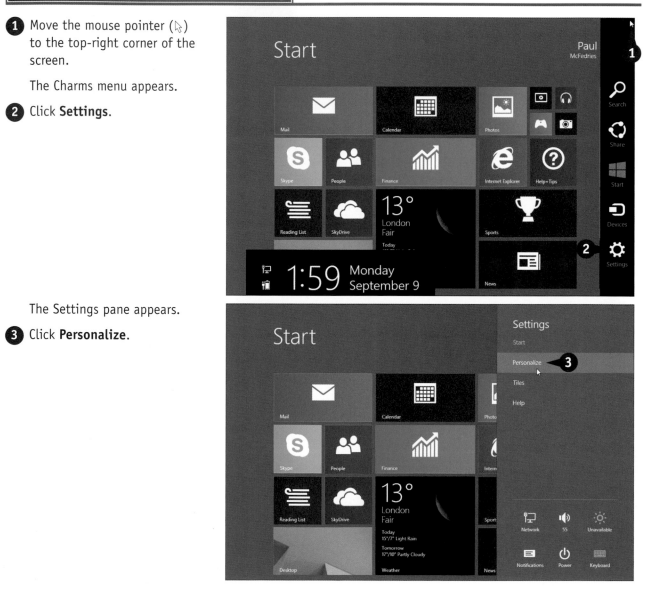

The Settings pane appears.

3 Click **Personalize**.

The Personalize pane appears.

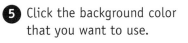 Click the background image that you want to use.

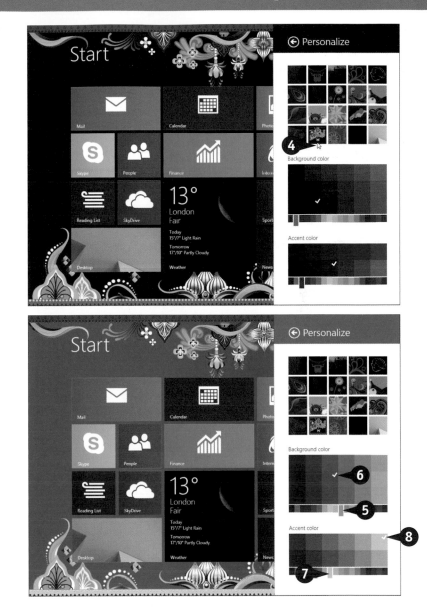

5 Click the background color that you want to use.

6 Click the shade of the background color that you want to use.

7 Click the accent color that you want to use.

8 Click the shade of the accent color that you want to use.

The background image and color that you chose appear on your Start screen.

TIP

My eyesight is not what it used to be. Is there a way to make the Start screen more readable?
Windows tends to use subtle colors, so the screen can be hard to read if your eyesight is poor. The solution is to switch to High Contrast mode, which uses white text on a black background. To set this up, open the PC Settings app, click the **Ease of Access** tab, and then click **High contrast**. Select a high contrast theme, click each item to set the color for text, hyperlinks, and so on, and then click **Apply**.

Change the Lock Screen Background

You can make your Lock screen more interesting by changing the image that appears as its background. Locking your computer is a useful safety feature because it prevents unauthorized users from accessing your files and your network. If you find yourself looking at the Lock screen frequently, you might prefer to see something other than the default image. Windows comes with several system pictures that you can use, or you can use one of your own pictures.

Change the Lock Screen Background

Display the Lock Screen Settings

1 Open the PC Settings app.

Note: See the section, "Open the PC Settings App," in this chapter.

2 Click **Lock screen**.

The Lock screen settings appear.

Choose a System Picture

1 Click the picture that you want to use.

The image appears the next time that you lock your computer.

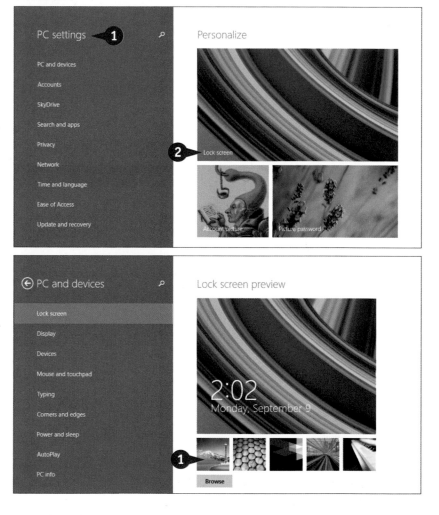

Choose One of Your Own Pictures

1 Click **Browse**.

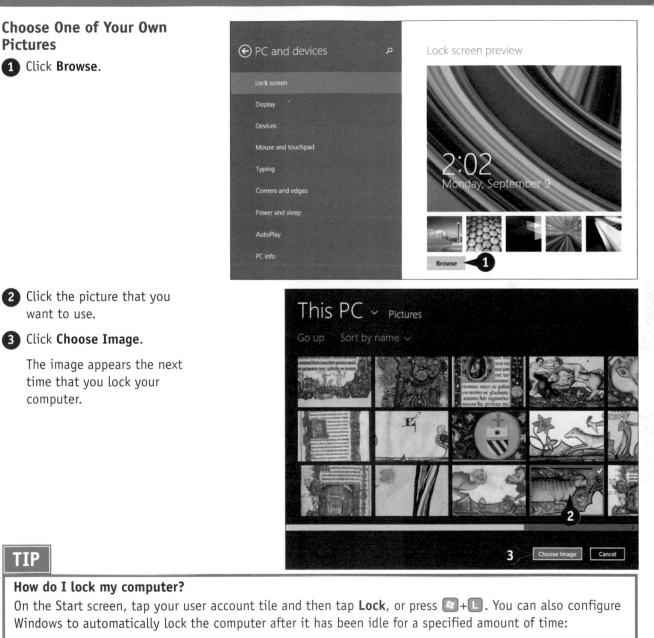

2 Click the picture that you want to use.

3 Click **Choose Image**.

The image appears the next time that you lock your computer.

TIP

How do I lock my computer?

On the Start screen, tap your user account tile and then tap **Lock**, or press ⊞+🅛. You can also configure Windows to automatically lock the computer after it has been idle for a specified amount of time:

1 From the Start screen, type **lock pc**.

2 Click **Lock the computer when I leave it alone for a period of time**.

3 Click **On resume, display logon screen** (☐ changes to ☑).

4 Use the **Wait** text box to set the number of minutes of idle time after which Windows locks your PC.

5 Click **OK**.

Add an App to the Lock Screen

When you lock your PC, Windows displays status icons for some apps. For example, the status icon for the Mail app shows the number of unread messages. The Lock screen also shows any new notifications that appear for the Calendar app, such as an upcoming appointment. If you lock your computer frequently, you can make the Lock screen even more useful by adding icons for other apps, including ones that support notifications.

Add an App to the Lock Screen

1 Open the PC Settings app.

Note: See the section, "Open the PC Settings App," in this chapter.

2 Click **Lock screen**.

The Lock screen settings appear.

3 To add a status icon for an app, click an **Add** button (+).

The Choose an app window appears.

4 Click the app for which you want to add a status icon to the Lock screen.

5 To choose which app displays a detailed status, click here.

6 Click the app.

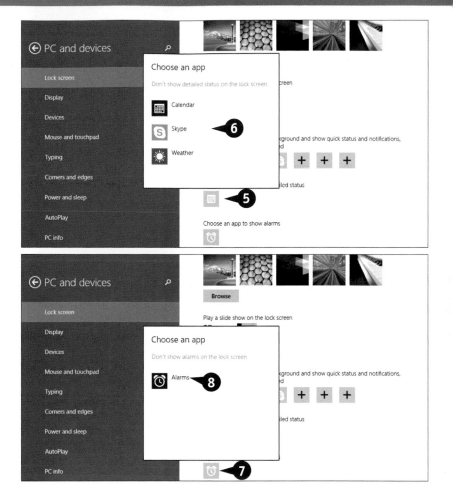

7 To add recent alarms to the Lock screen, click the existing alarm button.

8 Click the app.

Windows puts the new settings into effect, and the apps appear on the Lock screen the next time that you use it.

TIP

What is the difference between a quick status and detailed status?
A *quick status* means that the Lock screen shows only a small icon for an app, and that icon displays the number of recent or unread items, such as the number of unread e-mail messages in the Mail app. A *detailed status* means that the Lock screen shows more information from the app. For example, if you have an upcoming event in the Calendar app, the lock screen shows the details of that event, including the event title, location, and time.

Synchronize Settings Between PCs

If, besides your Windows desktop computer, you also have a Windows notebook, a Windows tablet, and a Windows smartphone, using the same Microsoft account on each platform means that you can synchronize data among them. You can synchronize customizations, such as backgrounds and themes; system settings, such as languages and regional settings; Internet Explorer data, such as favorites and history; app settings, and more. This gives you a consistent interface across your devices and consistent data so that you can be more productive.

Synchronize Settings Between PCs

1 Open the PC Settings app.

Note: See the section, "Open the PC Settings App," in this chapter.

2 Click **SkyDrive**.

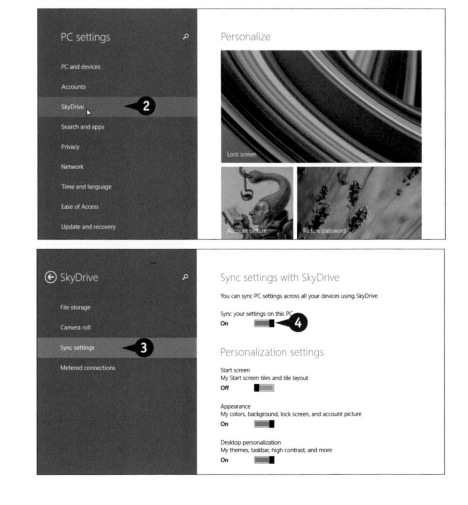

3 Click **Sync settings**.

The Sync screen appears.

4 Click the **Sync your settings on this PC** switch to **On**.

Under **Personalization settings**, click the switch to **Off** beside each type of setting that you do not want to include in the sync.

⑥ Click the **Apps** switch to **Off** if you do not want to sync your installed apps.

⑦ Click the **App data** switch to **Off** if you do not want to sync your app data.

⑧ Under **Other Windows settings**, click the switch to **Off** beside each type of setting that you do not want to include in the sync.

The next time Windows syncs, it does not include the settings that you turned off.

TIPS

Can I prevent syncing during those times when I am using a metered Internet connection that allows me only so much data?

Yes. By default, Windows syncs with other PCs when you are using a metered Internet connection. To turn this off, follow steps **1** to **3** in this section to display the Sync screen, scroll to the bottom, and then click the **Sync and back up settings over metered connections** switch to **Off.**

How does Windows know when I am using a metered Internet connection?

You have to tell Windows when you are using a metered connection. Display the PC Settings app, click **Network**, click **Connections**, click your Internet connection, and then click the **Set as a metered connection** switch to **On.**

Access an App's Features

By design, apps appear simple and uncomplicated. They take up the entire screen, and when you first launch them, you usually see a basic interface. However, almost all apps include a number of features — commands, settings, views, and so on — that you cannot see at first. To access these features, you must display the application bar (sometimes called the *app bar*), a strip that appears along the bottom or top of the screen. You can then click the feature that you want to use.

Access an App's Features

Display the Application Bar

1 Open the app that you want to work with.

2 Right-click the screen.

On a tablet PC, swipe up from the bottom edge of the screen.

A The application bar appears.

B The application bar's icons represent the app's features.

Hide the Application Bar

Note: If you click an application bar feature, the app automatically hides the application bar. You need to manually hide the application bar if you decide not to select a feature.

1 Click an empty section of the app screen outside of the application bar.

C The app hides the application bar.

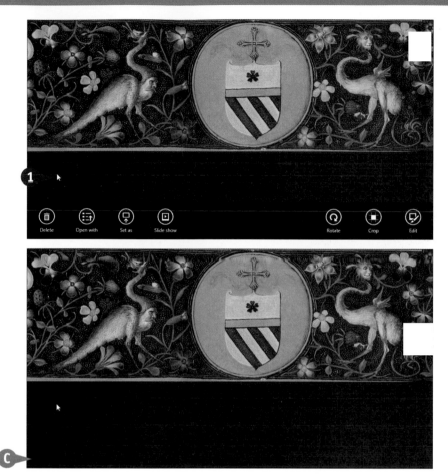

Do apps always display a single application bar at the bottom of the screen?

No. In some apps, the application bar appears at the top of the screen, and in other apps, you see *two* application bars — one on the bottom and one on the top of the screen.

Are there more app features that I can access?

Yes, you can also display the Settings pane for each app. The layout of the Settings pane varies between apps, but it usually includes commands for setting app preferences and options. To display an app's Settings pane, move the mouse pointer (⬡) to the top-right or bottom-right corner of the screen (or swipe left from the right edge of the screen) and then click **Settings**.

Pin an App to the Taskbar

Pinning an app to the Start screen is helpful only if you use the Start screen regularly. If you use the desktop more often and you have an app that you use frequently, you might prefer to have that app just a single click away. You can achieve this by pinning the app to the taskbar. You can pin an app to the taskbar either from the Start screen or from the desktop.

Pin an App to the Taskbar

Using the Start Screen

1 Display the Charms menu and then click **Search**.

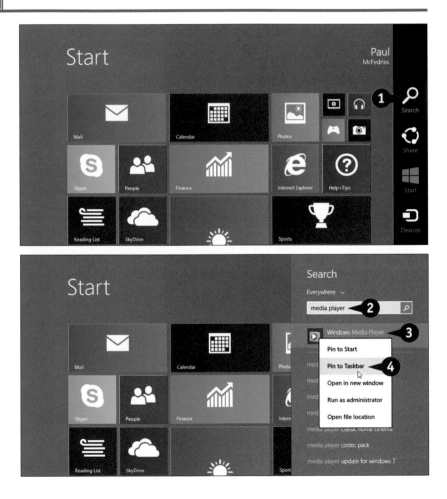

2 Type the name of the app that you want to pin to the taskbar.

Windows displays the search results.

3 Right-click the app.

4 Click **Pin to Taskbar**.

Ⓐ An icon for the app now appears in the taskbar.

From the Desktop

❶ Launch the app that you want to pin to the taskbar.

❷ Right-click the running app's taskbar icon.

❸ Click **Pin this program to taskbar**.

❹ Click **Close** (✖).

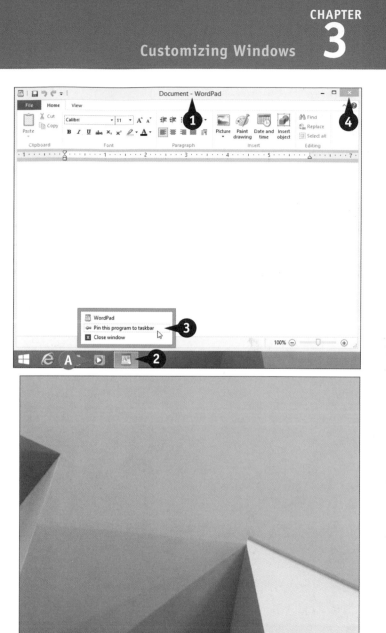

Ⓑ An icon for the app remains on the taskbar.

TIPS

Can I change the order of the taskbar icons?
Yes. Click and drag a taskbar icon to the left or right and then drop it in the new position. Note that this technique applies not only to the icons pinned to the taskbar, but also to the icons for any running programs.

How do I remove an app icon from the taskbar?
If you decide that you no longer require an app to be pinned to the taskbar, you should remove it to reduce taskbar clutter and provide more room for other app icons. To remove a pinned app icon, right-click the icon and then click **Unpin this program from taskbar**.

Adjust the Volume

While an audio or video file is playing, you can adjust the volume up or down to get its audio just right. If you are listening to media by yourself, you can adjust the volume to suit the music and your mood. However, if there are other people nearby, you will probably want to use the volume control to keep the playback volume low to avoid disturbing them. If you need to silence the media temporarily, you can mute the playback.

Adjust the Volume

 Display the Charms menu and then click **Settings**.

The Settings pane appears.

2 Click the **Volume** icon (🔊).

3 Click and drag the slider to set the volume level that you want.

A You can also click **Mute** (🔇) to mute the volume.

Windows sets the system volume to the new level.

Set the Time Zone

To ensure that your system clock is accurate, you should set the time zone to correspond to your location. When Windows configures your computer, it performs a number of chores, including setting the current system time and time zone. However, for the time zone, Windows defaults to Pacific Time in North America. If this is not the time zone used where you live, you must select the correct one to ensure that you have the accurate system time.

Set the Time Zone

1 Open the PC Settings app.

Note: See the section, "Open the PC Settings App," in this chapter.

2 Click **Time and language**.

3 Click the **Time zone** ☑.

4 Click your time zone.

Windows adjusts the time to the new time zone.

CHAPTER 4

Surfing the World Wide Web

This chapter discusses the web and shows you how to use Internet Explorer to navigate from site to site. You also learn how to select links, enter web page addresses, work with tabs, save your favorite sites, search for information, and more.

Understanding the World Wide Web

The *World Wide Web* — the *web,* for short — is a massive storehouse of information that resides on computers called *web servers,* located all over the world. You will probably find that you spend the majority of your online time browsing the web. That is not surprising because the web is useful, entertaining, fun, interesting, and provocative.

Web Pages

World Wide Web information is presented on *web pages,* which you download to your computer using a web browser program, such as Windows 8 Internet Explorer. Each web page can combine text with images, sounds, music, and even video to present you with information on a particular subject.

Websites

A *website* is a collection of web pages associated with a particular person, business, service, government, school, or organization. Websites are stored on a *web server,* a special computer that makes web pages available for people to browse.

Web Addresses

Every web page has its own *web address* that uniquely identifies the page. This address is

sometimes called a *URL* (pronounced *yoo-ar-ell* or *erl*), which is short for *Uniform Resource Locator.*

Links

A *link* (also called a *hyperlink*) is a cross-reference to another web page. Each link is a bit of text — usually shown underlined and in a different color — or an image that, when you click it, loads the other page into your web browser.

Start Internet Explorer

To access websites and view web pages, you must use a web browser program. In Windows 8, the default web browser is Internet Explorer, which you can use to surf websites when your computer is connected to the Internet. The desktop version of Internet Explorer offers a number of features that make it easy to browse the web. For example, you can open multiple pages in a single window, save your favorite sites for easier access, and perform Internet searches from the Internet Explorer window.

Start Internet Explorer

1 On the Start screen, click **Internet Explorer**.

The Internet Explorer window appears.

Navigate Internet Explorer

You can easily surf the web if you know your way around the Internet Explorer web browser. You need to familiarize yourself with important Internet Explorer features, such as the address bar and the web page title. You also need to understand links, recognize the current link, and determine where a link will take you before clicking it.

Ⓐ Web Page Title

This part of Internet Explorer shows the title of the displayed web page. You see this only when you display the tabs, as described in the "Open a Web Page in a Tab" section.

Ⓑ Links

Links appear as either text or images. On most pages, although not the page shown here, text links appear underlined and in a different color — usually blue — than the regular page text.

Ⓒ Current Link

This is the link that you are currently pointing to with your mouse. The mouse pointer changes to a pointing finger (🖑). On some pages, such as this one, the link text also becomes underlined.

Ⓓ Address Bar

This text box displays the address of the current web page. You can also use the address bar to type the address of a web page that you want to visit to search for information on the web. You see this only when you right-click the screen or swipe up from the bottom on a tablet.

Ⓔ Link Address

When you point at a link, Internet Explorer displays a tooltip that shows you the address of the page associated with the link.

Select a Link

Almost all web pages include links to pages that contain related information. When you select a link, your browser loads the other page. Links come in two forms: text and images. Text links consist of a word or phrase that usually appears underlined and in a different color from the normal page text. However, web designers can control the look of their links, so text links may not always stand out like this. The only way to tell is to position the mouse pointer over the text or image. If the pointer changes to a pointing finger, the item is a link.

Select a Link

1 Position the mouse pointer over the link (the pointer changes to a pointing finger (👆)).

This tooltip shows the
A address of the linked page.

2 Click the text or image.

Note: The link address shown when you point at a link may be different from the one shown when the page is downloading. This happens when the website redirects the link, which occurs frequently.

The linked web page appears.

B The web page address changes after the linked page loads in your browser.

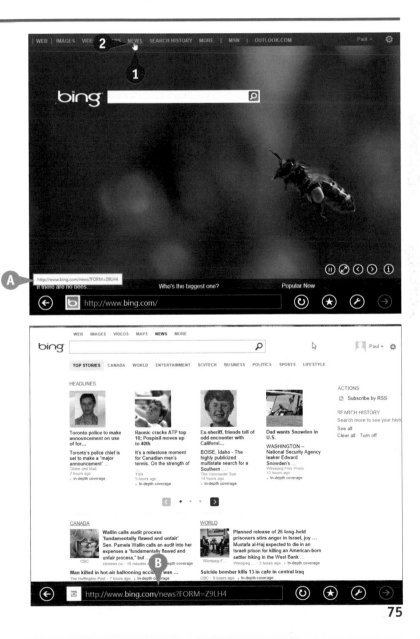

Enter a Web Page Address

If you know the address of a specific web page, you can type it into the web browser to display it. Every web page is uniquely identified by an address called the *Uniform Resource Locator,* or *URL.* The URL is composed of four basic parts: the transfer method (usually http, which stands for *Hypertext Transfer Protocol*), the website domain name, the directory where the web page is located on the server, and the web page filename. The website domain name suffix most often used is .com (commercial), but other common suffixes include .gov (government), .org (nonprofit organization), .edu (education), and country domains such as .ca (Canada).

Enter a Web Page Address

1 Click in the address bar.

Note: If you do not see the address bar, right-click or swipe up from the bottom edge of the screen.

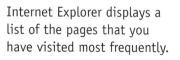

Internet Explorer displays a list of the pages that you have visited most frequently.

A If you see the page that you want, click it and skip the rest of these steps.

2 Press `Delete`.

Internet Explorer clears the address bar.

Note: Step 2 is optional.

Type the address of the web page.

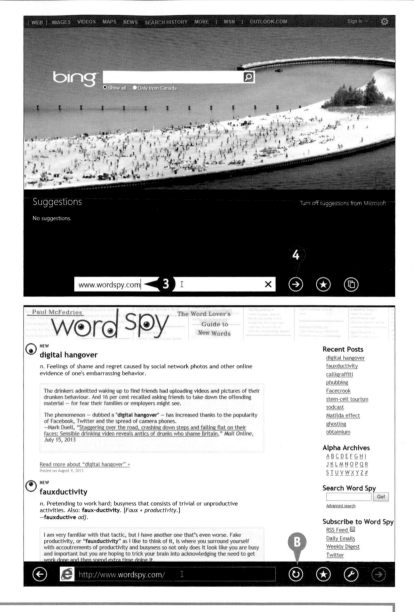

④ Click the **Go** button (◉).

The web page appears.

Ⓑ If you find that Internet Explorer cannot display the page, this is usually a temporary glitch, so click **Refresh** (◉) to try loading the page again.

TIP

Are there any shortcuts that I can use to enter web page addresses?

Yes. Here are some useful keyboard techniques:

- After you finish typing the address, press Enter instead of clicking **Go** (◉).
- Most web addresses begin with *http://*. You can leave off these characters when you type your address.
- If the address uses the form http://www.something.com, type just the *something* part and then press Ctrl + Enter. Internet Explorer automatically adds *http://www.* at the beginning and *.com* at the end.

Open a Web Page in a Tab

As you surf the web, you may come upon a page that you want to keep available while you visit other sites. That page may contain important information that you need to reference or read later on.

Instead of leaving the page and trying to find it again later, Internet Explorer lets you keep the page open in a special section of the browser screen called a *tab*. You can use a second tab to visit your other sites and then resume viewing the first site by clicking its tab.

Open a Web Page in a Tab

Open a Web Page in a Tab

1. Right-click the screen.

   A The tab bar appears.

2. Click the **New Tab** button (⊕).

   Internet Explorer prompts you for the web page address.

3. Follow the steps in the "Enter a Web Page Address" section to display the page.

Open a Link in a Tab

1. Right-click the link that you want to open.

   B Internet Explorer displays a list of actions for the link.

2. Click **Open link in new tab**.

Internet Explorer loads the page in a new tab.

3 Click the tab.

Internet Explorer switches to the tab and displays the web page.

Work with Tabs

1 Right-click the screen.

C The tab bar appears.

D You can click a tab to switch to that page.

E You can click **Close** (![x]) to close a tab.

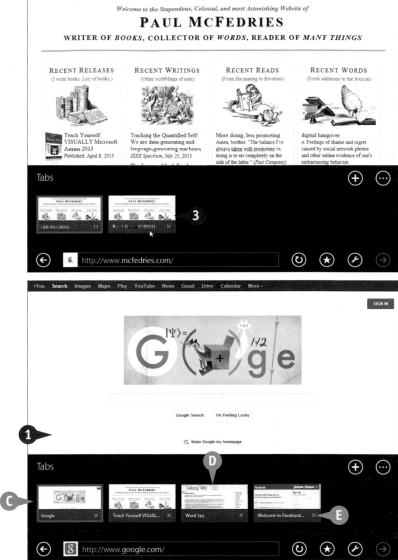

TIP

Is there an easy way to close all my tabs except the one that I am currently using?

Yes, you can do so by following these steps:

1 Switch to the tab that you want to leave open.

2 Right-click the screen.

The tab bar appears.

3 Right-click the tab you want to keep open.

4 Click **Close other tabs**.

Internet Explorer closes all the tabs except the current one.

Navigate Web Pages

After you have visited several pages, you can return to a page that you visited earlier. Instead of retyping the address or looking for the link, Internet Explorer gives you some easier methods.

When you navigate from page to page, you create a kind of "path" through the web. Internet Explorer keeps track of this path by maintaining a list of the pages that you have visited. You can use that list to go back to a page. After you have gone back, you can also use that same list to go forward through the pages again.

Navigate Web Pages

Go Back One Page

1 Right-click the screen.

The address bar appears.

2 Click the **Back** button (⊙).

The previous page that you visited appears.

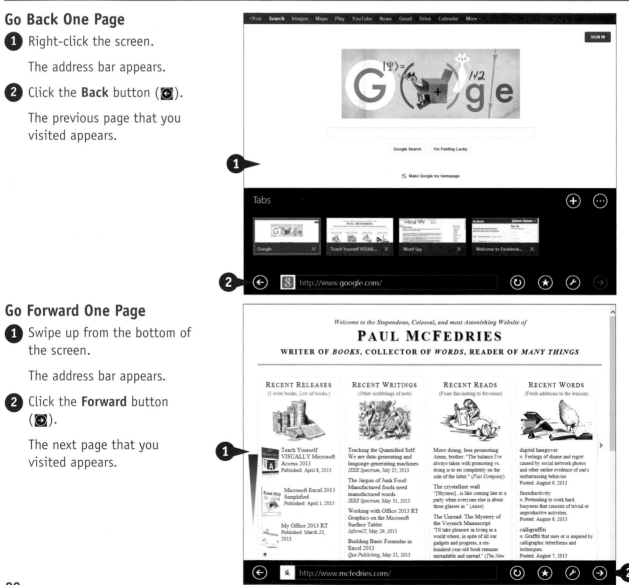

Go Forward One Page

1 Swipe up from the bottom of the screen.

The address bar appears.

2 Click the **Forward** button (⊙).

The next page that you visited appears.

Find Text on a Page

When you are reading a page on the web, it is not unusual to be looking for specific information. In those situations, rather than read through the entire page to find the information that you are looking for, you can search the web page text for the data. The Find on Page feature in Internet Explorer lets you to do that by enabling you to search through the current page text for a specific word or phrase.

Find Text on a Page

1 Right-click the screen.

The address bar appears.

2 Click the **Tools** button (⚙).

3 Click **Find on page**.

The Find on Page bar appears.

4 Click inside the text box.

5 Type the word or phrase that you want to locate.

A Internet Explorer highlights the matching text on the page.

B You can click **Next** to cycle forward through the matches.

C You can click **Previous** to cycle backward through the matches.

6 When you are done, click **Close**.

Save Favorite Web Pages

If you have web pages that you visit frequently, you can save yourself time by saving those pages as favorites within Internet Explorer. This enables you to display the pages with just a couple of clicks.

You save favorite pages in Internet Explorer by adding them to a special section of the app called the Favorites list. Instead of typing an address or searching for one of these pages, you can display the web page by clicking it in the Favorites list.

Save Favorite Web Pages

1 Display the web page that you want to save.

2 Right-click the screen.

The address bar appears.

3 Click **Favorites** (⊙) (⊙ changes to ⊙).

A Internet Explorer displays the Favorites list.

4 Click **Add to Favorites** (⊙).

5 Edit the page name, as necessary.

6 Click **Add**.

Internet Explorer adds the page to the Pinned list.

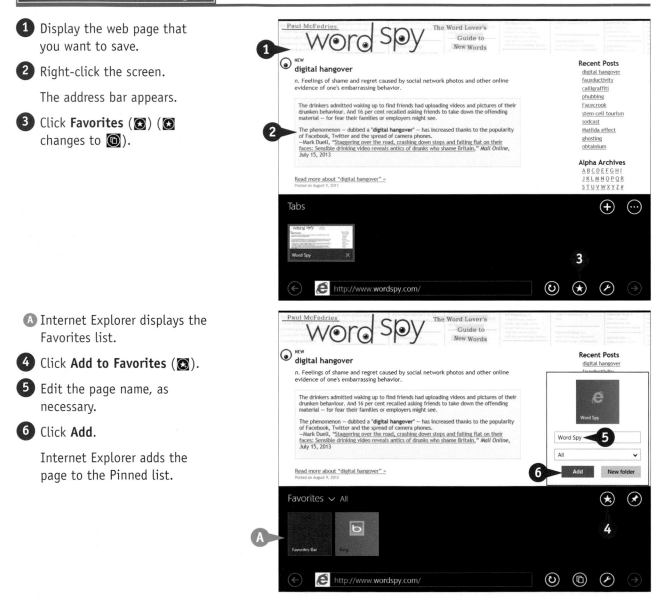

Display a Favorite Web Page

1 Right-click the screen.

The address bar appears.

2 Click **Favorites** (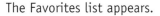).

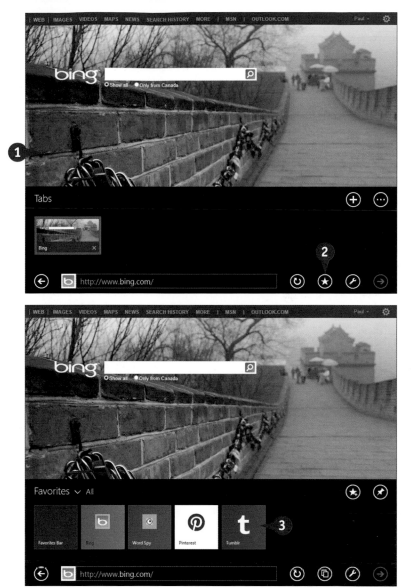

The Favorites list appears.

3 Click the web page that you want to display.

The web page appears.

TIPS

What does the Pin site button do?

You use the Pin Site button to create a tile for a web page on the Start screen. This means that you can display a pinned page in Internet Explorer by clicking its Start screen tile. To pin a page to the Start screen, navigate to the page, right-click the screen, click **Favorites** (⊙), and then click **Pin site** (⊙). Edit the page name, if desired, and then click **Pin to Start**.

How do I delete a favorite?

Right-click the screen and then click **Favorites** (⊙) to display the Favorites list. Right-click the favorite you want to delete, and then click **Remove**.

Search for Sites

If you need information on a specific topic, Internet Explorer has a built-in feature that enables you to quickly search the web for sites that have the information you require. The web has a number of sites called *search engines* that enable you to find what you are looking for. By default, Internet Explorer uses the Bing search site. You use the Internet Explorer address bar to enter a word or phrase representing the information you are seeking. Internet Explorer passes the word or phrase to Bing, which then looks for pages that match your text.

Search for Sites

1 Right-click the screen.

2 Click inside the address bar.

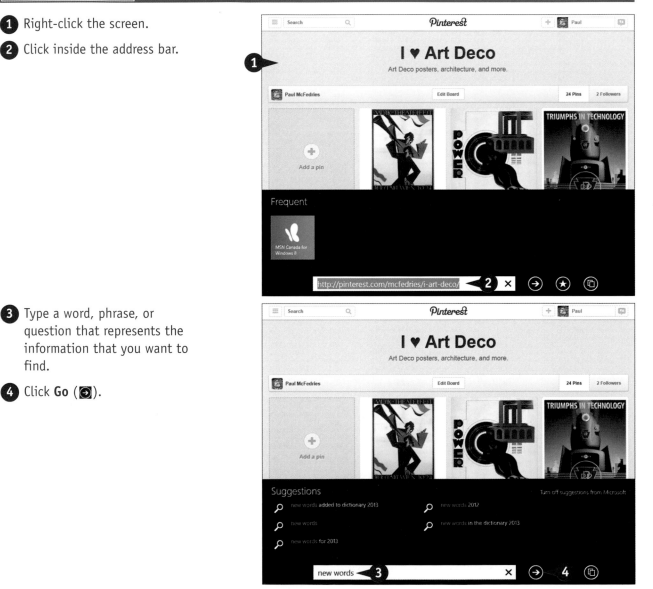

3 Type a word, phrase, or question that represents the information that you want to find.

4 Click **Go** (➡).

Ⓐ A list of pages that match your search text appears.

❺ Click a web page.

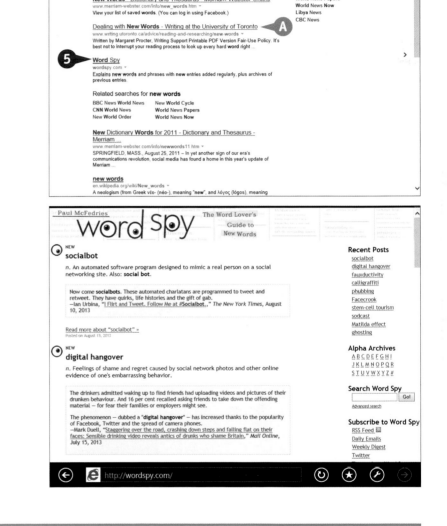

The page appears.

How can I get better search results?
Simple, one-word searches often return tens of thousands of *hits*, or matching sites. To improve your searching, type multiple search terms that define what you are looking for. To search for an exact phrase, enclose the words in quotation marks. If you want to find a page that includes one term or another, separate the two terms with the word OR (in capitals). If you want the results to exclude pages that contain a particular term, precede that term with a minus sign (–).

Download a File

Many websites make files available for you to use on your computer, so you need to know how to save them to your PC, a process known as *downloading*. Once you have downloaded a file, you can open it on your computer as long as you have an app that can work with the type of file you downloaded. For example, if the file is an Excel workbook, you need either Excel or a compatible program. You can either open the downloaded file right away, or open it later by displaying your downloaded files.

Download a File

Download and Open a File

1 Navigate to the page that contains the link to the file.

2 Click the link to the file.

Internet Explorer asks what you want to do with the file.

3 Click **Save**.

Internet Explorer downloads the file to your PC.

4 Click **Open**.

A If you do not want to work with the file right away, click **Close**, instead.

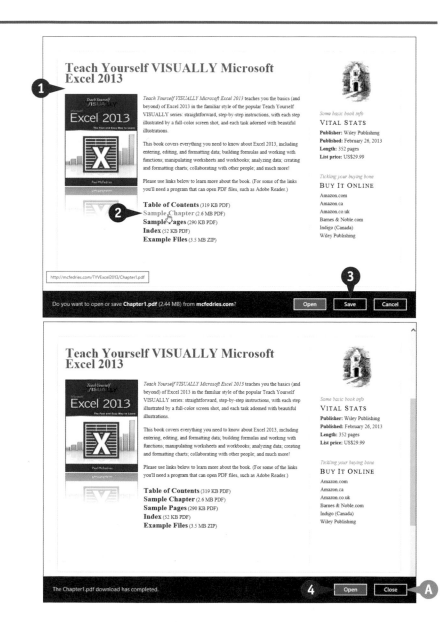

View Your Downloaded Files

1 Right-click the screen.

2 Click **Tools** (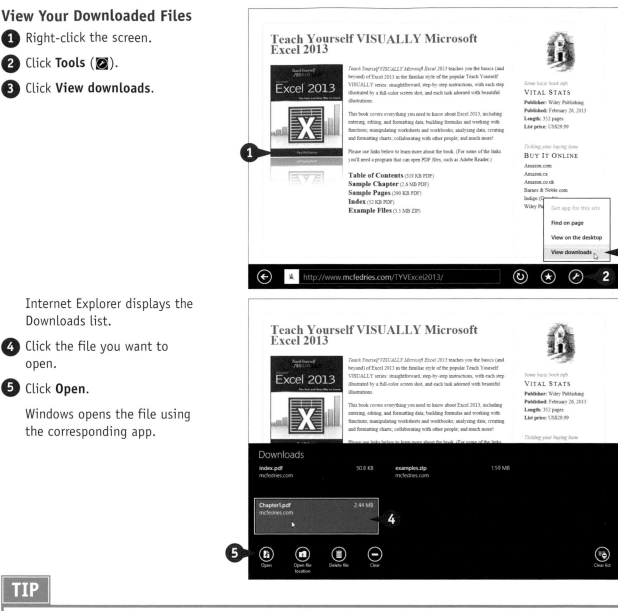).

3 Click **View downloads**.

Internet Explorer displays the Downloads list.

4 Click the file you want to open.

5 Click **Open**.

Windows opens the file using the corresponding app.

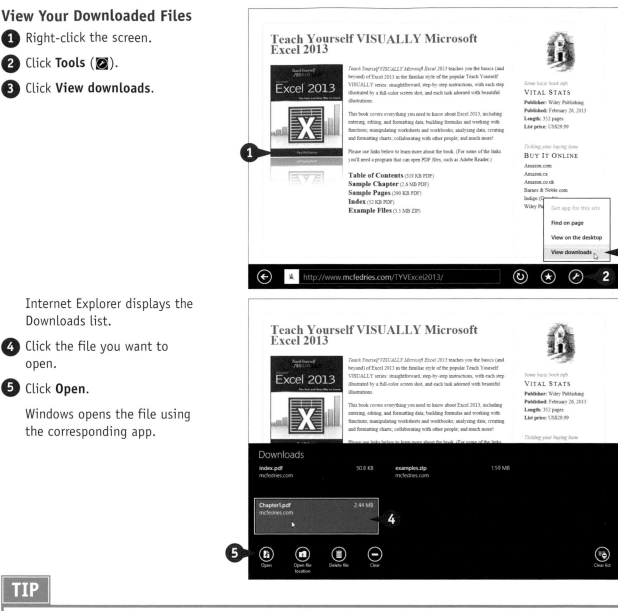

Is it safe to download files from the web?

Yes, as long as you only download files from sites you trust. If you ever notice that Internet Explorer is attempting to download a file without your permission, cancel the download immediately because it is likely that the file contains a virus or other malware.

If you do not completely trust a file that you have downloaded, use an antivirus program such as Avast! Antivirus (www.avast.com) or AVG Internet Security (http://free.avg.com/) to scan the file before you open it.

CHAPTER 5

Sending and Receiving E-mail

You can use the Mail app to work with your e-mail account. You can use Mail to send e-mail messages and file attachments. You can also use Mail to receive and read incoming messages.

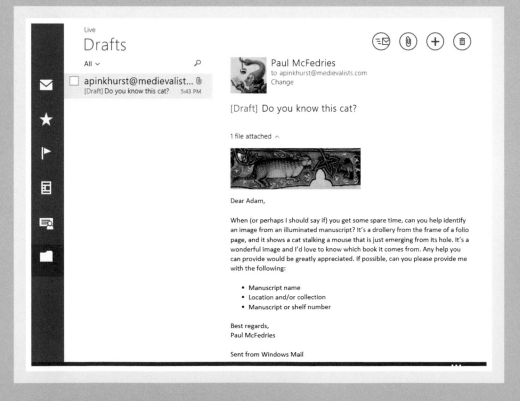

Configure an E-mail Account

Before you can send an e-mail message, you must add your e-mail account to the Mail application. This also enables you to use Mail to retrieve the messages that others have sent to your account.

You use Mail to set up web-based e-mail accounts with services such as Hotmail and Gmail. Note, however, that if you are already signing in to Windows using a Microsoft account, then Windows automatically adds that account to the Mail app — so you need to follow the steps in this section only if you want to add another account to Mail.

Configure an E-mail Account

1 On the Start screen, click **Mail** (not shown).

2 Position the mouse pointer (⏳) at the top-right corner of the screen.

The Charms menu appears.

3 Click **Settings**.

The Settings menu appears.

4 Click **Accounts**.

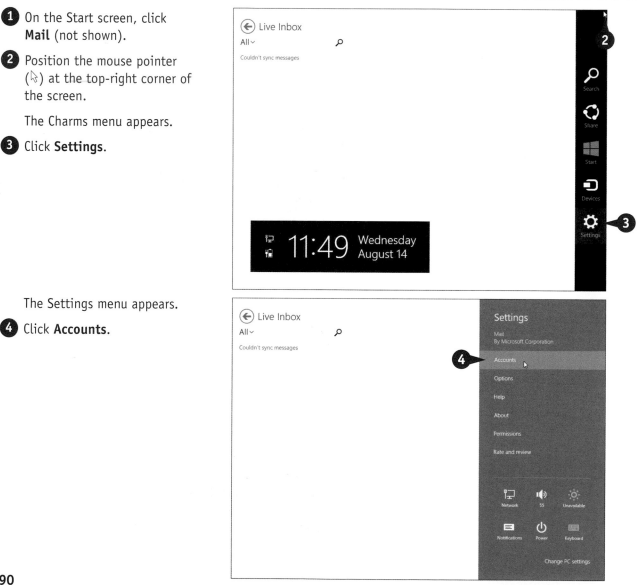

The Accounts pane appears.

 5 Click **Add an account**.

The Add an Account menu appears.

6 Click the type of account that you want to add.

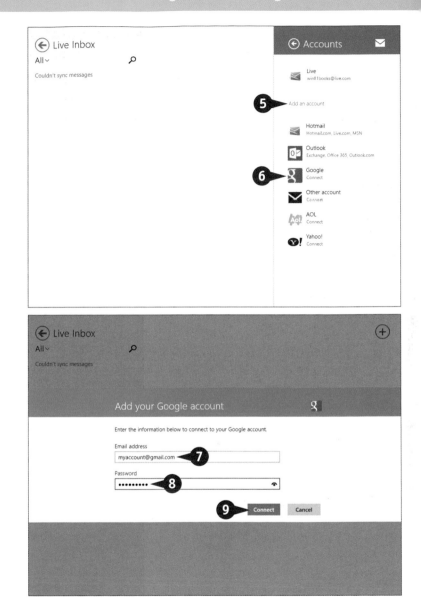

Mail asks for your account e-mail address and password.

7 Type your e-mail address.

8 Type your e-mail password.

 9 Click **Connect**.

Mail adds your e-mail account to the Accounts pane.

TIP

How do I add my Exchange account to Mail?

You will need to obtain from your Exchange administrator or provider the account's server address, domain name, and username — and you will need to know your account's e-mail address and password, of course. In many cases, you can follow steps **1** to **5**. Click **Other account**, click **Exchange ActiveSync (EAS)** (○ changes to ●), click **Connect**, follow steps **7** to **9**, and then click **Show more details**. You use the extra text boxes to enter the server address, domain, and username and then click **Connect**.

Send an E-mail Message

If you know the e-mail address of a person or organization, you can send an e-mail message to that address. Each address uniquely identifies the location of an Internet mailbox. An address takes the form *username@domain*, where *username* is the name of the person's account, and *domain* is the Internet name of the company that provides the person's e-mail account. When you send an e-mail message, it travels through your Internet service provider's (ISP) outgoing mail server. This server routes the message to the recipient's incoming mail server, which then stores the message in the recipient's mailbox.

Send an E-mail Message

1 In Mail, click **New** (⊞).

A message window appears.

2 Type the e-mail address of the recipient.

Ⓐ To send a copy of the message to another person, type that person's e-mail address in the **Cc** field.

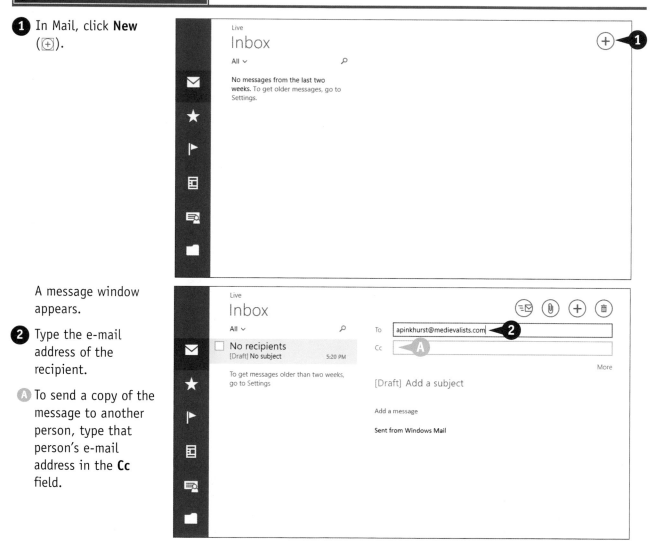

3 Type a subject for the message.

To   apinkhurst@medievalists.com

Cc

More

[Draft] Do you know this cat? **3**

Add a message

Sent from Windows Mail

4 Type the message.

Note: See the following section, "Format the Message Text," to learn how to apply formatting to your message.

5 Click **Send** (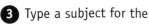).

Mail sends your message.

5

To   apinkhurst@medievalists.com

Cc

More

[Draft] Do you know this cat?

Dear Adam,

When (or perhaps I should say if) you get some spare time, can you help identify an image from an illuminated manuscript? It's a drollery from the frame of a folio page, and it shows a cat stalking a mouse that is just emerging from its hole. It's a wonderful image and I'd love to know which book it comes from. Any help you can provide would be greatly appreciated. **4**

Best regards,
Paul McFedries

Sent from Windows Mail

TIPS

Can I send my message to several people?
Yes. Besides adding a single address to each of the To and Cc lines, you can add multiple e-mail addresses to both To and Cc. After each address is complete, press Enter to begin a new line and then type the next address.

Can I send a copy to someone but not let the other recipients see that person's address?
Yes, this is known as a *blind carbon copy* (Bcc, sometimes also called a *blind courtesy copy*). To include a blind carbon copy with your message, click **More** to add the Bcc field and then use that field to type the person's address.

Format the Message Text

You can add visual interest and make your message easier to read by formatting your message text. A plain e-mail message is quick to compose, but it is often worth the extra time to add formatting to your text. For example, you can add bold or italic formatting to highlight a word or phrase. Mail supports a wide range of formatting options, including font colors, highlights, emoticons, bulleted lists, and numbered lists. All of these formatting options have their place, but be careful not to overdo it, or you may make your message *harder* to read.

Format the Message Text

1 Select the text that you want to format.

A Mail displays its formatting options.

2 Click the formatting that you want to apply to the text.

Mail applies the formatting to the text.

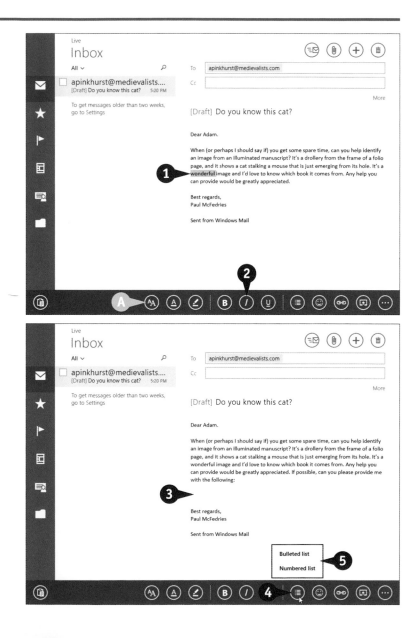

3 To add a list, right-click where you want the list to appear.

4 Click **List.**

5 Click the type of list that you want to insert.

Mail adds the bullet or number for the first item in the list. To complete the list, type each item and then press Enter. When you are done, press Enter twice.

Set the Message Priority

You can set the priority level of your outgoing message to let the recipient know whether to handle your message with a high or low priority. If you are sending a message that has important information or that requires a fast response, set the message's priority to high. When the recipient receives the message, his or her e-mail program indicates the high priority. Alternatively, you can set the priority to low for unimportant messages so that the recipient knows that she does not need to handle the message immediately.

Set the Message Priority

1 Click **More**.

To apinkhurst@medievalists.com

Cc

More ← **1**

[Draft] Do you know this cat?

Dear Adam.

When (or perhaps I should say if) you get some spare time, can you help identify an image from an illuminated manuscript? It's a drollery from the frame of a folio page, and it shows a cat stalking a mouse that is just emerging from its hole. It's a wonderful image and I'd love to know which book it comes from. Any help you can provide would be greatly appreciated. If possible, can you please provide me with the following:

- Manuscript name
- Location and/or collection
- Manuscript or shelf number

2 In the Priority list, click the priority that you want to use.

Paul McFedries
win81books@live.com

To apinkhurst@medievalists.com

Cc

Bcc | High

Priority | Normal ← **2**

| Low

[Draft] Do you know this cat?

Dear Adam.

When (or perhaps I should say if) you get some spare time, can you help identify an image from an illuminated manuscript? It's a drollery from the frame of a folio page, and it shows a cat stalking a mouse that is just emerging from its hole. It's a wonderful image and I'd love to know which book it comes from. Any help you can provide would be greatly appreciated. If possible, can you please provide me with the following:

Add a File Attachment

If you have a document that you want to send to another person, you can attach the document to an e-mail message. A typical e-mail message is fine for short notes, but you may have something more complex to communicate, such as budget numbers or a slide show, or some form of media that you want to share, such as an image or a song. Because these more complex types of data usually come in a separate file — such as a spreadsheet, presentation file, or picture file — it makes sense to send that file to your recipient as an attachment.

Add a File Attachment

1 Click **Attachments** (⬓).

The file selection screen appears.

2 Select the folder that contains the file you want to attach.

3 Click the file that you want to attach.

4 Click **Attach.**

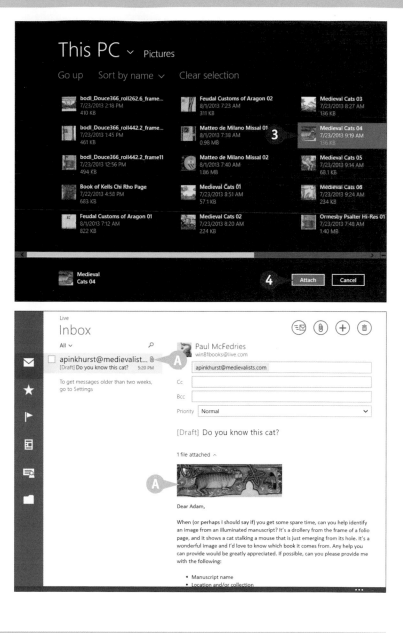

Ⓐ Mail attaches the file to the message.

Is there a limit to the number of files that I can attach to a message?
There is no practical limit to the number of files that you can attach to a message. However, you should be careful with the total *size* of the files that you send. If you or the recipient has a slow Internet connection, sending or receiving the message can take an extremely long time. Also, many Internet service providers (ISPs) place a limit on the size of a message's attachments, which is usually between 2MB and 10MB. In general, use e-mail to send only a few small files at a time.

Save a Draft of a Message

If you cannot complete or send your message right away, you can save it as a draft and open it again later. As you work on an e-mail message, you might find that you need to give it more thought or that you have to do more research. Rather than discard your work, you can close the message and have Mail save it for you. Mail stores the saved message in your account's Drafts folder. When you are ready to resume editing the message, you can open it from the Drafts folder.

Save a Draft of a Message

Save the Draft

1 Right-click the message.

2 Click **Save draft**.

Mail saves the message to your Drafts folder.

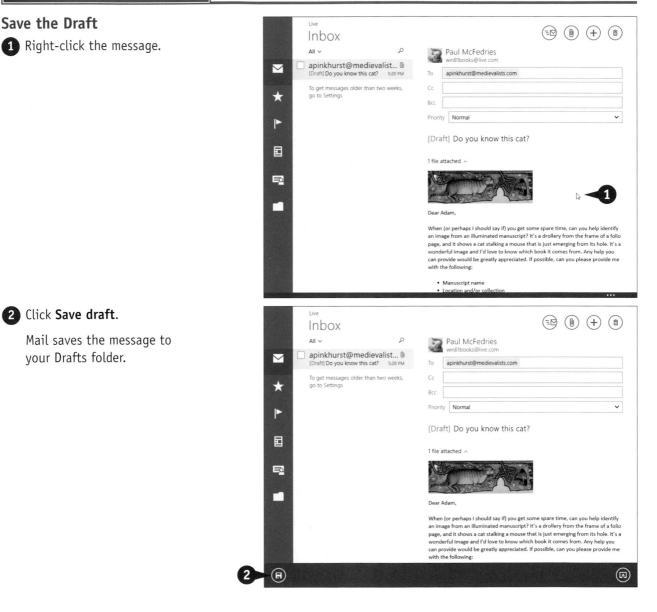

Open the Draft

1 From the Mail Inbox folder, click **Folders** (⬜).

A You can click here and then click **All** to display your saved drafts in the Inbox folder.

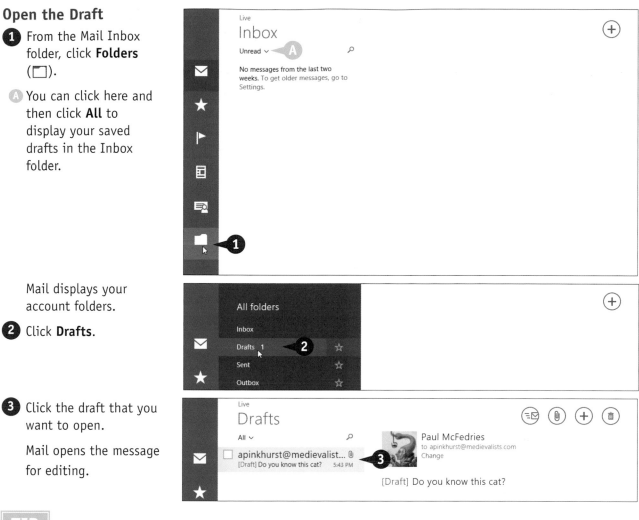

Mail displays your account folders.

2 Click **Drafts**.

3 Click the draft that you want to open.

Mail opens the message for editing.

What are the other account folders used for?

Flagged	Displays messages that you have flagged for follow-up.	Junk	Holds incoming messages that Mail has deemed to be unsolicited commercial e-mails, also known as *junk mail* or *spam*.
Sent	Holds copies of outgoing messages that you have sent.	Deleted	Holds messages that you have deleted from other folders.
Outbox	Holds outgoing messages that are in the process of being sent.	Archive	Displays messages that are more than two weeks old.

Receive and Read E-mail Messages

When another person sends you an e-mail message, the message ends up in your e-mail account's mailbox on the incoming mail server that is maintained by your ISP or e-mail provider. However, that company does not automatically pass along that message to you. Instead, you must use Mail to connect to your mailbox on the incoming mail server and then retrieve any messages waiting for you. By default, Mail automatically checks for new messages every ten minutes while you are online, but you can also check for new messages at any time.

Receive and Read E-mail Messages

Receive E-mail Messages

1 Right-click the screen.

A The application bar appears.

2 Click **More**

3 Click **Sync.**

B If you have new messages, they appear in your Inbox folder in bold type.

C A number tells you how many messages are in the conversation, which is a series of messages and replies.

D The **!** symbol means that the message was sent with a high priority.

E The ⬇ symbol means that the message was sent with a low priority.

F The ⓘ symbol means that the message has an attachment.

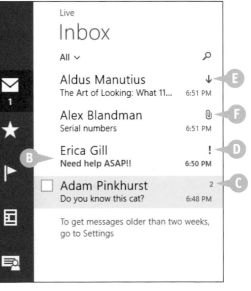

Read a Message

1 Click the message.

Live

Inbox

All ⌄   🔍

☐ **Aldus Manutius**   ↓
   The Art of Looking: What 11... 6:51 PM

Alex Blandman   📎
Serial numbers   6:51 PM

Erica Gill   !
Need help ASAP!!   6:50 PM

Adam Pinkhurst
Do you know this cat?   6:48 PM

To get messages older than two weeks,
go to Settings

Aldus Manutius   9/9/2013 6:51 PM
to Paul McFedries

Fwd: The Art of Looking: What 11 Experts Teach Us
about Seeing Our Familiar City Block with New Eyes

Paul,

I think you'll really like this...

Begin forwarded message:

**The Art of Looking: What 11 Experts Teach Us about Seeing Our Familiar City
Block with New Eyes**

http://rdd.me/9ytidhvn

(Sent from Readability)

The message text
appears in the
preview pane.

2 Read the message
text.

Live

Inbox

All ⌄   🔍

Aldus Manutius   ↓
The Art of Looking: What 11... 6:51 PM

Alex Blandman   📎
Serial numbers   6:51 PM

Erica Gill   !
Need help ASAP!!   6:50 PM

☐ **Adam Pinkhurst**
   Do you know this cat?   6:48 PM

To get messages older than two weeks,
go to Settings

Adam Pinkhurst   9/9/2013 6:48 PM
to Paul McFedries

Re: Do you know this cat?

Hi Paul,

Nice to hear from you and I'm happy to help. I do, indeed, know this cat. It comes
from a manuscript called The Ormesby Psalter, produced ca. 1300, now residing
in the Bodleian Library at the University of Oxford, where it's shelved as MS.
Douce 366. The cat resides on folio 131 recto.

I hope this helps!

Cheers,
Adam

On 2013-09-9, at 1:03 PM, Paul McFedries wrote:

Dear Adam,

TIP

Why do new messages sometimes appear in my Inbox when I have not clicked the Sync button?
For specific types of accounts, Mail supports a feature called *push* that can send new messages to your
Inbox automatically. In this case, when the mail server receives a new message, it immediately sends the
message to your Inbox without your having to run the Sync command. Note that this feature works only if
you are using a Hotmail, Live.com, or Outlook.com e-mail account.

Reply to a Message

When a message you receive requires some kind of response — whether it is answering a question, supplying information, or providing comments — you can reply to that message. Most replies go only to the person who sent the original message. However, you can also send the reply to all the people who were included in the original message's To and Cc lines. Mail includes the text of the original message in the reply, but you might want to edit the original message text to include only enough of the original message to put your reply into context.

Reply to a Message

1 Click the message to which you want to reply.

2 Click **Respond** (⤺).

3 Click the reply type that you want to use.

A message window appears.

A Mail automatically inserts the sender of the original message as the recipient.

B Mail also inserts the subject line, preceded by "Re:."

C Mail includes the original message's addresses (To and From), date, subject, and text at the bottom of the reply.

④ Edit the original message to include only the text relevant to your reply.

⑤ Click the area above the original message text.

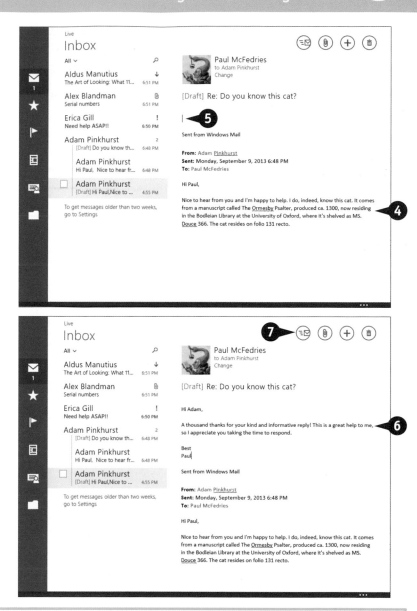

⑥ Type your reply.

⑦ Click **Send** (🖅).

Mail sends your reply.

Mail stores a copy of your reply in the Sent folder.

What is the difference between Reply and Reply all?

Reply responds to the sender only. Reply all responds to both the sender and the revealed recipients of the e-mail. You can click **Reply** to respond only to the person who sent the message, or click **Reply all** to respond to the sender as well as any other addresses in the fields.

Do I have to edit the original message text when I am composing my reply?

If the original message is short, you usually do not need to edit the text. However, if the original message is long, and your response deals only with part of that message, you will save the recipient time by deleting everything except the relevant portion of the text.

Forward a Message

If a message has information that is relevant to or concerns another person, you can forward a copy of the message to that person. You can also include your own comments in the forward.

In the body of the forward, Mail includes the original message's addresses, date, and subject line. Below this information, Mail also includes the text of the original message. In most cases, you will leave the entire message intact so that your recipient can see it. However, if only part of the message is relevant to the recipient, you should edit the original message accordingly.

Forward a Message

1 Click the message that you want to forward.

2 Click **Respond** (⊜).

3 Click **Forward**.

A message window appears.

Ⓐ Mail inserts the subject line, preceded by "Fw:."

Ⓑ The original message's addresses (To and From), date, subject, and text are included at the bottom of the forward.

4 Select or type the e-mail address of the person to whom you are forwarding the message.

Ⓒ To send a copy of the message to another person, select or type that person's e-mail address in the **Cc** field.

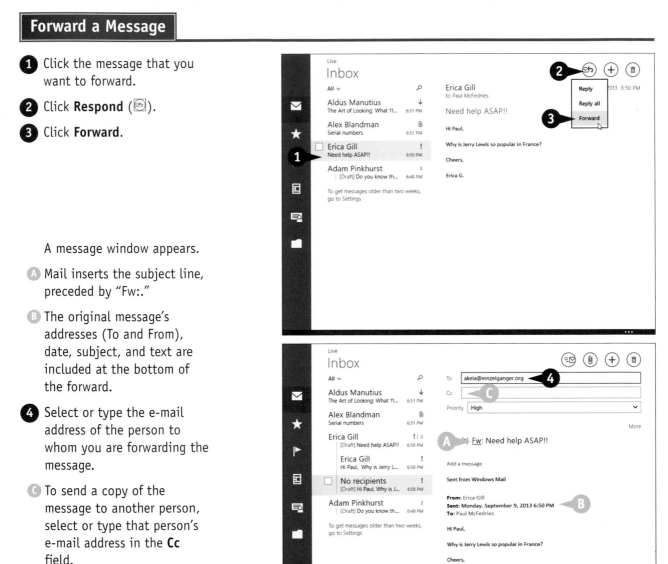

5 If necessary, edit the original message to include only the text relevant to your forward.

6 Click the area above the original message text.

Live

Inbox

All ⌄   🔍

Aldus Manutius   ↓
The Art of Looking: What 11...   6:51 PM

Alex Blandman   📎
Serial numbers   6:51 PM

Erica Gill   ! | 2
[Draft] Need help ASAP!!   6:50 PM

    Erica Gill   !
    Hi Paul, Why is Jerry L...   6:50 PM

☐ No recipients   !
[Draft] Hi Paul, Why is J...   4:58 PM

Adam Pinkhurst   2
[Draft] Do you know th...   6:48 PM

To get messages older than two weeks, go to Settings

To   akela@einzelganger.org

Cc

Priority   High   ⌄

More

[Draft] <u>Fw</u>: Need help ASAP!!

|

Sent from Windows Mail

From: Erica Gill
Sent: Monday, September 9, 2013 6:50 PM
To: Paul McFedries

Hi Paul,

Why is Jerry Lewis so popular in France?

Cheers,

Erica G.

7 Type your comments.

8 Click **Send** (🖃).

Mail sends your forward.

Mail stores a copy of your forward in the Sent Items folder.

Live

Inbox

All ⌄   🔍

Aldus Manutius   ↓
The Art of Looking: What 11...   6:51 PM

Alex Blandman   📎
Serial numbers   6:51 PM

Erica Gill   ! | 2
[Draft] Need help ASAP!!   6:50 PM

    Erica Gill   !
    Hi Paul, Why is Jerry L...   6:50 PM

☐ No recipients   !
[Draft] Hi Paul, Why is J...   4:58 PM

Adam Pinkhurst   2
[Draft] Do you know th...   6:48 PM

To get messages older than two weeks, go to Settings

To   akela@einzelganger.org

Cc

Priority   High   ⌄

More

[Draft] <u>Fw</u>: Need help ASAP!!

Hi Akela,

Care to answer this one?

Cheers,
Paul

Sent from Windows Mail

From: Erica Gill
Sent: Monday, September 9, 2013 6:50 PM
To: Paul McFedries

Hi Paul,

Why is Jerry Lewis so popular in France?

Cheers,

Erica G.

TIP

Why does Mail sometimes set the priority of a forward or reply?
Mail forwards or replies to a message using the same priority as the original. This is rarely useful, so in most cases, you will want to set the priority to Normal before sending the forward or reply. To do this, click the **Priority** ☑ and then click **Normal**.

Open and Save an Attachment

When a message comes in and displays the attachment symbol (a paper clip), it means that the sender has included a file as an attachment to the message. If you just want to take a quick look at the file, you can open the attachment directly from Mail. Alternatively, if you want to keep a copy of the file on your computer, you can save the attachment to your hard drive.

Be careful when dealing with attached files. Computer viruses are often transmitted by e-mail attachments.

Open and Save an Attachment

Open an Attachment

1 Click the message that has the attachment, as indicated by a paper clip icon (📎).

A A list of the message attachments appears.

2 Click the attachment that you want to open.

The file opens in the appropriate program.

Note: Instead of opening the file, you may see a message that says, "Windows can't open this type of file." This means that you need to install the appropriate program for the type of file. If you are not sure, ask the person who sent you the file what program you need.

Save an Attachment

① Click the message that has the attachment, as indicated by a paper clip icon (📎).

Ⓑ A list of the message attachments appears.

② Right-click the attachment that you want to save.

③ Click **Save.**

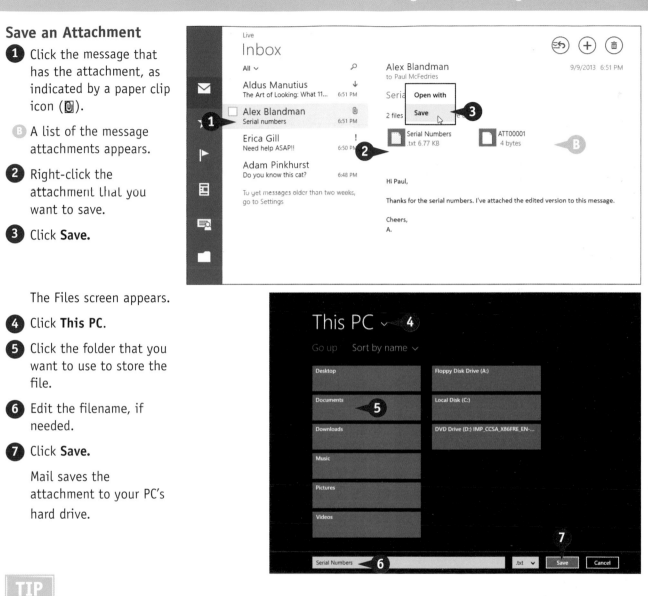

The Files screen appears.

④ Click **This PC.**

⑤ Click the folder that you want to use to store the file.

⑥ Edit the filename, if needed.

⑦ Click **Save.**

Mail saves the attachment to your PC's hard drive.

TIP

Can I open an attachment using some other program than the one Mail chooses?
Yes. When you click the attachment, Mail automatically opens the file in the app associated with that type of file. For example, text files open in the Notepad app. However, you can tell Mail to open the file using a different app, if you prefer. Click the message that contains the attachment, right-click the attachment that you want to open, and then click **Open with**. Mail displays a list of apps that you can use to open the file. Click the app that you want to use. If you do not see the app that you want, click **More options** to expand the list.

Delete a Message

After you have used Mail for a while, you may find that you have many messages in your Inbox folder. The more messages you have, the more time-consuming it is to navigate the messages and find the message that you want. To keep the Inbox uncluttered and easier to navigate, you should delete any messages that you have already read and do not need to keep.

Note that when you delete a message, Mail actually sends it to the Deleted folder. If you delete a message accidentally, you can retrieve it from the Deleted folder.

Delete a Message

Delete a Message from the Inbox

1 Click the message that you want to delete.

2 Click **Delete** (🗑).

Mail removes the message from the Inbox and moves it to the Deleted folder.

Restore a Deleted Message

1 Click **Folders** (🗀).

Mail displays the folders list.

2 Click **Deleted**.

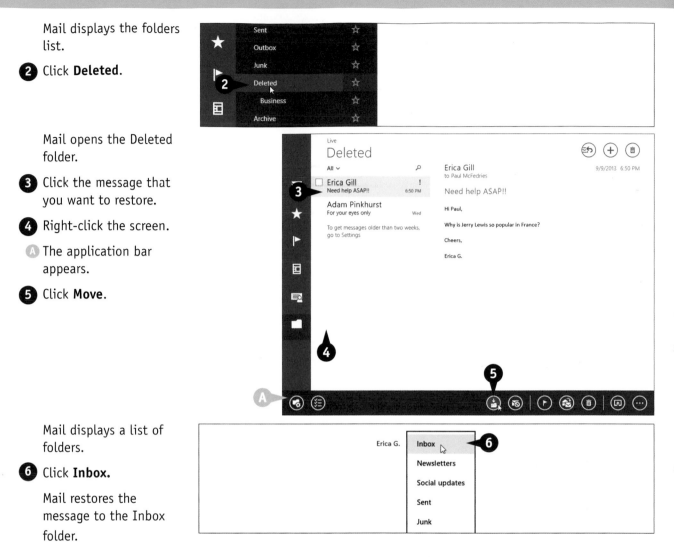

Mail opens the Deleted folder.

3 Click the message that you want to restore.

4 Right-click the screen.

Ⓐ The application bar appears.

5 Click **Move**.

Mail displays a list of folders.

6 Click **Inbox.**

Mail restores the message to the Inbox folder.

TIP

Can I restore more than one message at a time?

Yes, you can restore as many messages as you want. With the Deleted folder displayed, hold down the `Ctrl` key and click each message you want to restore. If you want to restore all the messages, right-click the screen and then click **Select all** (or press `Ctrl`+`A`). Follow steps **4** to **6** to restore the selected messages.

Create a Folder for Saving Messages

After you have used Mail for a while, you may find that you have many messages in your Inbox folder. To keep the Inbox uncluttered, you can create new folders and then move messages from the Inbox to the new folders.

To help keep your messages organized, you should use each folder you create to save related messages. For example, you could create separate folders for people you correspond with regularly, projects you are working on, different work departments, and so on. By saving each message to the appropriate folder, you make it easier to find your messages in the future.

Create a Folder for Saving Messages

Create a Folder

1 Right-click the screen.

2 Click **Manage folders** (icon).

3 Click **Create folder**.

The Create folder dialog box appears.

4 Type the name of the new folder.

5 Click **OK**.

Mail creates the new folder.

6 Click **OK** (not shown).

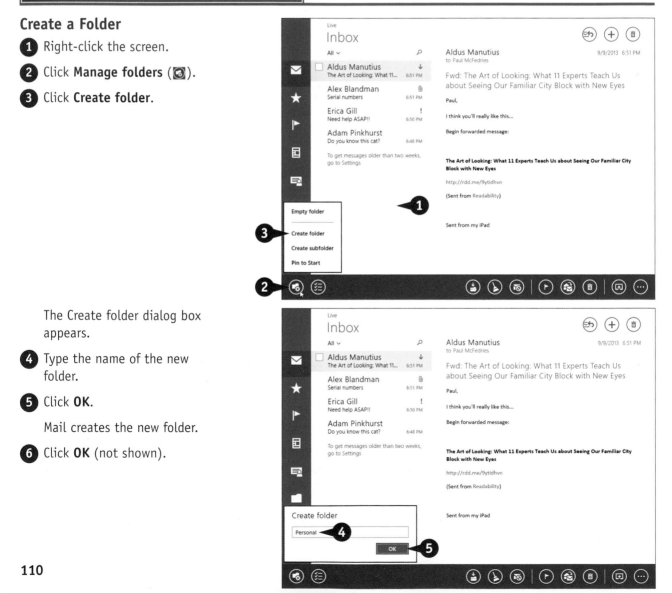

Move a Message to Another Folder

1 Click the message you want to move.

2 Right-click the screen.

3 Click **Move**.

Mail displays the list of folders.

4 Click the folder you want to use as the destination.

Mail moves the message.

TIPS

How do I rename a folder?

Click **Folders** (📁) to display the list of Mail folders, click the folder you want to rename, click **Manage folders** (⚙️), and then click **Rename folder**. In the dialog box that appears, type the new name and then click **OK**. Note that Mail only allows you to rename folders that you have created.

How do I delete a folder?

Click **Folders** (📁) to display the list of Mail folders, right-click the folder you want to delete, click **Manage folders** (⚙️), and then click **Delete folder**. Note that Mail only allows you to delete folders that you have created. Remember, too, that when you delete a folder, you also delete any messages stored in that folder.

CHAPTER 6

Getting Social with Windows

You can use Windows to manage your social schedule. You can use the People app to store contact information, connect to social networks, and keep track of friends. You can use the Calendar app to schedule meetings, appointments, and other events.

October 2013

Sunday	Monday	Tuesday	Wednesday	Thursday	Friday	Saturday
29	30	1	2	3	4	5
Ed Bott's birth... Running... 9AM						Glen Moore's... Iain Switzer's...
6	7	8	9	10	11	12
Running... 9AM						
13	14	15	16	17	18	19
Running... 9AM	Olivia Mellan'... Columbus Day					
20	21	22	23	24	25	26
Running... 9AM			Bob Mecoy's...			
27	28	29	30	31	1	2
Graeme McFe... Running... 9AM	Book Club... 4PM	Gord Naunton...		Halloween		

Create a Contact

You can easily store information about your friends, family, and colleagues, as well as send messages to them, by using the People app to create a contact for each person. Each contact can store a wide variety of information, such as a person's first and last names, company name, e-mail address, phone number, and street address.

If you already have contacts on a social network such as Facebook or LinkedIn, you do not need to enter those contacts manually. Instead, you can connect your social network account to your Microsoft account, as described in the next few sections.

Create a Contact

① On the Start screen, click **People**.

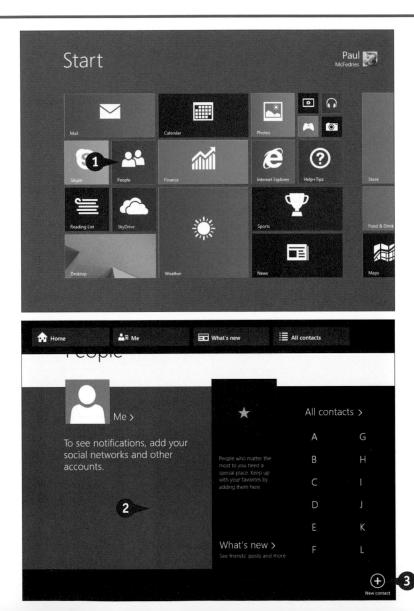

The People app loads.

② Right-click the screen.

③ Click **New contact**.

The New contact screen appears.

4 Type the contact's first name.

5 Type the contact's last name.

6 Type the contact's company name.

7 Click the **Email** label and then click the type of e-mail address that you want to enter.

8 Type the contact's e-mail address.

9 Click the **Phone** label and then click the type of phone number that you want to enter.

10 Type the contact's phone number.

11 To add an address for the contact, click the **Add** button (⊕).

Ⓐ To add another field for the contact, click ⊕, click a label, and then type the data in the field that appears.

12 Click **Save** (🖫).

The People app creates the new contact.

New contact 🖫 ✕

Account
Live ⌄

Name

First name
Robert ◄4

Last name
Cotton ◄5

Company
The Cottonian Bookshop ◄6

⊕ Name

Email
7► Work ⌄
rbcotton@cottonianbooks.com ◄8

⊕ Email

Phone
Mobile ⌄

⊕ Phone

Address
⊕ Address

Other info
⊕ Other info

New contact 12► 🖫 ✕

Account
Live ⌄

Name

First name
Robert

Last name
Cotton

Company
The Cottonian Bookshop

⊕ Name

Email
Work ⌄
rbcotton@cottonianbooks.com

⊕ Email

Phone
9► Mobile ⌄
317-555-8642 ◄10 ✕

⊕ Phone
Ⓐ

Address
11► ⊕ Address

Other info
⊕ Other info

TIPS

Is there an easy way to send an e-mail to a contact?

Yes. Normally, you would use the Mail app, as described in Chapter 5. If you are already working in the People app, however, it is easier to click the person's tile to open the contact and then click **Send email**.

Are there other types of information that I can record for a contact?

Yes, you can also add notes, the contact's job title, the contact's website address, and the name of the contact's significant other. To add one of these categories, click the **Other info** ⊕, click the category you want to add, and then type the information in the field that appears.

Connect to Facebook

If you are using a Microsoft account with Windows, you can connect your Facebook account to your Microsoft account and see your Facebook friends in the People app. To do so, you must tell Facebook that you give permission to connect your Microsoft and Facebook accounts.

After you have connected your accounts, you can use the People app to view your friends' Facebook profiles, see the latest status updates and photos from your Facebook friends, and send messages to online Facebook friends.

Connect to Facebook

1 On the Start screen, click **People** (not shown).

The People app loads.

2 Click **Connected to**.

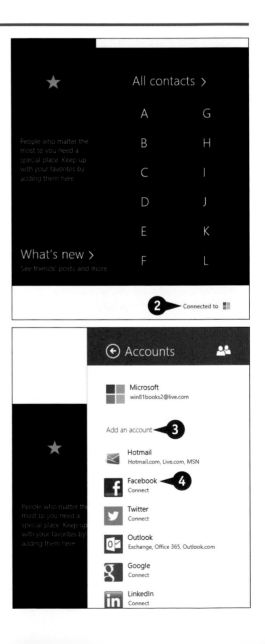

The Accounts pane appears.

3 Click **Add an account**.

4 Click **Facebook**.

The People app displays a description of the Facebook connection.

5 Click **Connect**.

See your Facebook friends and their updates here, and in other apps and websites where you use this Microsoft account. Just connect **Facebook** to win81books@live.com.

What else happens when I connect? ⌄

5 → Connect   Cancel

Facebook prompts you to log in to your account.

6 Type your Facebook e-mail address.

7 Type your Facebook password.

8 Select the **Keep me logged in** check box (☐ changes to ☑).

9 Click **Log In**.

f Facebook

Log in to use your Facebook account with Microsoft.

Email or Phone: myfb@myisp.com ← **6**

Password: ●●●●●●●●●●●● ← **7**

8 → ☑ Keep me logged in

Forgot your password?

Sign up for Facebook   **9** → Log In   Cancel

Windows connects your Facebook account to your Microsoft account.

10 Click **Done**.

If Windows asks for permission to remember your Facebook sign-in name and password, click **Yes**.

10 → Done

TIP

Can I interact with the Facebook messages that I receive in the People app?
Yes. See the section, "View Your Contacts' Activities," later in this chapter to learn how to view Facebook posts. To like a Facebook post, locate it and then click **Like**. To comment on a Facebook post, locate it, click **Comment**, type your feedback, and then click **Comment**.

Connect to Twitter

If you are using a Microsoft account with Windows, you can connect your Twitter account to your Microsoft account and see the people that you follow in the People app. To do so, you must tell Twitter that you give permission to connect your Microsoft and Twitter accounts.

After you have connected your accounts, you can use the People app to view the Twitter profiles of the people you follow, see their latest tweets, retweet posts, and send replies.

Connect to Twitter

 On the Start screen, click **People** (not shown).

The People app loads.

 Click **Connected to**.

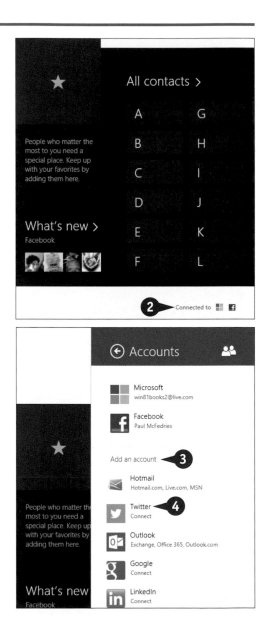

The Accounts pane appears.

3 Click **Add an account**.

4 Click **Twitter**.

The People app displays a description of the Twitter connection.

5 Click **Connect**.

See your Twitter contacts and their Tweets here, and in other apps and websites where you use this Microsoft account. Just connect **Twitter** to win81books@live.com.

What else happens when I connect? ⌄

5 ➤ Connect   Cancel

Twitter prompts you to authorize the connection.

6 Type your Twitter username.

7 Type your Twitter password.

8 Select the **Remember me** check box (☐ changes to ☑).

9 Click **Authorize app**.

use your account?

This application **will be able to:**

- Read Tweets from your timeline.
- See who you follow, and follow new people.
- Update your profile.
- Post Tweets for you.

Microsoft
By Microsoft Corporation
www.microsoft.com/

Application for connecting Microsoft products to Twitter

paulmcf **6**

•••••••••••• **7**

8 ☑ Remember me · Forgot password?

Sign up for Twitter   **9** ➤ Authorize app ⌄

Windows connects your Twitter account to your Microsoft account.

10 Click **Done**.

If Windows asks for permission to remember your Twitter sign-in name and password, click **Yes**.

10 ➤ Done

TIP

Can I interact with the Twitter messages that I receive in the People app?
Yes. See the section, "View Your Contacts' Activities," later in this chapter to learn how to view Twitter messages. To retweet a post, locate it and then click **Retweet**. To set a tweet as a favorite, locate it and then click **Favorite**. To send a message to the person who posted a tweet, locate the tweet, click **Reply**, type your message, and then click **Reply**.

Connect to LinkedIn

If you are using a Microsoft account with Windows, you can connect your LinkedIn account to your Microsoft account and see your LinkedIn connections in the People app. To do so, you must tell LinkedIn that you give permission to connect your Microsoft and LinkedIn accounts.

After you have connected your accounts, you can use the People app to view the LinkedIn profiles of the people to whom you are connected. You can also send an e-mail message to a connection and map a connection's address.

Connect to LinkedIn

1 On the Start screen, click **People** (not shown).

The People app loads.

2 Click **Connected to**.

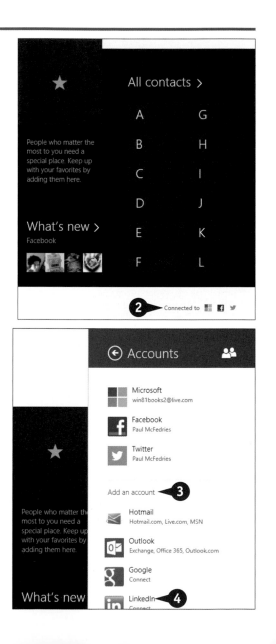

The Accounts pane appears.

3 Click **Add an account**.

4 Click **LinkedIn**.

The People app displays a description of the LinkedIn connection.

5 Click **Connect**.

See your LinkedIn contacts here, and in other apps and websites where you use this Microsoft account. Just connect **LinkedIn** to **win81books@live.com**.

What else happens when I connect? ⌄

LinkedIn prompts you to authorize the connection.

6 Type your LinkedIn e-mail address.

7 Type your LinkedIn password.

8 Click **Ok, I'll Allow It**.

If you see a security check screen, type the words you see displayed and then click **Continue**.

Windows connects your LinkedIn account to your Microsoft account.

9 Click **Done**.

If Windows asks for permission to remember your LinkedIn sign-in name and password, click **Yes**.

5 ► Connect   Cancel

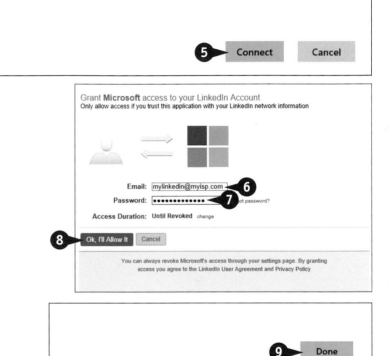

Grant **Microsoft** access to your LinkedIn Account
Only allow access if you trust this application with your LinkedIn network information

Email: mylinkedin@myisp.com **6**
Password: ••••••••••• **7** ot password?
Access Duration: Until Revoked change

8 ► Ok, I'll Allow It   Cancel

You can always revoke Microsoft's access through your settings page. By granting access you agree to the LinkedIn User Agreement and Privacy Policy

9 ► Done

TIPS

Can I adjust the permissions set up between my Microsoft account and a social networking account?
Yes. Open the People app, click **Connected to**, click the account that you want to adjust, and then click **Manage this account online**. Use the check boxes to turn permissions on (☑) and off (☐) and then click **Save**.

How do I disconnect a social network?
Open the People app, click **Connected to**, click the account that you want to remove, click **Manage this account online**, click **Remove this connection completely**, and then click **Remove**.

Add Your Google Account

You can add your Google account to Windows to access your Google contacts, e-mail, and calendar from your Windows computer. To do so, you must provide Windows with your Google account login data.

After you have added your Google account, you can use the People app to view your Google contacts. You can use the Calendar app to view your Google events and appointments, and you can use the Mail app to view your Gmail messages.

Add Your Google Account

 1 On the Start screen, click **People** (not shown).

The People app loads.

2 Click **Connected to**.

The Accounts pane appears.

 3 Click **Add an account**.

4 Click **Google**.

The People app displays a description of the Google connection.

 Click **Connect**.

See your Google friends here, and in other apps and websites where you use this Microsoft account. Just connect **Google** to **win81books@live.com**.

What else happens when I connect? ∨

⑤ ▸ Connect   Cancel

The People app prompts you for your Google login data.

⑥ Type your Google e-mail address.

⑦ Type your Google password.

⑧ Click **Sign in**.

The People app shows you what it will do with your Google data.

⑨ Click **Accept**.

Windows connects your Google account to your Microsoft account.

 Click **Done** (not shown).

If Windows asks for permission to remember your Google sign-in name and password, click **Yes**.

Google   SIGN UP

Sign in   Google

Email
mygoogle@gmail.com ◂ ⑥

Password
•••••••••••• ◂ ⑦

⑧ ▸ Sign in

Can't access your account?

This app would like to:

8 Manage your contacts   ⓘ

8 View basic information about your account ⓘ

Microsoft and Google will use this information in accordance with their respective terms of service and privacy policies.

c ⑨ Accept

TIP

Can I control what type of Google content appears in Windows?
Yes, you can configure the type of content to synchronize between Google and Windows and how much of that content to sync. In the People app, click **Connected to**, click **Google**, and then click **Manage this account online**.

View a Contact

After you have added contacts and connected your other accounts to Windows, you can use the People app to view your contacts. The information that you see when you view a contact depends on how the contact was added to Windows 8. If you added the contact yourself, you see the information that you entered. If the contact was added by connecting another account to Windows, you see the data provided by that account. After you have a contact displayed, you can edit the contact's data to update existing information or add new information.

View a Contact

View a Contact

1 On the Start screen, click **People** (not shown).

The People app loads.

2 Click **All contacts**.

A You can also click the letter that corresponds to the first letter of the contact's first name.

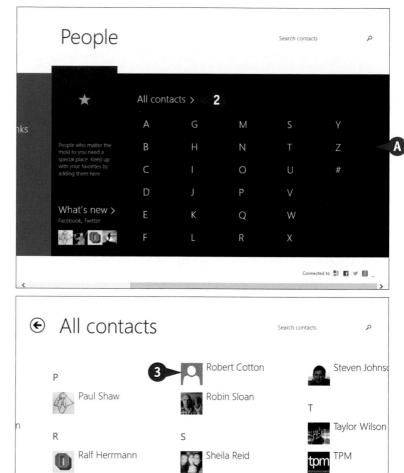

3 Click the contact.

The People app displays the contact's data.

Note: When you are done with the contact, click the **Back** button (⊙) to return to the main People screen.

Edit a Contact

1 Right-click the screen.

2 Click **Edit**.

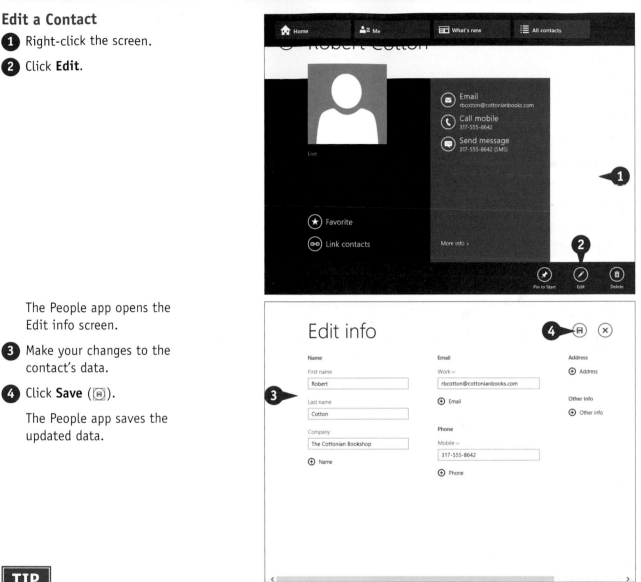

The People app opens the Edit info screen.

3 Make your changes to the contact's data.

4 Click **Save** (💾).

The People app saves the updated data.

TIP

Is there an easier way to view a contact that I use frequently?

Yes, the People app gives you a couple of methods for quickly accessing frequently used contacts. Follow steps **1** to **3** in the "View a Contact" subsection to open the contact and then right-click the screen. Click **Pin to Start**, edit the contact name as necessary, and then click **Pin to Start**. This adds a tile for the contact to the Start screen.

Alternatively, follow steps **1** to **3** in the "View a Contact" subsection to open the contact, right-click the screen, and then click **Favorite**. This adds the contact to the beginning of the People tab.

View Your Contacts' Activities

After you have connected your Microsoft account to one or more social network accounts, you can use the People app to view contact activities such as Facebook posts and photos and Twitter updates. When designing the Windows Start screen, one of the goals of Microsoft was to give you a single place that shows you what is happening in your life. The People app can show you the latest messages from your social networks. You can view these messages using the People tile, or you can open the People app and view messages for all contacts or just a single contact.

View Your Contacts' Activities

View All Contacts' Activities

1 In the People app, click **What's new**.

A Your contacts' latest messages appear.

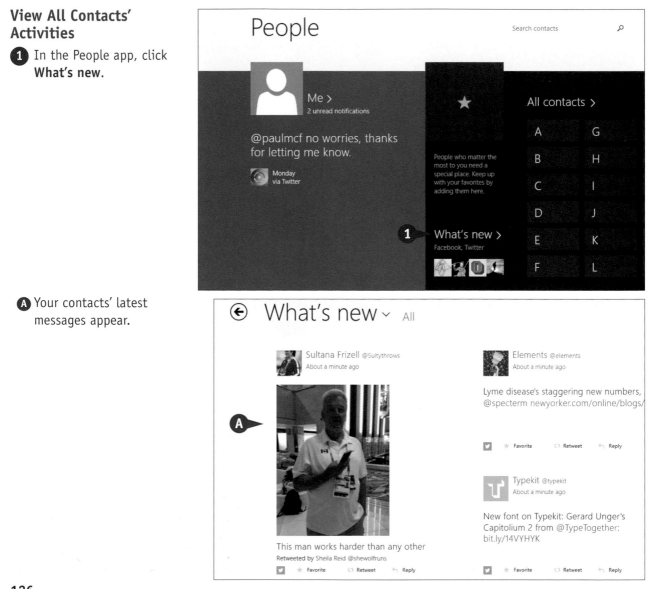

View One Contact's Activities

1 In the People app, click the contact.

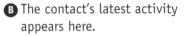

People

All

A
Alex Witchel

1 Alphabout

Amira Skomorows...

C
Cam Levins

Clerk of Oxford

Cooper-Hewitt

Cooper-Hewitt La...

D
D.T. Max

Discarding Images

B The contact's latest activity appears here.

2 Click **What's new** to see more activities.

What's new > **2**

Twitter

@Alphabout

0/140

Alphabout @Alphabout
8/6/2013

B New X posts! Judge them!
alphabout.com

Favorite   Retweet   Reply

TIPS

Can I see a friend's Facebook photos in the People app?

Yes, the People app shows each friend's Facebook photo albums. To view a friend's Facebook photos, open the contact for your Facebook friend, scroll to the Photos section, and then click the album that you want to view.

Can I view a contact's Facebook or Twitter profile?

Yes. In the What's New section, click the person's name or Twitter handle to open his or her data screen. Otherwise, use the People section to click the contact. Then click **View profile** to switch to Internet Explorer and display the contact's profile.

View Your Social Networking Activity

After you have connected your Microsoft account to one or more social network accounts, you can use the People app to view your recent social networking activity.

Your social networking activity includes your Facebook status updates, posts, and photos, as well as your Twitter updates and retweets. Your activity also includes any notifications that a social networking service sends you. These notifications include comments on your Facebook posts, Twitter mentions, and service messages.

View Your Social Networking Activity

① Open the People app.

Ⓐ If you are viewing the People app's Home screen, this number tells you how many of your recent updates you have yet to view.

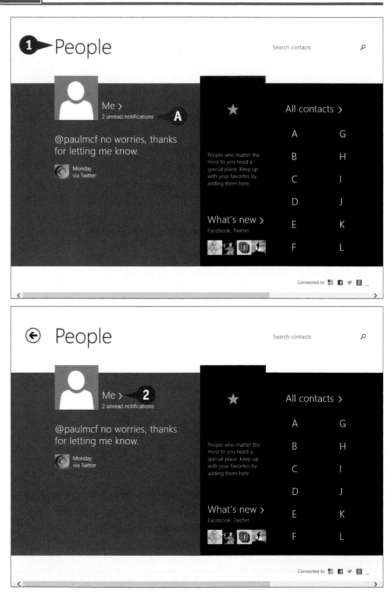

② Click **Me.**

Note: From any People app screen, you can also right-click the screen and then click **Me** in the app bar.

B Your latest social network post appears here.

C Click **What's new** to see all your recent posts.

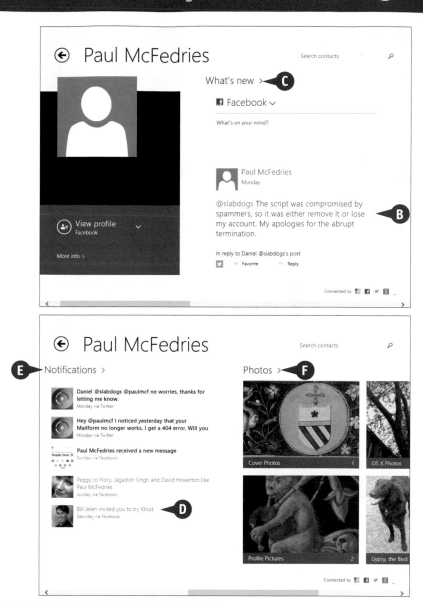

D The Notifications section shows the most recent notifications sent by your social networks.

E Click **Notifications** to see all your recent notifications.

F The Photos section shows your social network photo albums.

TIPS

Can I use the People app to post a message on a friend's Facebook wall?

Yes. Open the People app, click the friend to open that contact's screen, and then scroll to the What's New section. In the Facebook text box, type your message, and then click **Send** (⊞).

Is there an easy way to view my notifications as they appear on the social network?

Yes. Open the People app, right-click the screen, and then click **Me** to open your social information. Scroll to the Notifications section and click the notification you want to view. Windows splits the screen between the People app and Internet Explorer, and uses Internet Explorer to display the notification on the social network.

Post a Link to a Social Network

If you come across an interesting, useful, or entertaining web page, you can share that page by posting the link to a social network. Windows does not offer any way to post a text-only Facebook status update or tweet. However, you can use the Share feature to post links to interesting web pages. You can post a link and a short message describing the web page to your Facebook feed or to your Twitter followers.

Post a Link to a Social Network

1 Use Internet Explorer to open the web page that you want to share.

2 Position the mouse pointer (⬚) in the top-right corner of the screen.

The Charms menu appears.

3 Click **Share**.

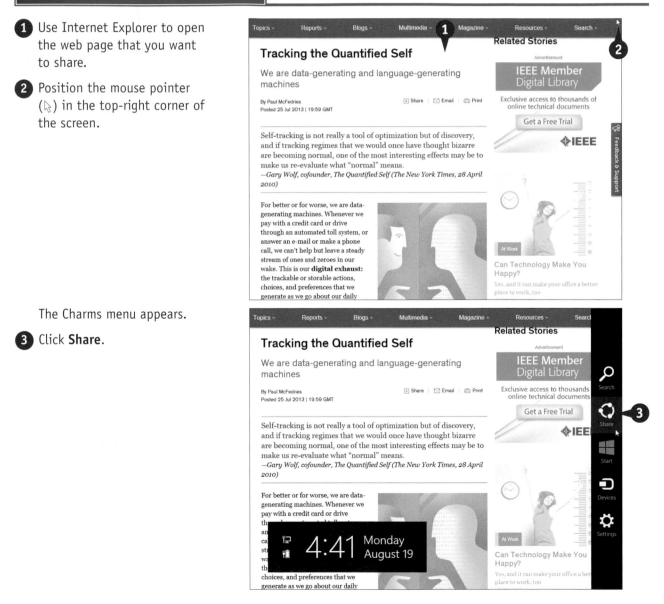

The Share pane appears.

4 Click **People**.

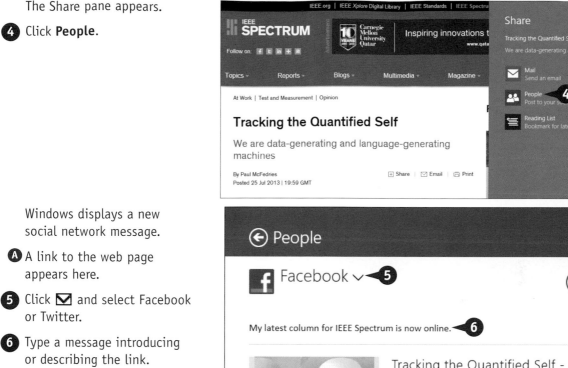

Windows displays a new social network message.

A A link to the web page appears here.

5 Click ☑ and select Facebook or Twitter.

6 Type a message introducing or describing the link.

7 Click **Send** (⊕).

Windows posts the link to the social network.

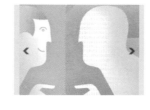

Can I share other types of content in addition to links to my social networks?

Yes, several other apps support sharing data to Facebook and Twitter. For example, you can use the Music app to open an album — either one of your own or one in the store — and then post information about the artist to your friends or followers. You can also use the Video app to share information about a movie or TV show, the Store app to share a link to an app in the Windows Store, and the Maps app to share a map or directions to a location.

View Your Calendar

Windows comes with a Calendar app to enable you to manage your schedule. To create an event such as an appointment or meeting, or an all-day event such as a conference or trip, first select the date when the event occurs.

Calendar lets you change the calendar view to suit your needs. For example, you can show just a single day's worth of events if you want to concentrate on that day's activities. Similarly, you can view a week's or a month's worth of events if you want to get a larger sense of what your overall schedule looks like.

View Your Calendar

View Events by Month

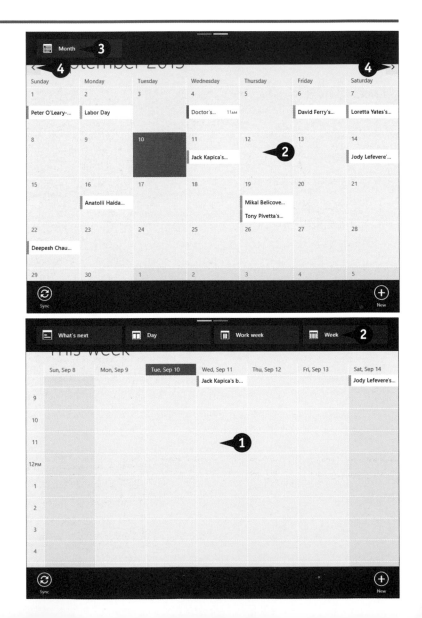

① On the Start screen, click the **Calendar** tile (not shown).

② Right-click the screen.

③ Click **Month**.

Your calendar for the month appears.

④ Click the screen and then click ◄ and ► to navigate the months.

View Events by Week

① Right-click the screen.

② Click **Week**.

Your events for the week appear.

View Events by Day

1 Right-click the screen.

2 Click **Day**.

The events for two days appear.

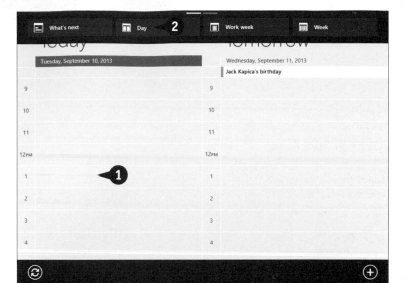

View Today's Events

1 Right-click the screen.

2 Click **What's next**.

Calendar navigates the current view to include today's date.

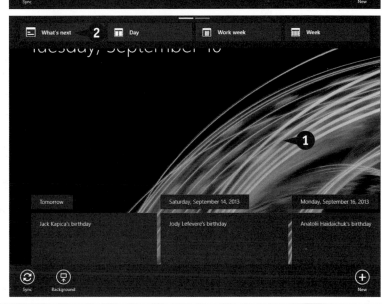

TIP

What shortcuts can I use to navigate the calendar?

Press	To	Press	To
Ctrl + 1	Switch to What's next.	Ctrl + 4	Switch to Week view.
Ctrl + 2	Switch to Day view.	Ctrl + 5	Switch to Month view.
Ctrl + 3	Switch to Weekday view.	Page down / Page up	Navigate to the next/previous screen in the current view.

Add an Event to Your Calendar

You can help organize your life by using the Calendar app to record your upcoming events — such as appointments, meetings, phone calls, and dates — on the date and time that they are scheduled to occur.

If the event has a set time and duration — for example, a meeting or a lunch date — you add the event directly to the calendar as a regular appointment. If the event has no set time — for example, a birthday, anniversary, or multiple-day event such as a sales meeting or vacation — you can create an all-day event.

Add an Event to Your Calendar

1 In the Calendar app, navigate to the date when the event occurs.

2 Click the time when the event starts.

Note: If you are currently in Month view, click the day the event occurs.

A You can click and drag these markers to adjust the event's start and end times.

3 Type a name for the event.

4 Type the event location.

5 Press **Enter**.

6 Click the event.

Calendar displays the event details screen.

7 If the start time is incorrect, use the **Start** controls to select the correct time.

8 Click the **How long** ☑.

9 Click the duration of the event.

B If the event is an anniversary or other event that lasts all day, click **All day**.

C To choose a specific end time, click **Custom**.

10 Use the large text area to type notes related to the event.

11 Click **Save this event** (🖫).

D Calendar adds the event to your schedule.

To make changes to the event, you can click it.

Paul's calendar
win81books@live.com

Lunch with Karen   🖫 — **11**

Add a message   — **10**

When

| 0 minutes |
| 30 minutes |
| 1 hour |
| 90 minutes |
| **9** — 2 hours |
| All day — **B** |
| **C** — Custom |

Who

Invite people

Show more

Saturday ˅   Sunday

October 26, 2013   October 27, 2013

                                    Graeme McFedries's birthday

9   9   **Running Group**
                                    Central Park

10   10

11   11

12PM   12PM   **Lunch with Karen**
                                    Gramercy Tavern   — **D**

1   1

2   2

TIP

How do I create a custom event duration?

With a custom event duration, you specify not only the date and time the event starts, but also the date and time the event ends. Here are the steps to follow:

1 Follow steps **1** to **5** to set up a new event or click an existing event.

2 Click the **How long** ☑.

3 Click **Custom**.

Calendar adds controls for the end of the event.

4 Use the **End** controls to set the end date and time.

Create a Recurring Event

If you have an activity or event that recurs at a regular interval, you can create an event and configure it to automatically repeat in the Calendar app. This saves you from having to repeatedly add the future events manually because Calendar adds them for you automatically.

You can repeat an event daily, weekly, monthly, or yearly. If your activity recurs every day only during the workweek, such as a staff meeting, you can also set up the event to repeat every weekday.

Create a Recurring Event

1. Follow the steps in the preceding section, "Add an Event to Your Calendar," to create an event.

2. Click **Show more**.

3. Click the **How often** ☑.

4. Click the repeat interval that you want to use.

5. Click **Save this event** (🖫).

   Calendar adds the future events using the interval that you specified.

Note: To edit a recurring event, click it and then click either **Open one** to edit just that occurrence or **Open series** to edit every occurrence.

Add an Event Reminder

We are all living hectic, busy lives, and with our schedules more crammed than ever, it is easy to forget about an upcoming appointment or anniversary. You can help make sure that you never miss a meeting, appointment, or other event by setting up the Calendar app to remind you before the event occurs. A *reminder* is a notification message that Windows displays at a specified time before the event occurs.

Add an Event Reminder

① Follow the steps in the section, "Add an Event to Your Calendar," earlier in this chapter, to create an event.

② Click **Show more**.

③ Click the **Reminder** ☑.

④ Click the length of time before the event that you want the reminder to appear.

⑤ Click **Save this event** (🖫).

Calendar saves the event and later reminds you of it beforehand, according to the time that you selected.

Send or Respond to an Event Invitation

The Calendar app has a feature that enables you to include people from your Contacts list in your event by sending them invitations to attend. If you receive an event invitation, you can respond to it to let the person organizing the event know whether you will be attending.

The advantage of this approach is that when other people respond to the invitation, Calendar automatically updates the event. When you receive an event invitation, the e-mail message contains buttons that enable you to respond quickly.

Send or Respond to an Event Invitation

Send an Event Invitation

1 Follow the steps in the section, "Add an Event to Your Calendar," earlier in this chapter, to create an event.

2 In the **Who** list, type the e-mail addresses of the people that you want to invite.

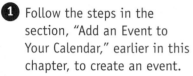

Note: To invite multiple people, press **Enter** after each address.

3 Type a note that will appear with the invitation.

4 Click **Send invite** (📧).

Calendar saves the event and sends the invitation.

Handle an Event Invitation

1 Click **Mail**.

Your Inbox appears.

2 Click the invitation message.

3 Click the button that represents your reply to the invitation:

A Click **Accept** if you can attend the event.

B Click **Tentative** if you are currently not sure whether you can attend.

C Click **Decline** if you cannot attend the event.

4 Click **Send now** to return your response to the event organizer.

TIPS

If I click Tentative, how do I later either accept or decline the invitation?

When you click **Tentative**, Windows temporarily adds the event to the Calendar at the date and time specified in the invitation. To respond definitively, open the event, click **Respond** (), and then click either **Accept** or **Decline**.

If I am not sure whether to accept or decline an invitation, is there a quick way to check my calendar?

Yes. The invitation message includes a link to your calendar that automatically displays the date on which the event occurs. Click the message and then click **View Calendar**. Windows splits the screen with the Calendar app and displays the event date so that you can check your schedule.

CHAPTER 7

Performing Day-to-Day Tasks

You can use the Windows apps to perform a number of useful day-to-day tasks, including searching for apps, settings, and files; getting directions to a location; looking up a weather forecast; planning a trip; tracking a stock; and getting the latest sports news.

Search Your PC

After you have used your PC for a while and have created many documents, you might have trouble locating a specific file. You can save a great deal of time by having Windows search for your document.

You can use the Windows Start screen to search for apps, system settings, and documents. If you are working with the Desktop app, you can also perform document searches using the Search box in a folder window.

Search Your PC

Search from the Start Screen

1 Display the Start screen.

2 Type your search text.

Ⓐ Windows displays the top apps, settings, and documents with names that include your search text.

Ⓑ Windows displays Internet search results here.

3 If you see the app, setting, or document that you want, click it.

4 If you do not see the item you want, click **Search** (🔍).

Windows displays a larger selection of search results.

5 If you see the app, setting, or document that you want, click it.

6 If you do not see the item you want, click a See all link:

Ⓒ Click **See all X apps** to see a complete list of matching apps.

Ⓓ Click **See all X settings** to see a complete list of matching settings.

Ⓔ Click **See all X documents** to see a complete list of matching files.

Windows displays the complete list of items that match your search text.

7 Click the item you want.

Windows opens the app, setting, or document.

Search from a Folder Window

1 Open the folder in which you want to search.

2 Type your search text in the Search box.

F As you type, Windows displays the folders and documents in the current folder with names, contents, or keywords that match your search text.

3 If you see the folder or document that you want, double-click it.

The folder or document opens.

How do I begin a Start screen search on my tablet PC?

A tablet PC does not have a keyboard and it does not display the on-screen keyboard when you display the Start screen, so you cannot initiate a search just by typing. Instead, swipe left from the right edge of the screen to display the Charms menu, and then tap **Search**.

Is there any way to tell Windows that I specifically want to search for settings, documents, or apps?

Yes. When the Search pane appears, click the **Everywhere** ☑ and then click either **Settings** or **Files**. If you want to search for apps only, click the screen, click **All apps** (◉), and then type your search text in the Search box that appears on the Apps screen.

Display a Location on a Map

You can use the Maps app to display a location on a map. *Maps* is a Metro app that displays digital maps that you can use to view just about any location by searching for an address or place name.

When you first start the Maps app, Windows asks if it can turn on location services, which are background features that help determine your current location and offer this information to apps such as Maps. For the best results with Maps, you should allow Windows to turn on location services.

Display a Location on a Map

1 On the Start screen, click the **Maps** tile.

The first time that you start Maps, the app asks if it can use your location (not shown). Click **Allow**.

2 Right-click the screen.

The application bar appears.

3 Click **Search**.

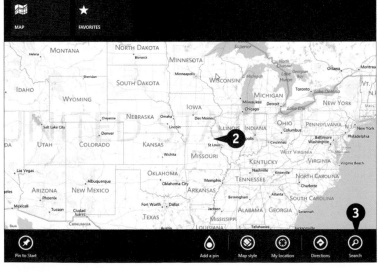

The Search pane appears.

④ Type the address or the name of the location.

⑤ Click **Search** (🔎).

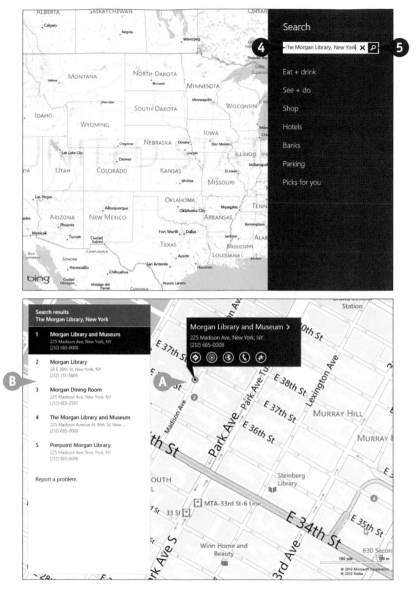

Ⓐ Maps displays the location on the map.

Ⓑ If Maps displays multiple locations, click the one that you want to view.

Note: To display your current location, right-click the screen and then click **My location**.

TIPS

How does Maps know my location?

Maps uses several bits of data to determine your location. First, it looks for known *Wi-Fi hotspots,* which are commercial establishments that offer wireless Internet access. Second, if you are connected to the Internet, Maps uses the location information embedded in your unique Internet Protocol (IP) address. Third, if your PC has a Global Positioning System (GPS) receiver, Maps uses this GPS data to pinpoint your location to within a few feet.

Can I turn off location services?

Yes. Display the Charms menu, click **Settings**, and then click **Change PC Settings**. In the PC Settings app, click **Privacy**, click **Location**, and then click the **Let Windows and apps use my location** switch to **Off**.

Get Directions to a Location

Besides displaying locations, Maps also recognizes the roads and highways found in most cities, states, and countries. This means that you can use the Maps app to get specific directions for traveling from one location to another.

You specify a starting point and destination for a trip, and Maps then provides you with directions for getting from one point to the other. Maps highlights the trip route on a digital map and gives you specific details for negotiating each leg of the trip.

Get Directions to a Location

1 Right-click the screen.

The application bar appears.

2 Click **Directions**.

Ⓐ If you already have your destination location on the map, click **Directions** (Ⓞ); you can then skip step **4**.

Note: Maps assumes that you want to start at your current location. If that is true, skip step **3**.

3 Type the name or address of the location where your journey will begin.

4 Type the name or address of your destination.

5 Click the travel method: **Driving** (🚗), **Transit** (🚌), or **Walking** (🚶).

6 Click **Get Directions** (➡).

B Maps displays an overview of your journey.

C This area tells the distance and approximate traveling time by the chosen travel method.

D This area displays the various legs of the journey.

7 Click the first leg of the trip.

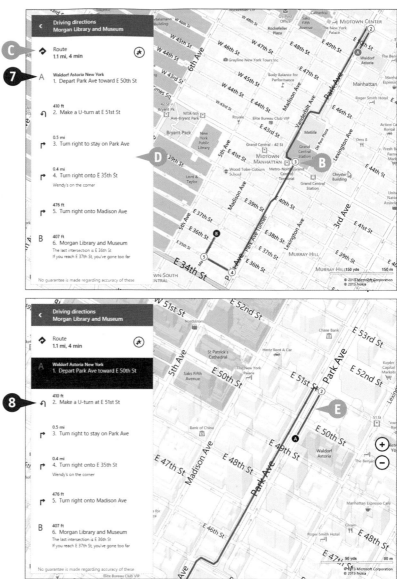

E Maps zooms in to show you just that leg of the trip.

8 As you complete each leg of the trip, click the next leg for further instructions.

TIP

Can I get traffic information as I follow the directions provided by Maps?

Yes. Right-click the screen to display the application bar. Click **Map style** and then click **Show traffic** to see the current traffic conditions:

- Green means traffic is moving normally on that route.
- Orange tells you that traffic is slow.
- Red means traffic is heavy.

Check Your Weather Forecast

You can use the Weather app to view your city's current conditions and five-day forecast. The Weather app takes advantage of the Bing Weather service provided by Microsoft, which uses several online weather resources to obtain up-to-the minute conditions and forecasts.

The Weather app includes a feature that uses Windows location services to determine your location and display the forecast for your city. If you would prefer to see the forecast for some other city, see the following section, "Check Another City's Weather Forecast."

Check Your Weather Forecast

1 On the Start screen, click **Weather**.

The first time that you start Weather, the app asks if it can use your location (not shown). Click **Allow**.

The Weather app appears.

2 Right-click the screen.

The application bar appears.

3 Click **Places**.

The Places screen appears.

④ Click **Add** (⊕).

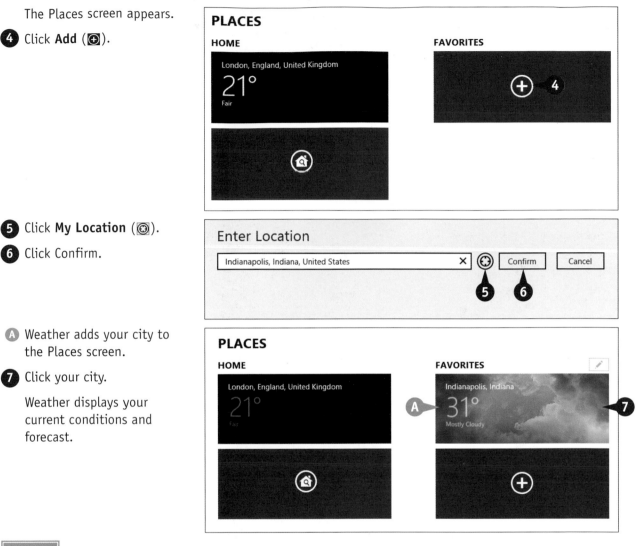

⑤ Click **My Location** (◎).

⑥ Click Confirm.

Ⓐ Weather adds your city to the Places screen.

⑦ Click your city.

Weather displays your current conditions and forecast.

Why does the Weather app say, "Your location cannot be found"?

It means you have turned off location services. Open the Charms menu, click **Settings**, and then click **Change PC Settings**. In the PC Settings app, click **Privacy**, click **Location**, and then click the **Let Windows and apps use my location** switch to **On**.

I would like to see my city's forecast when I start the Weather app. How can I set this up?

If your city is the only one added to Weather, then you see your forecast as soon as you start the app. Otherwise, you need to make your location the default. To do this, open Weather, right-click the screen, click **Change Home**, and then click your location.

Check Another City's Weather Forecast

You can use the Weather app to view another city's current conditions and five-day forecast. The Bing Weather service uses online resources to obtain up-to-the minute information on the current conditions and weather forecasts for hundreds of locations around the world. If you are going to be traveling to another city or if you are simply curious about the weather conditions elsewhere, you can use Maps to look up the weather forecast for most cities around the world.

Check Another City's Weather Forecast

① In the Weather app, right-click the screen.

The application bar appears.

② Click **Places**.

The Places screen appears.

③ Click **Add** ().

150

④ Type the name of the city whose weather you want to view.

Ⓐ As you type, Weather displays place names that match.

⑤ When you see the location that you want, click it.

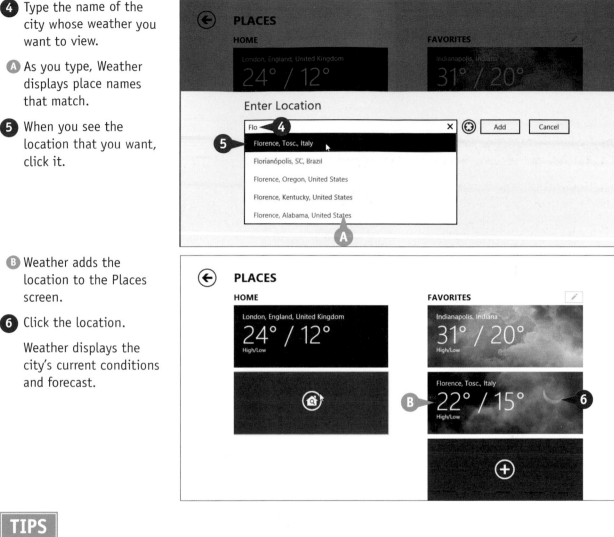

Ⓑ Weather adds the location to the Places screen.

⑥ Click the location.

Weather displays the city's current conditions and forecast.

TIPS

Can I show the weather for more than one city on the Start screen?
Yes. By default, the Weather tile shows the current conditions for whatever city you have set up as the default location. To add a second Weather tile that shows the current conditions for another city, follow the steps in this section to display the weather for the city that you want to add, right-click the screen, click **Pin to Start**, adjust the place name if needed, and then click **Pin to Start**.

How do I remove a city?
To remove a location from the Places screen, follow the steps in this section to display the city that you want to remove, right-click the screen, and then click **Remove**.

Plan a Trip

You can use the Travel app to plan your next vacation or business trip. For the most part, we make our own travel arrangements nowadays, so it is useful to have tools such as this that can help plan each aspect of a trip. The Travel app offers features that enable you to research destinations and search for the best flights and hotels. The Travel app also offers travel articles, news, and tips; destination photos; lists of hotels and restaurants; travel guides, and more.

Plan a Trip

Start the Travel App

1 At the Start screen, type **travel**.

2 Click **Travel**.

The Travel app appears.

Note: On the Travel app Home page, you can slide left to see links to highlighted destinations, photos, and articles.

Research a Destination

1 Right-click the screen.

2 Click the **Destinations** ☑.

3 To narrow down the location, click a region, such as **Caribbean** or **Europe**.

4 Click the destination.

The Travel app displays a screen that gives you an overview of the destination, as well as photos, lists of attractions, hotels, restaurants, and travel guides.

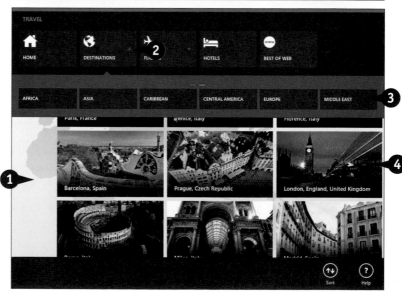

Search for Flights

1 Right-click the screen.

2 Click **Flights**.

3 Select your departure city.

4 Select your destination city.

5 Fill in your departure and return dates.

6 Select a cabin type.

7 Specify the number of passengers.

8 Click **Search Flights**.

The Travel app displays a list of matching flights.

Search for Hotels

1 Right-click the screen.

2 Click **Hotels**.

3 Select your destination city.

4 Fill in your check-in and check-out dates.

5 Specify the number of rooms.

6 Specify the number of guests.

7 Click **Search Hotels**.

The Travel app displays a list of matching hotels.

TIP

What is a more direct way to locate a travel destination?

1 In the Travel app, right-click the screen.

2 Click **Home** to open the home screen appears.

3 Use the **Search destinations** text box to type the name of the location, and then click **Search** ( ).

Travel displays a list of locations that match what you have typed.

4 Click the location that you want.

Get the Latest News

You can use the News app to read the latest news stories and to locate stories that are important to you. The News app aggregates news stories from a wide variety of web sources, including the Associated Press, Reuters, *The New York Times,* and CNN.

The News app's main page — called *Bing News* — displays stories in various categories, including Technology, Business, Politics, and Sports. If you are interested in other topics, you can customize Bing News to show stories related to those topics.

Get the Latest News

1 On the Start screen, click **News**.

The News app appears.

2 In the Bing News page, scroll left and right to see the main stories of the day in each category.

3 Right-click the screen.

The application bar appears.

4 Click **Customize**.

The Customize page appears.

5 To change the section order, drag an existing section and drop it in the new position.

6 To remove an existing section, click **Close** (✖).

7 To add a new section, click **Add** (+).

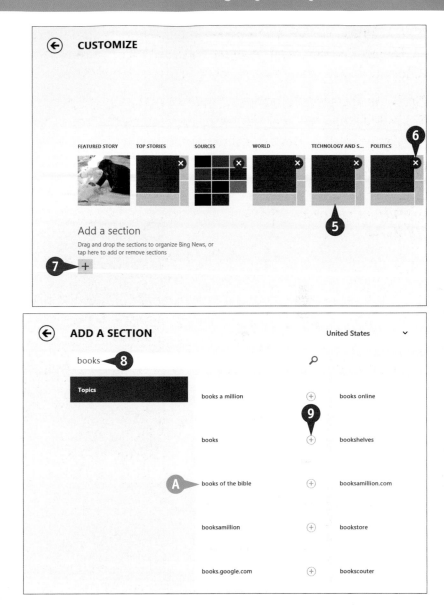

The Add a Section screen appears.

8 Type the name of the topic that you want to add and then press Enter.

A News displays topics that match.

9 Click **Add** (⊕) beside the topic that you want to add (⊕ changes to ✓).

News adds the topic to the Bing News page.

TIPS

Can I see news that focuses on a particular country?
Yes. To see news from a particular country, display the Charms menu, click **Settings** to open the News app's Settings pane, and then click **Options**. Use the **Change app language and content to** list to select the country.

Can I add a blog to Bing News?
Yes. The News app supports RSS (Real Simple Syndication) feeds to show the blog's most recent posts. Use Internet Explorer to visit the blog page and then copy the RSS address. Return to News, display the Add a Section screen, paste the RSS address, press Enter, and then click **Add** (⊕).

Track a Stock

You can use the Finance app to read the latest financial news stories, see the latest financial data, and create a list of stocks to track. The Finance app combines a wide variety of financial information in a single place.

The Finance app's main screen — called *Bing Finance* — displays financial news; Dow statistics, NASDAQ information, and other index values; major stock activity; bond prices; interest rates, and more. You can also use the Finance app to create a list — called a *watchlist* — of the stocks that you want to track.

Track a Stock

① On the Start screen, click **Finance**.

The Finance app appears.

Ⓐ On the Bing Finance screen, you can scroll left and right to see the latest financial news and data.

② Right-click the screen.

The application bar appears.

③ Click **Watchlist**.

The Watchlist screen appears.

④ Click **Add** (⊞).

WATCHLIST

Name	Last Price	Change	Volume	Day (Hi/Lo)	52 Wk (Hi/Lo)
XOM Exxon Mobil Corp	▲ 86.89	+0.06 +0.07%	1.92M 12.76M (avg)	87.10 86.65	95.49 84.70
SPY SPDR S&P 500	▼ 165.04	-0.54 -0.33%	21.07M 131.72M (avg)	165.45 164.91	170.97 134.70
VFINX Vanguard 500 Index Inv	▲ 152.74	+0.58 +0.38%			
FTSE 100	▼ 6,417.72	-35.74 -0.55%		6,453.55 6,392.63	6,875.62 5,605.59

④ ⊕

The Add to Watchlist screen appears.

⑤ Type the stock symbol or name of the stock that you want to add.

Ⓑ As you type, Finance displays stocks that match.

⑥ When you see the stock that you want, click it.

Finance adds the stock to the Watchlist screen.

Note: Your watchlist also appears on the Bing Finance screen.

WATCHLIST

Name	Last Price	Change	Volume	Day (Hi/Lo)	52 Wk (Hi/Lo)
XOM Exxon Mobil Corp	▲ 86.92	+0.09 +0.10%	1.98M 12.76M (avg)	87.10 86.65	95.49 84.70

Add to Watchlist

| MSFT ⑤ | | | ✕ | | Add | | Cancel |

⑥ | **MSFT** | Microsoft Corporation | Stock | NASDAQ |
| **MSFT** | Microsoft Corporation | Stock | Chile |
| **MSFT** | Microsoft Corporation | Stock | Mexico |
Ⓑ | **MSFT** | Microsoft Corporation | Stock | Merval... |
| **MSFT11B** | Microsoft Corporation | Stock | Sao Pau... |

TIPS

How do I remove a stock from my watchlist?

Follow steps **1** to **3** to display the Watchlist screen, click **Edit** (), and then click **Remove** (✕) beside each stock you no longer want on the watchlist.

Is there a way to keep my watchlist on-screen so that I can monitor it?

Yes, you can snap Finance to the edge of the screen. In Finance, display the Watchlist screen. Move the mouse pointer (↖) to the top of the screen (↖ changes to ✋), drag down until you see the app window, drag the window to the left or right edge of the screen, and then release.

Follow Your Favorite Teams

You can use the Sports app to catch up on all your sports news. The Sports app combines a wide variety of sports news and information in a single place.

The Sports app's main screen — called *Bing Sports* — displays the top story of the day, other sports news, the day's schedule of upcoming games, and the latest scores from those games. You can also use the Sports app to create a list — called *Favorite Teams* — of the teams that you want to follow.

Follow Your Favorite Teams

1 On the Start screen, click **Sports**.

The Sports app appears.

A On the Bing Sports screen, you can scroll left and right to see the latest sports news, schedules, and scores.

2 Scroll to the Favorite Teams section.

3 Click **Add** (⊞).

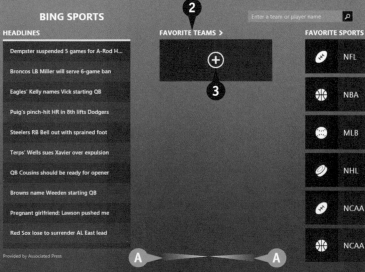

The Add to Favorite Teams screen appears.

④ Type the name of the team that you want to add.

Ⓑ As you type, Sports displays teams that match.

⑤ When you see the team that you want, click it.

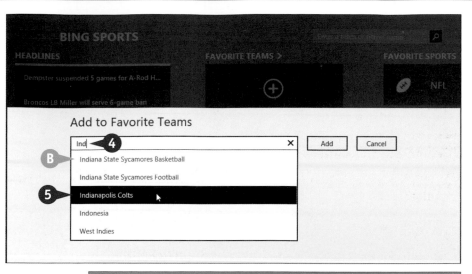

Ⓒ Sports adds the team to the Favorite Teams page.

⑥ Repeat steps **3** to **5** for every other team that you want to follow.

You can now see news, schedules, and stats by clicking a team in the Favorite Teams list.

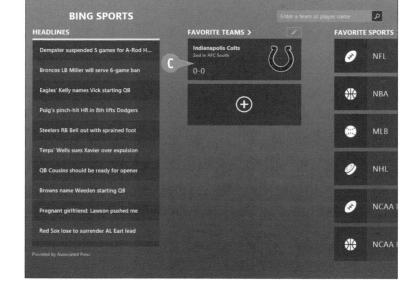

TIPS

How do I remove a team from my Favorite Teams list?

Follow steps **1** and **2** to display the Favorite Teams section. Click **Edit** (✏) and then click **Remove** (✖) beside each team you no longer want to follow.

Can I see more information about a particular sport?

Yes, the Sports app offers detailed information on a number of sports leagues, including the National Football League, the National Basketball Association, Major League Baseball, and the National Hockey League. For each league, you see the latest news stories, a schedule of upcoming games, recent results, current standings, player statistics, and more. To select a league, right-click the screen and then click a league in the application bar.

CHAPTER 8

Working with Images

Whether you load your images from a digital camera or a scanner, download them from the Internet, or draw them yourself, Windows 8 comes with a number of useful tools for working with those images. In this chapter, you learn how to import images from a camera, view your images, fix photo problems, and delete images.

Import Images from a Digital Camera

You can import photos from a digital camera and save them on your PC. If your camera stores the photos on a memory card, you can also use a memory card reader attached to your PC to upload the digital photos from the removable drive that Windows sets up when you insert the card.

To perform the import directly from your digital camera, you need a cable to connect your camera to your PC. Most digital cameras come with a USB cable. After you have the digital photos on your system, you can view or print the images.

Import Images from a Digital Camera

1 Plug in your camera or memory storage card reader.

A notification appears.

Note: If you have previously imported photos with this device, no notification appears, so skip to step **4**.

2 Click the notification.

Windows displays a list of actions that you can perform.

3 Click **Import photos and videos**.

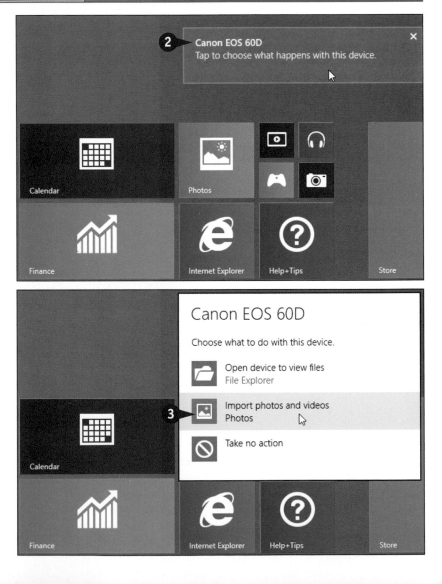

The Photos app loads and displays the photos that are on your camera.

4 Click each photo that you want to import.

A You can click **Select all** if you want to import all the photos.

5 Click **Import**.

Canon EOS 60D

Windows imports the photos.

When the import is complete, the Photos app displays your imported photos.

B The Photos app stores the imported photos in your Pictures library in a folder named after today's date.

TIPS

How can I import all but a few of the photos on my camera?
If you have many photos and you want to import all but a few of them, it can be time-consuming to select each photo that you want to import. Instead, click **Select all** and then click just the ones that you do not want to import.

I missed the notification. Can I still import photos from the camera?
Yes. Open the Photos app and then right-click the screen. In the app bar, click **Import** and then click your camera to display to the import screen.

Navigate the Pictures Library

Before you can work with your images, you need to view them on your PC. You do that by using the Photos app to open the Pictures library, which is a special folder designed specifically for storing images.

To get more out of the Pictures library, you need to know not only how to open it, but also the basic techniques for opening any albums that you have stored in the library.

Navigate the Pictures Library

1 On the Start Screen, click **Photos**.

The Photos app loads and displays the Pictures library.

A Items with names are albums that contain multiple images.

B Items without names are individual images.

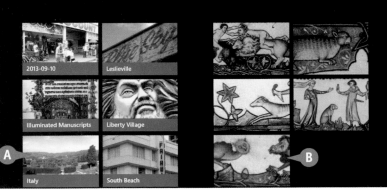

 Click an album.

The album appears.

③ If the album has subfolders, click a subfolder to open it.

 You can click to return to the previous section of the Photos app.

TIP

Can I change the image that appears as the background of the main Photos screen?

Yes. To do so, follow these steps:

① Follow the steps in this section to locate the image that you want to use.

② Click the image to open it.

③ Right-click the screen.

The Photos application bar appears.

④ Click **Set as**.

⑤ Click **Photos tile**.

The Photos app now uses your picture as its background image.

View Your Images

If you want to look at several images, the Photos app offers a couple of tools that you can use to navigate backward and forward through the images in the Pictures library. First, you can use the Photos app to open an album within your Pictures library, and you can then scroll through the images in that album. Second, you can open an album within your Pictures library and then open an individual image for viewing. You can then navigate through the other images in that album.

View Your Images

Scroll through an Album

 Open the album that contains the images you want to view.

Note: See the preceding section, "Navigate the Pictures Library," for details.

Ⓐ The Photos app displays the images in the album.

② Scroll right.

The Photos app displays the next screen of images from the album.

③ Repeat step **2** to continue viewing the album images.

Ⓑ You can return to the previous screen of images by scrolling left.

View Individual Images

1 Open the album that contains the images you want to view.

Note: See the preceding section, "Navigate the Pictures Library," for details.

2 Click the first image that you want to view.

The Photos app displays the image.

3 Press ⮕ to see the next image.

You can return to the previous image by pressing ⬅.

TIP

Can I zoom in and out of a photo?
Yes. Open the photo and then click the screen. In the bottom-right corner of the screen, click **Zoom In** (⊞) to increase the magnification, or **Zoom Out** (▢) to decrease the magnification. On a tablet PC, zoom in using the spread gesture — place two fingers close together on the screen and then spread them apart. To zoom out, use the pinch gesture — place two fingers relatively far apart on the screen and then bring them together. Note that you cannot navigate to the next or previous image while the image is zoomed in. Return to the normal magnification to continue navigating the images.

Start a Slide Show

Instead of viewing your photos one at a time, you can easily view multiple photos by running them in a slide show. You can run the slide show from within the Photos app. The slide show displays each photo for a few seconds and then automatically moves on to the next photo.

Alternatively, you can view a slide show of images using the Photos tile on the Start screen. This slide show uses random images from your Pictures library.

Start a Slide Show

In the Photos App

 In the Photos app, open the album that contains the photos you want to display in your slide show.

2 Click the first image you want to display in the slide show.

Photos opens the image.

3 Right-click the screen.

The Photos application bar appears.

4 Click **Slide show**.

The Photos app begins the slide show.

On the Photos Tile

1 In the Photos app, press + ▢.

The Settings pane appears.

2 Click **Options**.

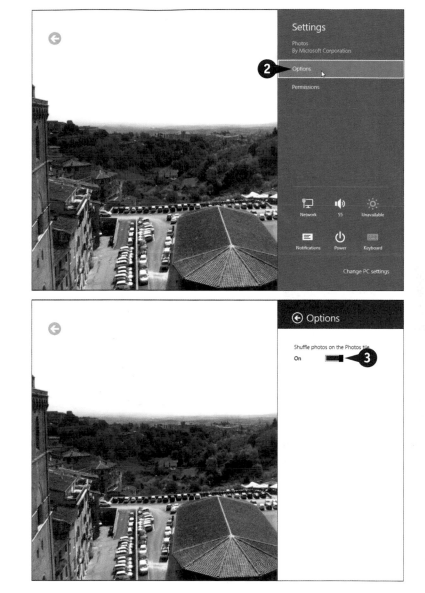

The Options pane appears.

3 Click **Shuffle photos on the Photos tile** to **On**.

The next time that you display the Start screen, the Photos tile displays a slide show of random images from your libraries.

Note: If you do not see the images on the Photos tile, make sure that the Photos tile is live. Right-click the **Photos** tile and then click **Turn live tile on**.

TIP

Can I change the speed at which the slide show displays the images?
No, not with the Photos app. However, you can adjust the speed if you start the slide show from File Explorer on the desktop. Click the **Desktop** tile, click the taskbar's **File Explorer** button (▢), open the **Pictures** library, and then double-click the folder that you want to view. In the ribbon, click the **Manage** tab and then click **Slide show** to start the show. To control the speed, right-click the screen to display the shortcut menu, and then click the speed that you want: **Slow**, **Medium**, or **Fast**.

Repair an Image

You can use Photos to improve the look of digital photos and other images. When you open an image in Photos, the application bar offers a number of tools for repairing various image attributes.

The easiest way to repair an image is to use the Auto Fix tool, which automatically adjusts an image's brightness, contrast, color temperature, tint, and saturation. You can also correct any of these elements manually, as well as remove red eye and hide photo flaws.

Repair an Image

Repair an Image Automatically

1 In Photos, display the image you want to repair.

2 Right-click the screen.

The application bar appears.

3 Click **Edit**.

Photos displays the image editing tools.

4 Click **Auto fix**.

5 Click the thumbnail that makes your image looks its best.

6 Right-click the screen.

7 Click **Update original**.

Photos saves your changes.

 If you prefer to leave the original as is, click **Save a copy**, instead.

Repair an Image Manually

1 Click **Light**.

2 For each light component, click the icon and then drag the circle that appears. Drag clockwise to increase the value; drag counterclockwise to decrease the value.

3 Click **Color**.

4 For each color component, click the icon and then drag the circle that appears.

Ⓑ You can also click **Effects** to apply a vignette effect or apply a selective focus.

5 Right-click the screen.

6 Click **Update original**.

Photos saves your changes.

Ⓒ If you prefer to leave the original as is, click **Save a copy**, instead.

TIPS

How do I remove red eye from a photo?
When you take a picture with a flash, the light may reflect off the subjects' retinas, resulting in *red eye*, where pupils appear red instead of black. To fix this, follow steps **1** to **3**, click **Basic fixes**, click **Red eye**, and then click each instance of red eye in your photo.

Can I remove a small flaw in a photo?
Yes. Photos offers a Retouch tool that enables you to perform a *spot fix*, which removes an element from the photo by replacing it with colors blended from the surrounding area. To perform a spot fix, follow steps **1** to **3**, click **Basic fixes**, click **Retouch**, and then click the flaw.

Crop an Image

If you have an image containing elements that you do not want or need to see, you can often cut out those elements. This is called *cropping*, and you can do this with Photos. When you crop a photo, you specify a rectangular area of the photo that you want to keep. Photos discards everything outside the rectangle.

Cropping is a useful skill to have because it can help give focus to the true subject of a photo. Cropping is also useful for removing extraneous elements that appear on or near the edges of a photo.

Crop an Image

1 In Photos, display the image you want to crop.

2 Right-click the screen.

The application bar appears.

3 Click **Edit**.

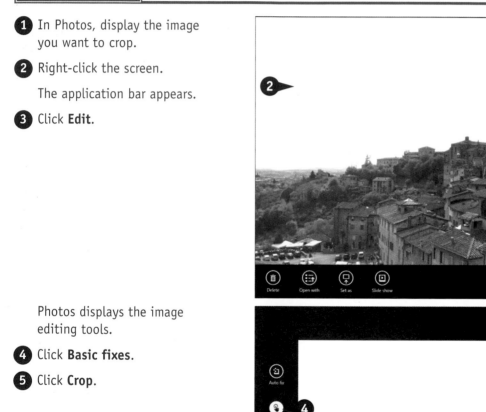

Photos displays the image editing tools.

4 Click **Basic fixes**.

5 Click **Crop**.

Photos displays a cropping rectangle on the photo.

6 Click and drag the entire rectangle or any corner to define the area you want to keep.

Note: Remember that Photos keeps the area inside the rectangle.

7 Click **Apply**.

Photos applies the cropping.

8 Right-click the screen.

9 Click **Update original**.

Photos saves your changes.

A If you prefer to leave the original as is, click **Save a copy**, instead.

TIP

Is there a quick way to crop a photo to a certain size?

Yes. Photos enables you to choose a specific ratio, such as 4 x 6 or 5 x 7. Follow these steps:

1 Repeat steps **1** to **5** to display the cropping rectangle over the image.

2 Click **Aspect ratio**.

3 Click the ratio you want to use, such as 4 x 6 or 5 x 7.

4 Repeat steps **7** to **9** to apply and save the cropping.

Rotate an Image

You can rotate and straighten an image using Photos. Depending on how you hold your camera when you take a shot, the resulting photo might show the subject sideways or upside down. To fix this problem, you can use Photos to rotate the photo so that the subject appears right-side up. You can rotate a photo either clockwise or counterclockwise.

Rotate an Image

1 Open the image you want to rotate.

2 Right-click the screen.

The application bar appears.

3 Click **Edit**.

Photos displays the image editing tools.

4 Click **Basic fixes**.

5 Click **Rotate** until the image is the way you want it.

6 Right-click the screen.

7 Click **Update original**.

Photos saves your changes.

Ⓐ If you prefer to leave the original as is, click **Save a copy**, instead.

Delete an Image

The images that you create may not always turn out perfectly. A photo may be blurry, or an edited image may not turn out the way that you want it to.

When you are viewing an album or watching a slide show, having a bad image turn up can make the experience less pleasant. You can prevent that from happening by deleting an image you no longer want to work with or view. You can delete a single image or multiple images with a single command.

Delete an Image

1 Open the album that contains the image or images you want to delete.

2 Right-click each image you want to delete.

A A check mark appears to indicate that you have selected the photo.

Note: If you select an image by accident, right-click it again to deselect it.

B To start over, click **Clear selection**.

The Photos application bar appears.

3 Click **Delete**.

Photos asks you to confirm the deletion.

4 Click **Delete**.

Photos deletes the selected image or images.

Print an Image

You can print an image from the Pictures library, or from any subfolder in the Pictures library. When you activate the Print command, the Print Pictures dialog box appears. You can use this dialog box to choose a printer and a layout, and to send the image to the printer.

You can print a single image or multiple images. If you work with multiple images, you can print them individually or print two or more images per sheet.

Print an Image

1 Open the image you want to print.

2 Move the mouse pointer (⌖) to the top-right corner of the screen.

The Charms menu appears.

3 Click **Devices**.

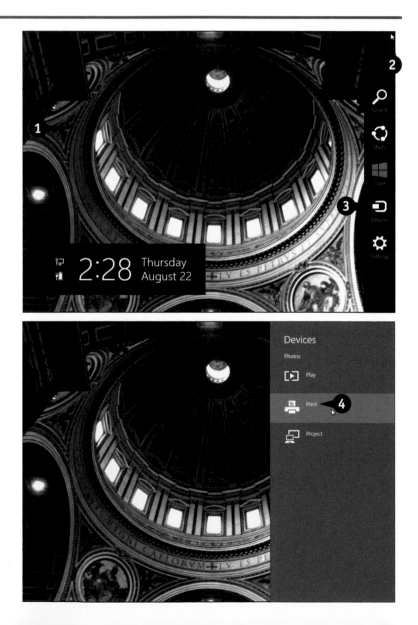

The Devices pane appears.

4 Click **Print**.

The Print pane appears.

5 Click the printer you want to use.

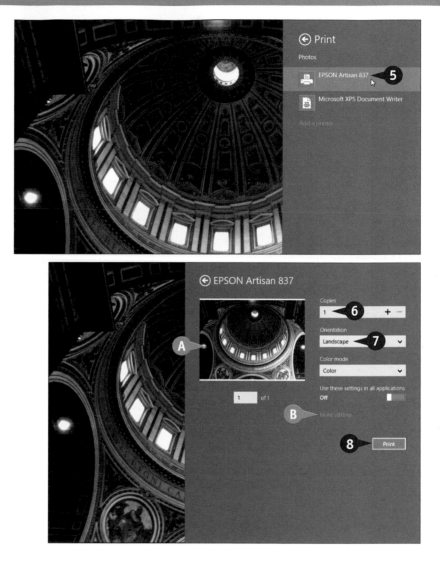

The printer pane appears.

Ⓐ Photos displays a preview of the printout.

6 Select the number of copies you want.

7 Select the orientation of the photo.

Ⓑ If you want to set extra options such as the paper size, paper type, or printout quality you prefer, click **More settings**.

8 Click **Print**.

Photos sends your image to the printer.

TIPS

Which orientation should I use?
The orientation determines how Photos lays out the image on the page. If your image has a greater height than width, choose Portrait; if your image has a greater width than height, choose Landscape.

What type of paper should I use for my photo printouts?
You can purchase a variety of photo-quality paper types for printing your digital photographs. Photo-quality paper, though more expensive than multipurpose paper, is designed to create a more permanent image and improve the resolution and color of the printed image. Photo-quality paper comes in glossy and matte finishes, as well as variations of each. Be sure to select a photo-quality paper that your printer manufacturer recommends.

Take a Picture with Your PC Camera

If your PC comes with a built-in camera or if you have an external camera attached to your PC, you can use the camera to take a picture of yourself, someone else, your surroundings — anything you want — using the Camera app.

The Camera app also gives you the option of recording a video. The Camera app stores each photo or video in a new album called *Camera Roll,* which appears in your Pictures library.

Take a Picture with Your PC Camera

1 On the Start screen, click **Camera**.

The first time that you start the Camera app, it asks for permission to use your location.

2 Click **Allow**.

The Camera app loads.

Ⓐ A live feed from the camera appears.

Ⓑ If you want the camera app to delay three seconds before taking the photo or starting the video recording, right-click the screen and then click **Timer** to select it.

❸ When you are ready to take the photo, click the screen.

Ⓒ If you want to record a video instead, click **Video**.

The Camera app takes the photo or starts the recording.

❹ If you are recording a video, click the **Stop** button when you are finished.

The Camera app saves your photo or video.

TIPS

I accidentally clicked Block when I first started the Camera app. How can I change this?
Open the Camera app, press ⊞+🅸 to open the Settings pane, click **Options**, and then click the **Location info** switch to **On**.

My video recordings are shaky. Can I fix this?
Yes, in many cases. However, this depends on whether your PC supports a feature called *video stabilization*, which can remove most of the artifacts caused by a shaking camera. To activate this feature, press ⊞+🅸 to open the Settings pane, click **Options**, and then click the **Video Stabilization** switch to **On**.

CHAPTER 9

Working with Multimedia

If you are into movies, TV shows, or music, you will appreciate the Windows apps that help you play, organize, edit, and generally get the most out of your multimedia. This chapter gives you the details on all of the Windows media apps.

Import Videos from a Digital Camera

You can import videos from a digital camera and save them on your computer. If your camera stores the videos on a memory card, you can also use a memory card reader attached to your PC to upload the digital videos from the removable drive that Windows sets up when you insert the card.

To perform the import directly from your digital camera, you need a cable to connect your camera to your PC. Most digital cameras come with a USB cable. After you have the digital videos on your system, you can view them.

Import Videos from a Digital Camera

1 Plug in your camera or memory storage card reader.

A notification appears.

2 Click the notification.

Windows displays a list of actions that you can perform.

3 Click **Import photos and videos**.

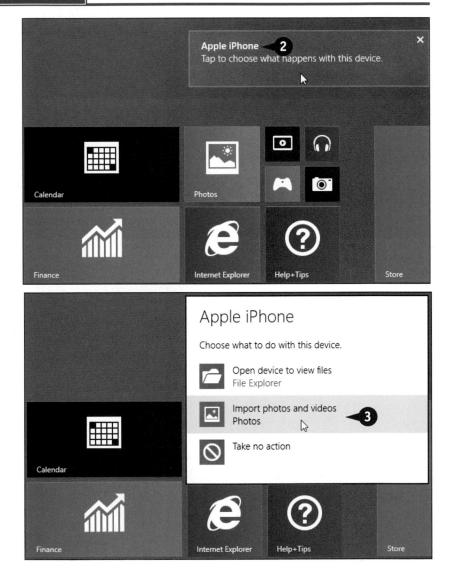

The Photos app loads and displays the videos that are on your camera.

④ Click each video that you want to import.

Ⓐ You can click **Select all** if you want to import all the videos.

⑤ Click **Import**.

Windows imports the videos.

When the import is complete, the Photos app displays your imported videos.

Ⓑ The Photos app stores the imported photos in your Pictures library in a folder named after today's date.

TIPS

When I connect my video camera, why do I not see the notification?

If you have already imported photos or videos with the video camera, Windows 8.1 remembers your previous selection and automatically displays the Photos app's import screen. If this happens, you can skip steps **2** and **3**.

How can I get my imported videos to appear in the Video app?

At the Start screen, click Video, press ⊞+Ⅰ, click **Preferences**, click **Choose where we look for videos on this PC**, click **Add** (⊕), click **SkyDrive**, click **This PC**, and then click **Pictures**. Click the folder that Photos created when you imported your videos, click **Add this folder to Videos**, and then click **OK**.

Navigate the Videos Library

Before you can work with your videos, you need to locate them on your PC. You do that by using the Video app to open the Videos library, which is a special folder designed specifically for storing digital videos, movies, and TV shows.

To get more out of the Videos library, you need to know the basic techniques for opening any videos that you have stored in it. If you are looking for commercial movies or TV shows, you can also use the Video app to buy or rent a movie or to buy a TV show episode.

Navigate the Videos Library

1 On the Start screen, click **Video**.

The Video app loads.

2 Scroll left until you see the personal videos section.

Ⓐ The Video app displays a selection of the videos on your PC.

3 Click **personal videos**.

The Videos library appears.

4 Click the personal videos ☑ and then select a video type.

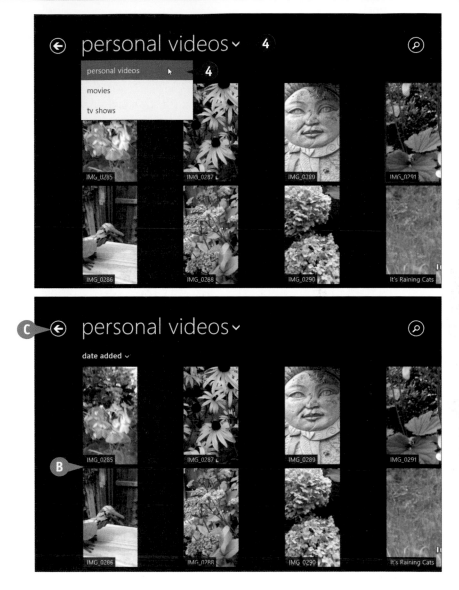

B The Video app displays the digital videos of that type that you have on your PC.

C You can click **Back** (◉) to return to the previous section of the Video app.

How can I get my Camera app videos to appear in the Video app?

Open the Video app, press ⊞+🔲, click **Preferences**, click **Choose where we look for videos on this PC**, click **Add** (⊕), click **SkyDrive**, click **This PC**, click **Pictures**, click **Camera Roll**, click **Add this folder to Videos**, and then click **OK**.

How do I get movies and TV shows?

You can use the Xbox Video Store to buy or rent movies or to buy TV show seasons or episodes. Return to the Main screen of the Video app; click a movie or TV section heading (such as new movies or featured TV shows); locate the movie, TV show season, or TV show episode; and then click either **Buy** or **Rent**.

Watch a Video

After you know how to use the Video app to navigate your Videos library, you can use the app to select and play a video that you have on your PC. The Video app plays the video full screen on your PC, so you get the best viewing experience. When you have the video playing, you can pause and restart the playback, and you can use a special tool called the *scrubber* to quickly fast-forward or rewind the video to the spot that you want.

Watch a Video

Start a Video

1 In the Video app, scroll left until you see the personal videos section.

A If you see the video that you want to watch, click it, and skip steps **2** and **3**.

2 Click **personal videos**.

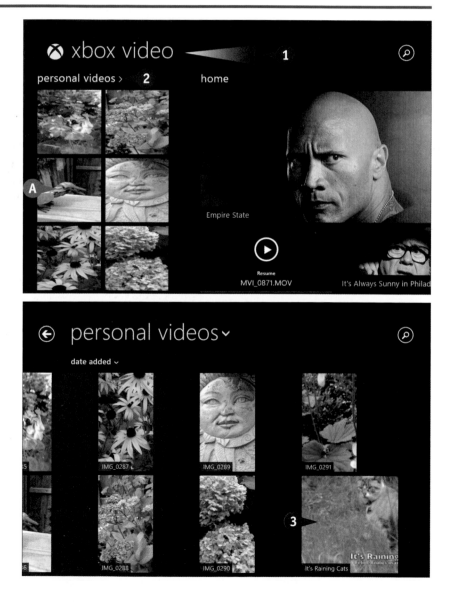

3 Click the video.

The Video app begins playing the video.

Control the Video Playback

1 Click the screen.

The Video app displays the playback controls.

B Click the **Pause** button to stop and restart the playback.

C Click and drag the scrubber to rewind or fast-forward the video.

D Click the timeline to jump to that position in the video.

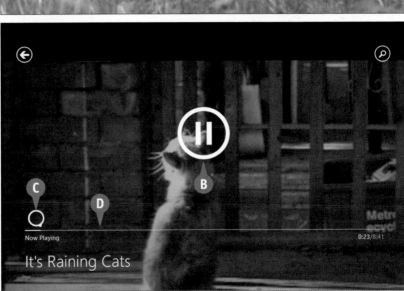

 TIP

Is there a way to get the video to automatically start over from the beginning?

Yes, the Video app offers a Repeat feature that automatically restarts the current video from the beginning as soon as the video ends. To activate this feature, follow these steps:

1 Start the video playback.

2 Right-click the screen.

3 Click **Playback options**.

4 Click **Repeat**.

Play a Music CD

Y ou can play music CDs in Windows Media Player. When you first insert an audio disc in your PC's optical drive (that is, a drive capable of reading CDs and DVDs), Windows asks what action you want to perform with audio CDs, and you can tell it to play them using Windows Media Player.

The CD appears in the Now Playing window. If you have an Internet connection, you will see the name of each track as well as other track data. You can control some playback options using the Now Playing window, but you can also switch to the Media Player library for more options.

Play a Music CD

Play a CD

1 Insert a music CD into your computer's optical drive.

A Windows displays an audio CD notification.

2 Click the notification.

Windows displays a list of actions you can take when you insert an audio CD.

3 Click **Play audio CD**.

The Windows Media Player Now Playing window appears and begins playing the audio CD.

Skip a Track

4 Click **Next** (▶▶|) to skip to the next track.

5 Click **Previous** (|◀◀) to skip to the previous track.

Pause and Resume Play

6 Click **Pause** (▮▮).

Windows Media Player pauses playback.

7 Click **Play** (▶).

Windows Media Player resumes playback where you left off.

Can I change the CD's audio levels?
Yes, Windows Media Player has a graphic equalizer component you can work with. To display it, right-click the **Now Playing** window, click **Enhancements**, and then click **Graphic equalizer**. To choose a predefined set of levels, click **Default**, and then click a preset value such as Rock or Classical. Alternatively, you can use the sliders to set your own audio levels.

Can I display something other than album art during playback?
Yes. Right-click the **Now Playing** window and then click **Visualizations** to see a list of visualization categories. Click a category and then click the visualization you want to view.

continued ▶

Play a Music CD (continued)

You can use the playback buttons at the bottom of the Windows Media Player library to control how a CD plays. For example, you can easily switch from one song to another on the CD. You can also use the Repeat feature to tell Windows Media Player to start the CD over from the beginning after it has finished playing the CD. Windows Media Player also offers the Shuffle feature, which plays the CD's tracks in random order. If you want to learn how to import music from the CD to Windows Media Player, see the section, "Copy Tracks from a Music CD."

Play a Music CD (continued)

Stop Play

8 Click **Stop** (□).

Windows Media Player stops playback.

If you click **Play** (▶) after clicking **Stop** (□), the current song starts over again.

9 Click **Switch to Library** (▦) to open the Windows Media Player library window.

Play Another Song

10 In the details pane, double-click the song you want to play.

Windows Media Player begins playing the song.

A This area displays the current song title, the album title, and the song composer (if one is listed).

Repeat the CD

11 Click **Turn Repeat On** (⟳).

Windows Media Player restarts the CD after the last track finishes playing.

Note: To turn on Repeat from the Now Playing window, press `Ctrl`+`T`.

Play Songs Randomly

12 Click **Turn Shuffle On** (⤨).

Windows Media Player shuffles the order of play.

Note: To turn on Shuffle from the Now Playing window, press `Ctrl`+`H`.

TIPS

Why does my details pane not list the song titles?

Windows Media Player tries to gather information about the album from the Internet. If it cannot ascertain song titles, it displays track numbers instead. To add your own titles, right-click each song title you want to change, click **Edit**, type your text, and press `Enter`.

Can I keep the Now Playing window in view at all times?

Yes. You can configure the Now Playing window so that it stays on top of any other window that you have open on your desktop. This enables you to control the playback no matter what other programs are running on your PC. Right-click the Now Playing window and then click **Always show Now Playing on top**.

Copy Tracks from a Music CD

You can add tracks from a music CD to the library in Windows Media Player. This enables you to listen to an album without having to put the CD into your optical drive each time. The process of adding tracks from a CD is called *copying*, or *ripping*, in Windows.

You can either rip an entire CD directly from the Now Playing window, or rip selected tracks using the library. You can also use the tracks to create your own playlists and to create your own custom CDs.

Copy Tracks from a Music CD

Rip an Entire CD Using the Now Playing Window

1 Insert a CD into your computer's optical drive.

The Now Playing window appears.

2 Click **Rip CD** (🔘).

Windows Media Player begins ripping the entire CD.

Rip Selected Tracks Using the Library

1 Insert a CD into your computer's optical drive.

If the Now Playing window appears, click **Switch to Library** (▦).

A Windows Media Player displays a list of the CD's tracks.

2 Click the CD tracks that you do not want to copy (✔ changes to ☐).

3 Click **Rip CD**.

Windows Media Player begins copying the track or tracks.

Ⓑ The Rip Status column displays the copy progress.

Ⓒ After each file is copied, the Rip Status column displays a Ripped to library message.

Ⓓ The copy is complete when all the tracks you selected display the Ripped to library status.

How do I remove a track from the library?
In the library, click **Music**, click **Album**, and then double-click the album that you ripped to display a list of the tracks. Right-click the track that you want to remove, and then click **Delete** in the menu that appears.

Can I adjust the quality of the copies?
Yes, by changing the *bit rate*, which is a measure of how much of the CD's original data is copied to your computer. This is measured in kilobits per second (Kbps); the higher the value, the higher the quality, but the more disk space each track takes up. Click **Rip Settings**, click **Audio Quality** in the menu that appears, and then click the value you want.

Navigate the Music Library

Before you can work with your songs and albums, you need to locate them on your PC. You do that by using the Music app to open the Windows Music library, which is a special folder designed specifically for storing digital music.

To get more out of the Music library, you need to know the basic techniques for opening any albums that you have stored in it. You can also use the Music app to purchase commercial albums or songs.

Navigate the Music Library

1 On the Start screen, click **Music**.

The Music app loads.

2 Click **Collection**.

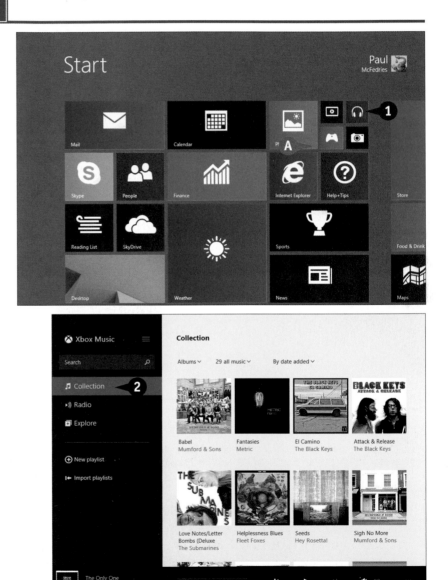

The Music library appears.

③ Click the down arrow (⌄) and then click a music category.

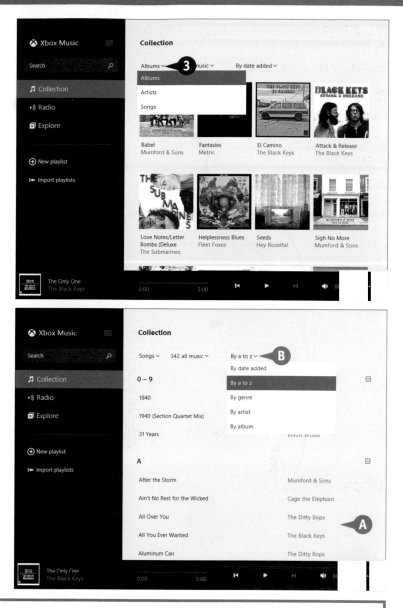

Ⓐ The music in that category appears.

Ⓑ You can click the down arrow (⌄) and then click a sort order for the category.

What if a song that I want to play does not appear in the Music library?

If your song is outside of the Music library, the Music app does not see it. Press ⊞+Ⅰ, click **Preferences**, click **Choose where we look for music on this PC**, click **Add** (⊕), click **SkyDrive**, click **This PC**, locate and click the folder that contains your music, then click **Add this folder to Music**.

How do I buy an album?

You can use the Xbox Music Store to purchase albums. Either use the Search box to look for the artist or album title, or click **Explore**, click a section heading such as New Albums, and locate the album. Click the album and then click **Buy album**.

Play Music

If you want to listen to music while using your PC and your PC has either built-in or connected speakers, you can use the Music app to play tunes from your Music library. You can listen to all the songs on an album, all the songs from a particular artist, or individual songs.

The Music app offers several features for controlling the music playback. You can also play albums, artists, and songs in random order and play albums and artists repeatedly.

Play Music

Start Music

1 Use the Music app to display your music.

Note: See the preceding section, "Navigate the Music Library," for details.

2 Click the item that contains the music you want to play.

The Music app opens the item and displays a list of songs.

3 Click **Play** (⊙).

Ⓐ You can also click a song and then click **Play** (⊙).

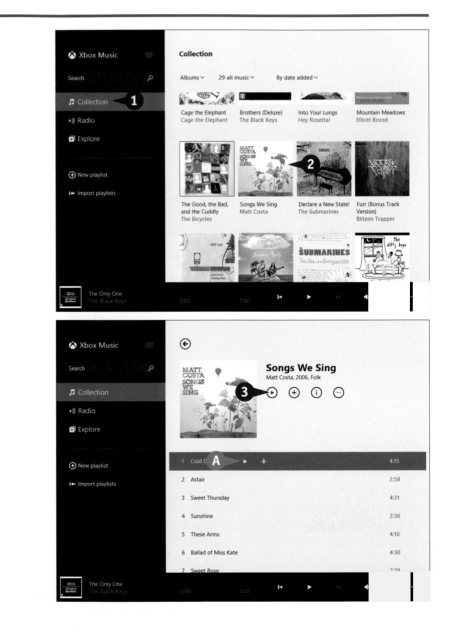

Control the Music Playback

ⓑ When you play music, the Music app displays the playback controls.

ⓒ Click **Pause** (⏸) to stop and restart the playback.

ⓓ Click and drag the scrubber to rewind or fast-forward the current song.

ⓔ To control the volume, click **Volume** (🔊) and then click and drag the black square.

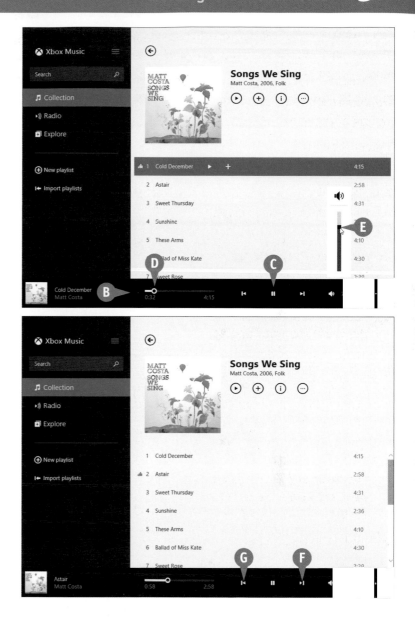

ⓕ Click **Next** (⏭) to jump to the next song.

ⓖ Click **Previous** (⏮) to return to the beginning of the current song. Click ⏮ again to jump to the previous song.

TIPS

Is there a way to get an album to automatically start over from the beginning?

Yes, the Music app offers a Repeat feature that automatically restarts the current album from the beginning as soon as the album ends. To activate this feature, start playing the album, click **More** (▪▪▪), and then click **Repeat**.

How do I play an album or artist's songs randomly?

You need to activate the Shuffle feature, which plays the songs for the current album or artist in random order. To activate this feature, start playing the album or artist, click **More** (▪▪▪), and then click **Shuffle**.

Create a Playlist

A *playlist* is a collection of songs that represents a subset of your total music collection. A playlist can include audio tracks you ripped from a music CD, songs downloaded from the Internet, or music purchased through the Xbox Music Store.

You can use the Music app to create customized playlists that include only the songs you want to hear. For example, you might want to create a playlist of upbeat or festive songs to play during a party or celebration. Similarly, you might want to create a playlist of your current favorite songs to play during a workout.

Create a Playlist

1 Click **New playlist**.

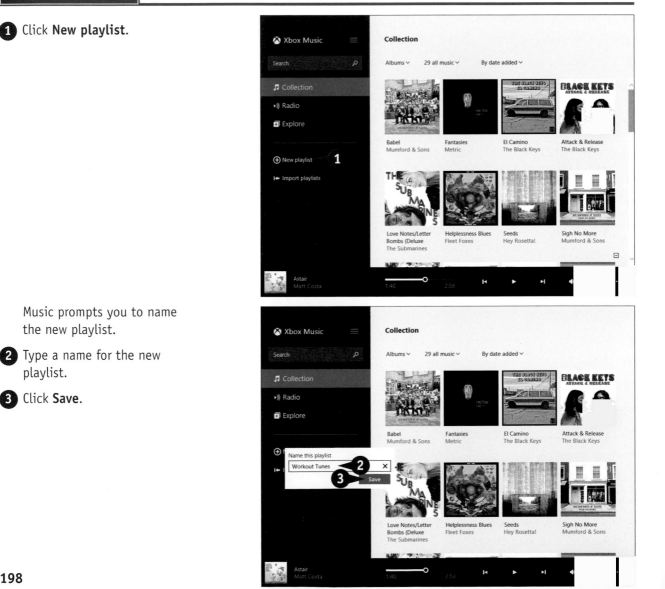

Music prompts you to name the new playlist.

2 Type a name for the new playlist.

3 Click **Save**.

4 Right-click a song that you want to add to the playlist.

5 Click **Add to**.

6 Click the name of your playlist.

Music adds the song to the playlist.

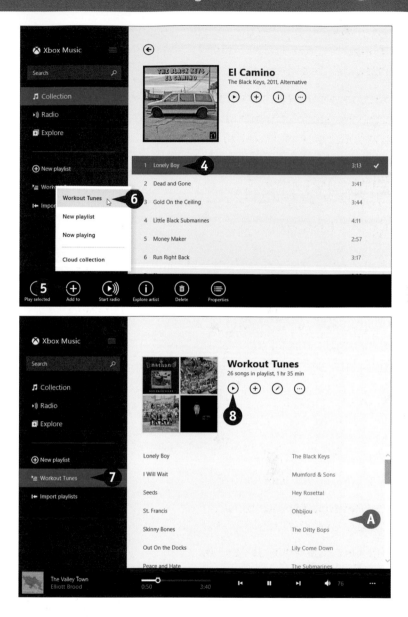

7 Click the playlist.

A Music displays a list of the songs you added.

8 Click **Play** (⊙) to listen to the playlist.

TIPS

How do I make changes to an existing playlist?
Click the playlist to open it. To change the playlist name, click **Edit** (⊘), type the new playlist name, and then click **Save**. To change the song order, right-click a song and then click either **Move up** or **Move down**. To delete a song from the playlist, right-click the song and then click **Remove from playlist**.

How do I delete a playlist?
Click the playlist to open it, click **More** (⊙), and then click **Delete**. When Music asks you to confirm, click **Delete**.

Create a Radio Station

To help you discover new music, you can create a radio station that plays songs that are similar to a particular artist, album, or song. That is, given a particular artist, album, or song, you can base a new radio station on that item, and Music plays a constant stream of songs that are similar.

The songs you hear come from the Xbox Music service, so you will likely hear many tunes and artists that you are not familiar with. If you like a particular song, you can buy it.

Create a Radio Station

Based on a Song

1 Right-click the song you want to use as the basis of your radio station.

2 Click **Start radio**.

Music creates and begins playing the radio station.

Based on an Album

1 Open the album you want to use as the basis of your radio station.

2 Click **More** (⬚).

3 Click **Start radio**.

Music creates and begins playing the radio station.

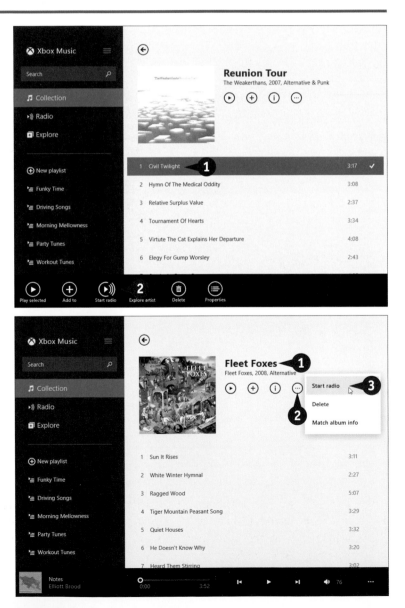

Based on an Artist

1 Open the artist you want to use as the basis of your radio station.

2 Click **Start radio** ().

Music creates and begins playing the radio station.

Based on Music in the Xbox Music Store

1 Click **Radio**.

2 Click **Start a station**.

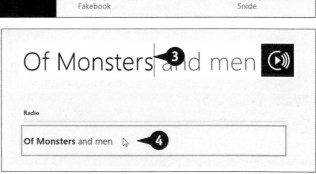

3 Type the name of an artist.

4 Click the artist.

Music creates and begins playing the radio station.

TIPS

Can I create a radio station based on an album that I do not own?

Yes. The easiest way to do this is to use the Search box to type the name of the album and then press `Enter`. In the search results, right-click the album you want to use as the basis for your radio station and then click **Start radio**.

How do I remove a radio station I no longer use?

Click **Radio** to display your radio stations. Right-click the radio station you no longer need, and then click **Delete**. Music removes the radio station.

CHAPTER 10

Editing Documents

To be productive with Windows, you need to know how to work with documents. In this chapter, you learn what documents are, as well as how to create, save, open, edit, and print documents.

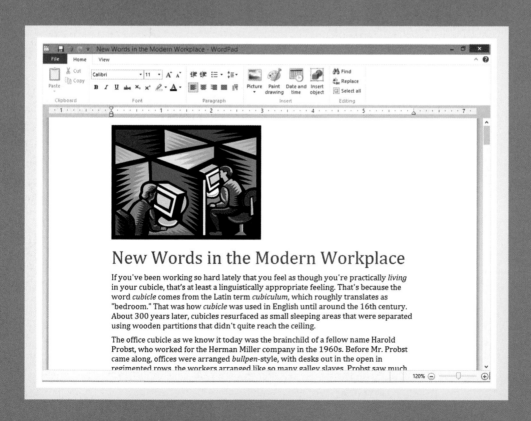

Understanding Documents

Documents are files that you create or edit yourself. The four examples shown here are the basic document types that you can create by using the programs that come with Windows.

Text Document

A text document is one that includes only the characters that you see on your keyboard, plus a few others. A text document contains no special formatting, such as colored text or bold formatting, although you can change the font. In Windows, you normally use the Notepad program to create text documents.

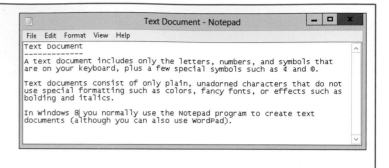

Word Processing Document

A word processing document contains text and other symbols, and you can format those characters to improve the look of the document. For example, you can change the size, color, and typeface, and you can make words bold or italic. In Windows, you use the WordPad program to create word processing — or Rich Text Format — documents.

Drawing

A drawing in this context is a digital image you create using special "tools" that create lines, boxes, polygons, special effects, and free-form shapes. In Windows, you use the Paint program to create drawings.

E-Mail Message

An e-mail message is a document that you send to another person via the Internet. Most e-mail messages use plain text, but some programs support formatted text, images, and other effects. In Windows, you create and send e-mail messages using the Mail app (see Chapter 5).

Create a Document

When you are ready to create something using Windows, in most cases you begin by launching a program and then using that program to create a new document to hold your work. Many Windows programs (such as WordPad and Paint) create a new document for you automatically when you begin the program. However, you can also use these programs to create another new document after you have started the program.

Create a Document

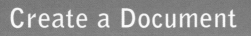

1 Click **File**.

2 Click **New**.

Ⓐ If the program supports more than one type of file, the program asks which type you want to create.

Note: Some programs display a dialog box with a list of document types.

3 Click the document type you want.

The program creates the new document.

Note: In most programs, you can also press Ctrl + N to create a new document.

Save a Document

After you create a document and make any changes to it, you can save the document to preserve your work. When you work on a document, Windows stores the changes in your computer's memory. However, Windows erases the contents of your PC's memory each time you shut down or restart the computer. This means that the changes you have made to your document are lost when you turn off or restart your PC. Saving the document preserves your changes on your computer's hard drive.

Save a Document

1 Click **File**.

2 Click **Save**.

Note: In most programs, you can also press **Ctrl**+**S** or click **Save** (🖫).

Note: If you saved the document previously, your changes are now preserved. You do not need to follow the rest of the steps in this section.

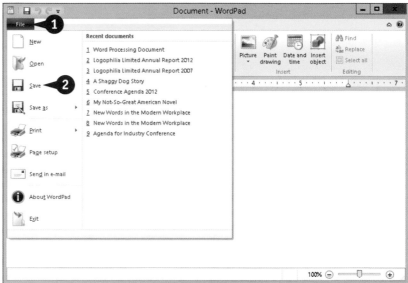

If this is a new document that you have never saved before, the Save As dialog box appears.

3 Click **Documents**.

Note: In most programs, the Documents library is selected automatically when you save a document.

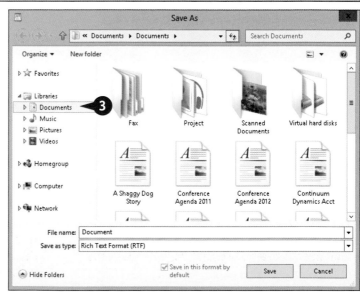

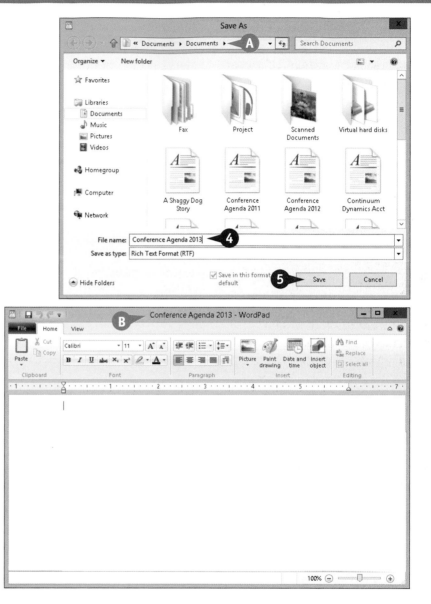

A Windows opens the Documents library.

4 Click in the **File name** text box and type the name you want to use for the document.

Note: The name you type can be up to 255 characters long, but it cannot include the following characters: < >, ?: " \ *.

5 Click **Save**.

B The filename you typed appears in the program's title bar.

TIPS

Can I create different types of documents in a program?

Yes, in most programs. If the program supports multiple document types, the Save As dialog box includes a drop-down list named Save As Type (or something similar). Use that list to choose the document type you want.

Do I have to save all my files to the Documents library?

No, not necessarily. You can create a subfolder within Documents and use it to store related files. In the Save As dialog box, click **New folder**, type the name of the folder, press **Enter**, double-click the new folder, and then follow steps **4** and **5**.

Open a Document

To work with a document that you have saved in the past, you typically need to open the document in the program that you used to create it. When you save a document, you save its contents to your PC's hard drive, and those contents are stored in a separate file. When you open the document using the same application that you used to save it, Windows loads the file's contents into memory and displays the document in the application. You can then view or edit the document as needed.

Open a Document

1 Start the program you want to work with.

2 Click **File**.

Ⓐ If you see the document you want in a list of the most recently used documents on the File menu, click the name to open it. You can then skip the rest of the steps in this section.

3 Click **Open**.

Note: In most programs, you can also press Ctrl+O or click **Open** (🖫).

The Open dialog box appears.

4 Click **Documents**.

Note: In most programs, the Documents library is selected automatically when you open a document.

Ⓑ If you want to open the document from some other folder, click here, click your username, and then double-click the folder.

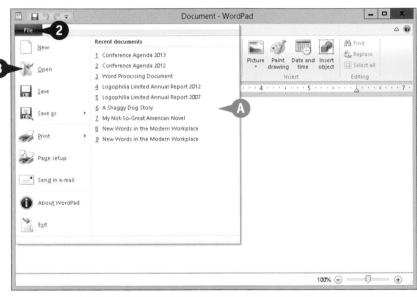

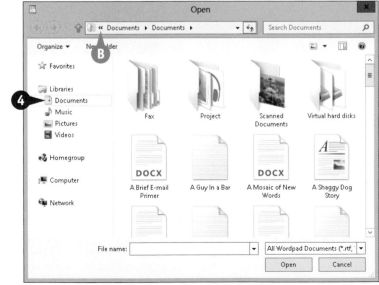

C Windows opens the Documents library.

5 Click the document name.

6 Click **Open**.

D The document appears in the program window.

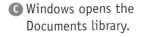

TIPS

Is there a more direct way to open a document?
Yes, there is. You do not always need to open the program first. Instead, open the folder that contains the document and then double-click the document. Windows automatically launches the program and opens the document.

Is there a quick way to locate a document?
Yes, Windows offers a file search feature, which is handy if your Documents library contains many files. On the Start screen, press ⊞+F to open the Files search pane. Type some or all of the document's filename and then double-click the document in the search results.

Edit Document Text

When you work with a character-based file, such as a text or word processing document or an e-mail message, you need to know the basic techniques for editing, selecting, copying, and moving text. Text you enter into a document is rarely perfect the first time through. The text likely contains errors that require correcting, or words, sentences, or paragraphs that appear in the wrong place. To get your document text the way you want it, you need to know how to edit text, including deleting characters, selecting the text you want to work with, and copying and moving text.

Edit Document Text

Delete Characters

1 Click immediately to the left of the first character you want to delete.

A The cursor appears before the character.

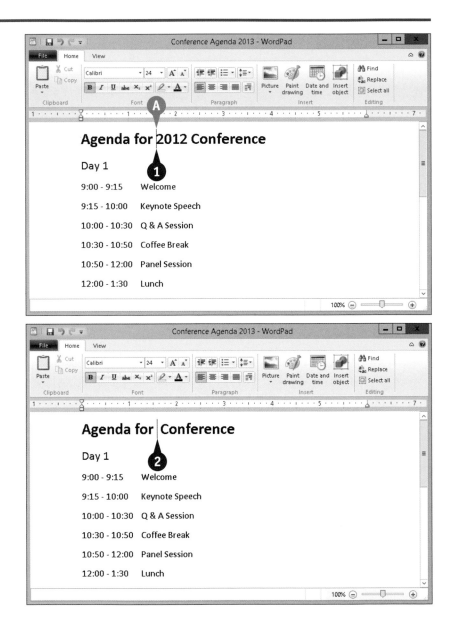

2 Press Delete until you have deleted all the characters you want.

Note: An alternative method is to click immediately to the right of the last character you want to delete and then press Backspace until you have deleted all the characters you want.

Note: If you make a mistake, immediately press Ctrl + Z or click **Undo** (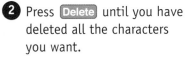). Alternatively, click **Edit** and then click **Undo**.

Select Text for Editing

1 Click and drag across the text you want to select.

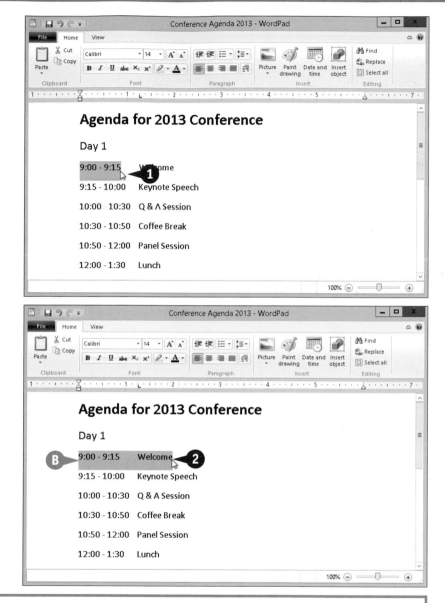

2 Release the mouse button.

B The program highlights the selected text.

Are there any shortcut methods I can use to select text in WordPad?

Yes. Here are the most useful ones:

- Click in the whitespace to the left of a line to select the line.

- Double-click a word to select it.

- Triple-click inside a paragraph to select it.

- Press **Ctrl**+**A** to select the entire document.

- For a long selection, click to the left of the first character, scroll to the end of the selection using the scroll bar, press and hold **Shift**, and then click to the right of the last character to select.

continued ▶

After you select some text, you can then copy or move the text to another location in your document. Copying text is often a useful way to save work instead of typing it from scratch. Likewise, if you need a similar passage in another part of the document, you can copy the original and then edit the copy as needed. If you enter a passage of text in the wrong position within the document, you can fix that by moving the text to the correct location.

Edit Document Text (continued)

Copy Text

1 Select the text you want to copy.

2 Click **Copy** (🗐).

A In WordPad, you display the Clipboard options by clicking the **Home** tab.

Note: In most programs, you can also press Ctrl + C or click the **Edit** menu and then click **Copy**.

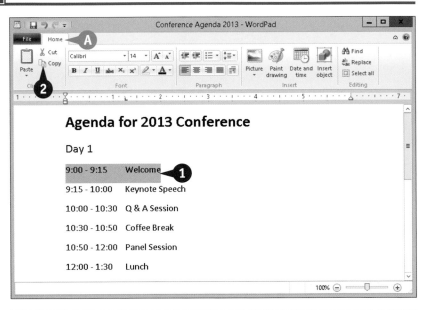

3 Click inside the document at the position where you want the copy of the text to appear.

The cursor appears in the position you click.

4 Click **Paste** (🗐).

Note: In most programs, you can also press Ctrl + V or click the **Edit** menu and then click **Paste**.

B The program inserts a copy of the selected text at the cursor position.

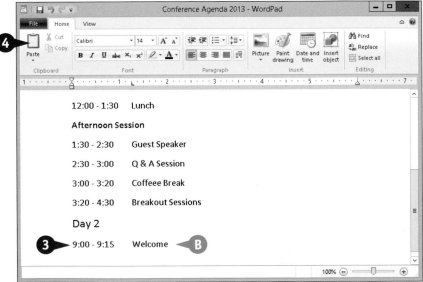

Move Text

1 Select the text you want to move.

2 Click **Cut** (✂).

C In WordPad, you display the Clipboard options by clicking the **Home** tab.

Note: In most programs, you can also press `Ctrl`+`X` or click the **Edit** menu and then click **Cut**.

The program removes the text from the document.

3 Click inside the document at the position where you want to move the text.

The cursor appears at the position you clicked.

4 Click **Paste** (📋).

Note: In most programs, you can also press `Ctrl`+`V`, or click the **Edit** menu and then click **Paste**.

D The program inserts the text at the cursor position.

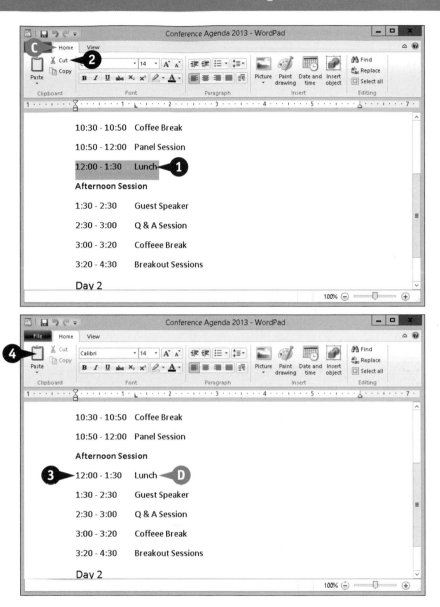

TIP

How do I move and copy text with my mouse?
First, select the text you want to work with. To move the selected text, position the mouse pointer (⇗) over the selection, and then click and drag the text to the new position within the document. To copy the selected text, position the mouse pointer (⇗) over the selection, press and hold `Ctrl`, and then click and drag the text to the desired position within the document.

Change the Text Font

When you work in a word processing document, you can add visual appeal by changing the font formatting. The font formatting includes attributes such as the typeface, style, size, or special effects. A *typeface* — also called a *font* — is a distinctive character design that you can apply to the selected text in a document. The *type style* refers to formatting applied to text, such as **bold** or *italics*. The *type size* refers to the height of each character, which is measured in *points*; 72 points equal one inch. *Special effects* are styles that change the appearance of the text. The most common examples are <u>underline</u> and ~~strikethrough~~.

Change the Text Font

1 Select the text you want to format.

2 Display the font options.

A In WordPad, you display the font options by clicking the **Home** tab.

Note: In many other programs, you display the font options by clicking **Format** in the menu bar and then clicking the **Font** command.

3 In the Font list, click ☑ and then click the typeface you want.

4 In the Size list, click the type size you want.

5 For bold text, click **Bold** (**B**).

6 For italics, click **Italic** (*I*).

7 For underlining, click **Underline** (U).

8 For color, click the **Font color** ☑ and then click a color.

B The program applies the font formatting to the selected text.

Note: Here are some shortcuts that work in most programs: For bold, press Ctrl + B; for italics, press Ctrl + I; for underline, press Ctrl + U.

TIP

How can I make the best use of fonts in my documents?

- Use one or two typefaces to avoid the ransom note look.

- Avoid overly decorative typefaces because they are often difficult to read.

- Use bold only for document titles, subtitles, and headings.

- Use italics only to emphasize words and phrases, or for the titles of books and magazines.

- Use larger type sizes only for document titles, subtitles, and, possibly, headings.

- In general, dark text on a light background is the easiest to read.

Find Text

In large documents, when you need to find specific text, you can save a lot of time by using the program's Find feature. In short documents that contain only a few dozen or even a few hundred words, finding a specific word or phrase is usually not difficult. However, many documents contain hundreds or even thousands of words, so finding a word or phrase becomes much more difficult and time consuming. You can work around this problem by using the Find feature, which searches the entire document in the blink of an eye.

Find Text

1 Click **Find** (⊞).

Ⓐ In WordPad, you display the Editing options by clicking the Home tab.

Note: In many programs, you run the Find command by clicking **Edit** in the menu bar and then clicking the **Find** command, or by pressing Ctrl+F.

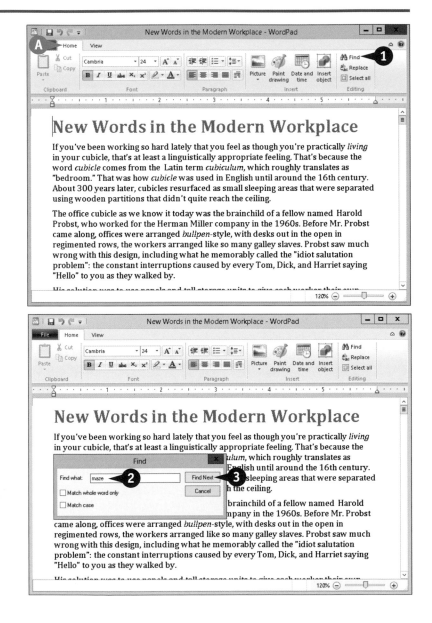

The Find dialog box appears.

2 Click in the **Find what** text box and type the text you want to find.

3 Click **Find Next**.

B The program selects the next instance of the search text.

Note: If the search text does not exist in the document, the program displays a dialog box to let you know.

4 If the selected instance is not the one you want, click **Find Next** until the program finds the correct instance.

5 Click **Close** (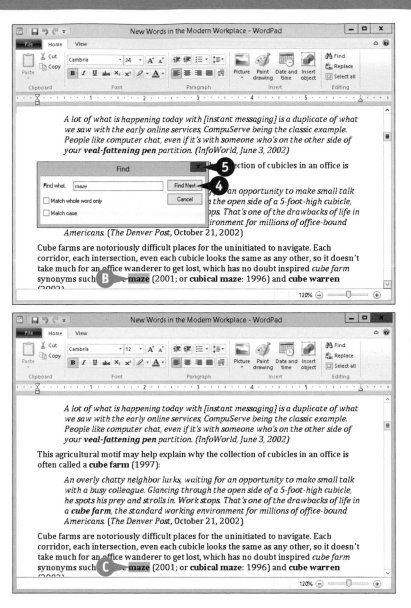) to close the Find dialog box.

C The program leaves the found text selected.

TIPS

A search for a word such as *the* also matches larger words such as *theme* and *bother*. How can I avoid this?

In the Find dialog box, click **Match whole word only** (☐ changes to ☑). This tells the program to match the search text only if it is a word on its own.

A search for a name such as *Bill* also matches the non-name *bill*. How do I fix this?

In the Find dialog box, click **Match case** (☐ changes to ☑). This tells the program to match the search text only if it has the same mix of uppercase and lowercase letters that you specify in the Find What text box.

Replace Text

You can make it easier to replace multiple instances of one word with another by taking advantage of the program's Replace feature. Do you need to replace a word or part of a word with some other text? If you have several instances to replace, you can save time and do a more accurate job if you let the program's Replace feature replace the word for you. Most programs that work with text — including the Windows WordPad and Notepad programs — have the Replace feature.

Replace Text

1 Click **Replace** (🖺).

A In WordPad, you display the Editing options by clicking the **Home** tab.

Note: In many programs, you run the Replace command by clicking **Edit** in the menu bar and then clicking the **Replace** command, or by pressing **Ctrl** + **H**.

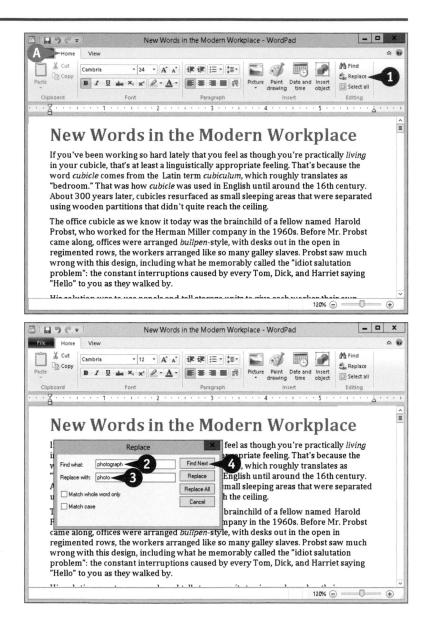

The Replace dialog box appears.

2 Click in the **Find what** text box, and type the text you want to find.

3 Click in the **Replace with** text box, and type the text you want to use as the replacement.

4 Click **Find Next**.

B The program selects the next instance of the search text.

Note: If the search text does not exist in the document, the program displays a dialog box to let you know.

5 If the selected instance is not the one you want, click **Find Next** until the program finds the correct instance.

6 Click **Replace**.

C The program replaces the selected text with the replacement text.

D The program selects the next instance of the search text.

7 Repeat steps **5** and **6** until you have replaced all the instances you want to replace.

8 Click **Close** (☒) to close the Replace dialog box.

TIP

Is there a faster way to replace every instance of the search text with the replacement text?
Yes. In the Replace dialog box, click **Replace All**. This tells the program to replace every instance of the search text with the replacement text. However, you should exercise some caution with this feature because it may make some replacements that you do not intend. Click **Find Next** a few times to make sure the matches are correct. Also, consider clicking the **Match whole word only** and **Match case** check boxes (☐ changes to ☑), as described in the "Find Text" section in this chapter.

Insert Special Symbols

You can make your documents more readable and more useful by inserting special symbols that are not available via your keyboard. The keyboard is home to a large number of letters, numbers, and symbols. However, the keyboard is missing some useful characters. For example, it is missing the foreign characters in words such as café and Köln. Similarly, your writing might require mathematical symbols such as ÷ and ½, financial symbols such as ¢ and ¥, or commercial symbols such as © and ®. These and many more symbols are available in Windows via the Character Map program.

Insert Special Symbols

1 On the Start screen, type **char**.

2 Click **Character Map**.

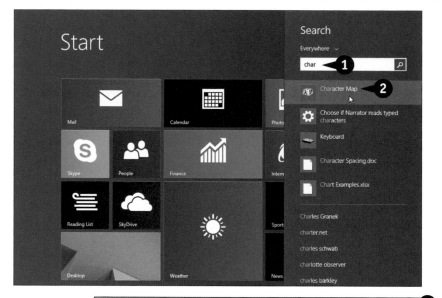

The Character Map window appears.

3 Click the symbol you want.

4 Click **Select**.

Ⓐ Character Map adds the symbol to the Characters to Copy text box.

5 Click **Copy**.

6 Click **Close** () to shut down Character Map after you choose all the characters you want.

7 In your document, position the cursor where you want to insert the symbol.

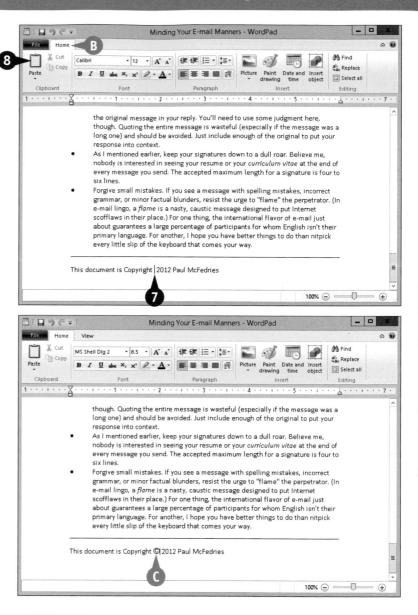

B In WordPad, you can display the Clipboard options by clicking the **Home** tab.

8 Click **Paste** (⬚).

C The program inserts the symbol.

When I click a symbol, Character Map sometimes displays a "keystroke" in the status bar. What does this mean?

This tells you that you can insert the symbol directly into your document by pressing the keystroke shown. For example, you can insert the copyright symbol (©) by pressing `Alt`+`0` `1` `6` `9`. When you type the numbers, be sure to use your keyboard's numeric keypad.

Are there even more symbols available?

Yes, dozens of extra symbols are available in the Character Map program's Webdings and Wingdings typefaces. To see these symbols, click the **Font** ⬇, and then click either **Webdings** or **Wingdings**.

Make a Copy of a Document

When you need to create a document that is nearly identical to an existing document, instead of creating the new document from scratch, you can save time by making a copy of the existing document and then modifying the copy as needed. For example, you might have a résumé cover letter that you want to modify for a different job application. Similarly, this year's conference agenda is likely to be similar to last year's conference. Instead of creating these new documents from scratch, it is much faster to copy the original document and then edit the copy as needed.

Make a Copy of a Document

1 Start the program you want to work with and open the original document.

2 Click **File**.

3 Click **Save as**.

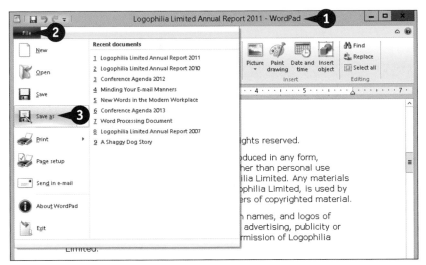

The Save As dialog box appears.

4 Click **Documents**.

Note: In most programs, the Documents library is selected automatically when you run the Save As command.

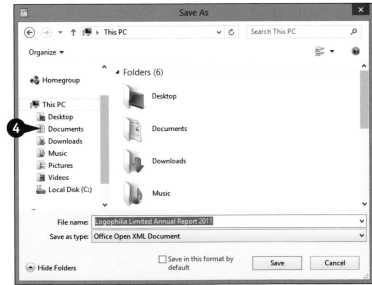

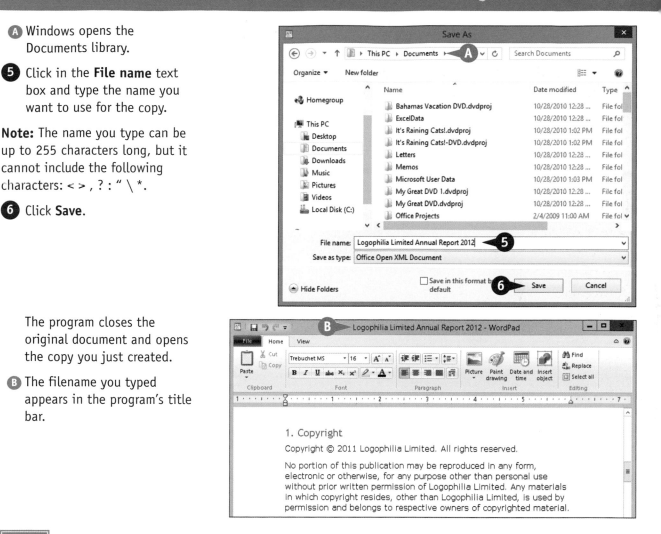

A Windows opens the Documents library.

5 Click in the **File name** text box and type the name you want to use for the copy.

Note: The name you type can be up to 255 characters long, but it cannot include the following characters: < > , ? : " \ *.

6 Click **Save**.

The program closes the original document and opens the copy you just created.

B The filename you typed appears in the program's title bar.

Print a Document

When you need a hard copy of your document to file or to distribute to someone else, you can obtain it by sending the document to your printer. Most applications that deal with documents also come with a Print command. When you run this command, the Print dialog box appears. You use the Print dialog box to choose the printer you want to use as well as to specify how many copies you want to print. Many Print dialog boxes also enable you to see a preview of your document before printing it.

Print a Document

1. Turn on your printer.

2. Open the document you want to print.

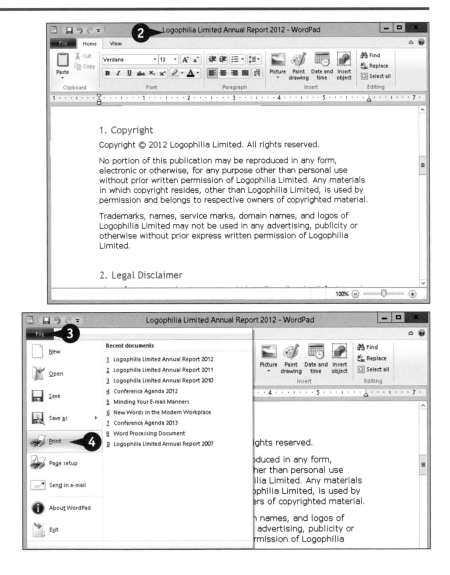

3. Click **File**.

4. Click **Print**.

Note: In many programs, you can select the Print command by pressing Ctrl+P or by clicking Print (▧).

The Print dialog box appears.

Note: The layout of the Print dialog box varies from program to program. The WordPad version shown here is a typical example.

5 If you have more than one printer, click the printer you want to use.

6 Use the **Number of copies** spin button (⬓) to specify the number of copies to print.

7 Click **Print**.

Ⓐ Windows prints the document. The print icon (🖶) appears in the taskbar's notification area while the document prints.

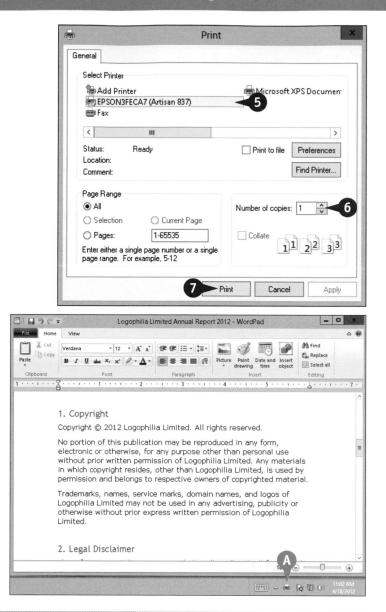

How do I print only part of a document?

- Print selected text. Select the text and then, in the Print dialog box, click **Selection** (◯ changes to ◉).

- Print a specific page. Place the cursor on the page and then, in the Print dialog box, click **Current Page** (◯ changes to ◉).

- Print a range of pages. In the Print dialog box, click **Pages** (◯ changes to ◉), type the first page number, a dash (–), and the last page number (for example, 1–5).

CHAPTER 11

Working with Files

This chapter shows you how to work with the files on your computer. These easy and efficient methods show you how to view, select, copy, move, rename, and delete files, as well as how to restore accidentally deleted files, how to copy files to a CD or DVD, and how to extract files from a compressed folder.

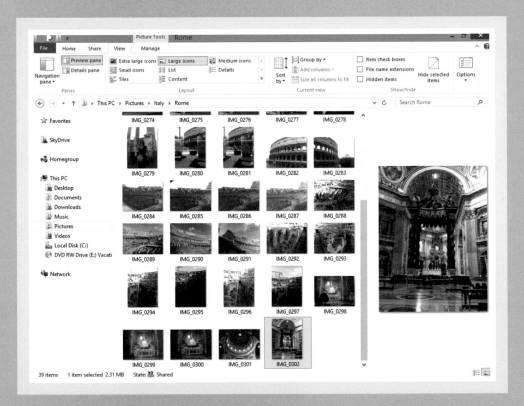

View Your Files

You can view the files you create, as well as those stored on your hard drive that you download and copy to your computer. If you want to open or work with those files, you first need to view them. Windows stores files on your hard drive using special storage areas called *folders*. A folder is a location on your hard drive that contains one or more related files. You can also store folders within folders, and these nested folders are known as *subfolders*. To view your files, you usually have to open one or more folders and subfolders.

View Your Files

1 Click **Desktop**.

2 Click **File Explorer** (![icon]).

Windows displays the This PC window.

3 Double-click the folder you want to view.

Windows displays the contents of the folder, including subfolders.

④ If the files you want to view are stored in a subfolder, double-click the subfolder.

Windows displays the contents of the subfolder.

How do I view the files I have on a disc, flash drive, memory card, or other media?

Insert the media into the appropriate drive or slot on your computer. If you see the AutoPlay notification, click it and then click **Open folder to view files**. Otherwise, open **File Explorer**, click **This PC**, and then double-click the drive or device that contains the files you want to view. Windows displays the contents of the media.

How do I navigate folders and subfolders?

Once you open a subfolder, you can usually return to its containing folder by clicking the name of the containing folder in the address bar. Otherwise, click the **Back** button (ⓖ) to retrace your steps.

Select a File

Before you can do any work with one or more files, you first have to select the files so that Windows knows which ones you want to work with. For example, before you can move files to a new location, you must first select the files you want to work with. You can select just a single file, two or more files, or group of files, or all the files in a folder. Although you learn specifically about selecting files in this section, the technique for selecting folders is the same.

Select a File

Select a Single File

1. Open the folder containing the file.

2. Click the file.

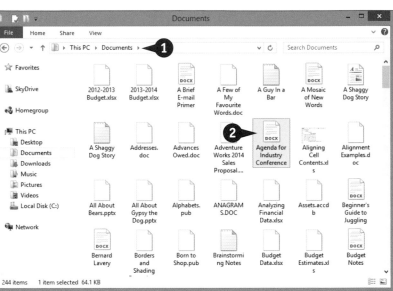

Select Multiple Files

1. Open the folder containing the files.

2. Click the first file you want to select.

3. Press and hold **Ctrl** and click each of the other files you want to select.

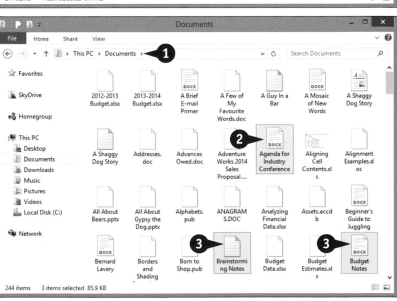

Select a Group of Files

1 Open the folder containing the files.

2 Position the mouse pointer (↖) slightly above and slightly to the left of the first file in the group.

3 Click and drag the mouse pointer (↖) down and to the right until all the files in the group are selected.

Select All Files

1 Open the folder containing the files.

2 Click the **Home** tab.

3 Click **Select all**.

Ⓐ File Explorer selects all the files in the folder.

Note: A quick way to select all the files in a folder is to press Ctrl + A.

TIP

How do I deselect a file?

Depending on the situation, there are a few ways to deselect files:

- To deselect a single file from a multiple-file selection, press and hold Ctrl and click the file that you want to deselect.

- To deselect all files, click an empty area within the folder.

- To reverse the selection — deselect the selected files and select the deselected files — click the **Home** tab, and then click **Invert selection**.

Change the File View

You can configure how Windows displays the files in a folder by changing the file view. This enables you to see larger or smaller icons or the details of each file.

You can choose a view such as Small Icons to see more files in the folder window. A view such as Large Icons or Extra Large Icons enables you to view images as thumbnail versions of each picture. If you want to see more information about the files, choose either the Tiles view or Details view.

Change the File View

1 Open the folder containing the files you want to view.

2 Click the **View** tab.

3 In the Layout section, click **More** (⬚).

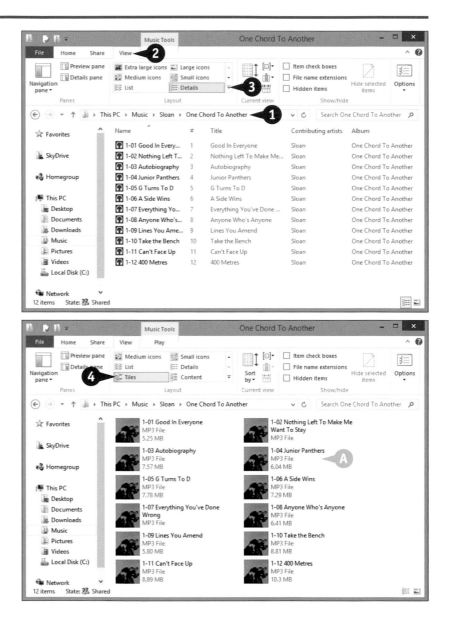

Windows displays the Layout gallery.

4 Click the view you want.

A File Explorer changes the file view (this example shows Tiles view).

Preview a File

Windows enables you to view the contents of some files without opening them. This makes it easier to select the file you want to work with because it means you do not have to run an application to see the file's contents. Previewing the file is faster and uses fewer system resources. Windows previews only certain types of files, such as text documents, rich text documents, web pages, images, and videos.

Preview a File

1 Open the folder containing the file you want to preview.

2 Click the **View** tab.

3 Click **Preview pane**.

A The Preview pane appears.

4 Click a file.

B The file's contents appear in the Preview pane.

C You can click and drag the left border of the Preview pane to change its size.

D When you are finished with the Preview pane, you can click the View tab's **Preview pane** button to close it.

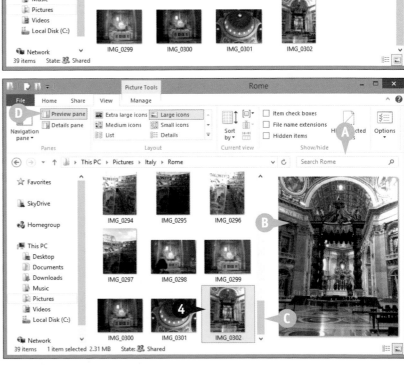

Copy a File

You can use Windows to make an exact copy of a file. This is useful if you want to back up an important file by making an extra copy on a flash drive, memory card, or other removable disk. Similarly, you might require a copy of a file if you want to send the copy on a disk to another person. This section shows you how to copy a single file, but the steps also work if you select multiple files. You can also use these steps to copy a folder.

Copy a File

1 Open the folder containing the file you want to copy.

2 Select the file.

3 Click the **Home** tab.

4 Click **Copy**.

Windows places a copy of the file in a special memory location called the *Clipboard*.

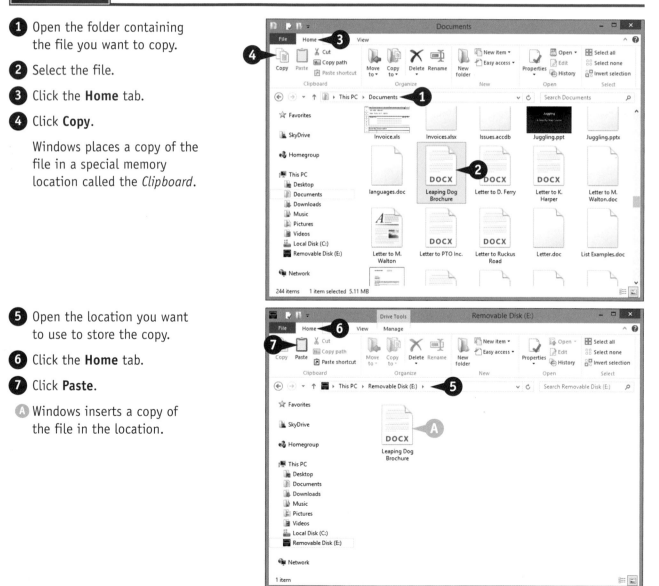

5 Open the location you want to use to store the copy.

6 Click the **Home** tab.

7 Click **Paste**.

Ⓐ Windows inserts a copy of the file in the location.

Move a File

W hen you need to store a file in a new location, the easiest way is to move the file from its current folder to another folder on your computer. When you save a file for the first time, you specify a folder on your PC's hard drive. This original location is not permanent; you can move the file to another location on the hard drive. This section shows you how to move a single file, but the steps also work if you select multiple files or move a folder.

Move a File

1 Open the folder containing the file you want to move.

2 Select the file.

3 Click the **Home** tab.

4 Click **Cut**.

Windows removes the file from the folder and places it in the Clipboard.

5 Click the new location you want to use for the file.

6 Click the **Home** tab.

7 Click **Paste**.

Ⓐ Windows inserts the file in the new location.

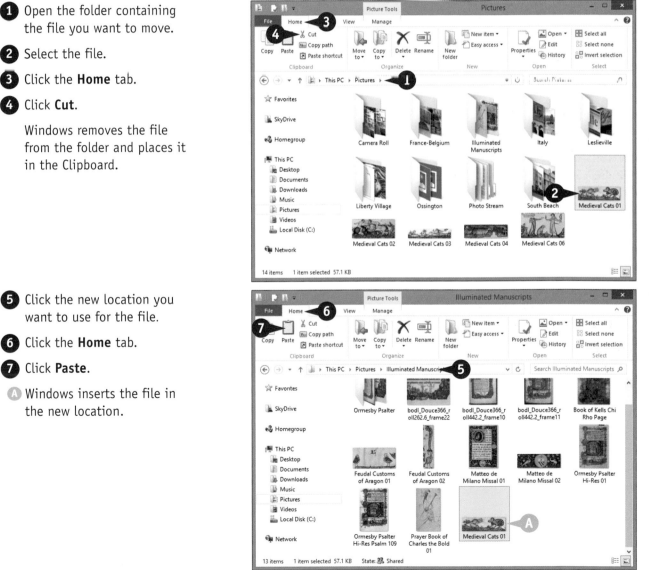

Rename a File

You can change the name of a file, which is useful if the current name of the file does not accurately describe the file's contents. By giving your document a descriptive name, you make it easier to find the file later.

Make sure that you rename only those documents that you have created or that someone else has given to you. Do not rename any of the Windows system files or any files associated with your programs, or your computer may behave erratically, or even crash.

Rename a File

1 Open the folder that contains the file you want to rename.

2 Click the file.

3 Click the **Home** tab.

Note: In addition to renaming files, you can also rename any folders that you have created.

4 Click **Rename** (or press F2).

A text box appears around the filename.

5 Type the new name you want to use for the file.

Note: If you decide that you do not want to rename the file after all, press Esc to cancel the operation.

Note: The name you type can be up to 255 characters long, but it cannot include the following characters: < >, ?: " \ *.

6 Press Enter or click an empty section of the folder.

The new name appears under the file's icon.

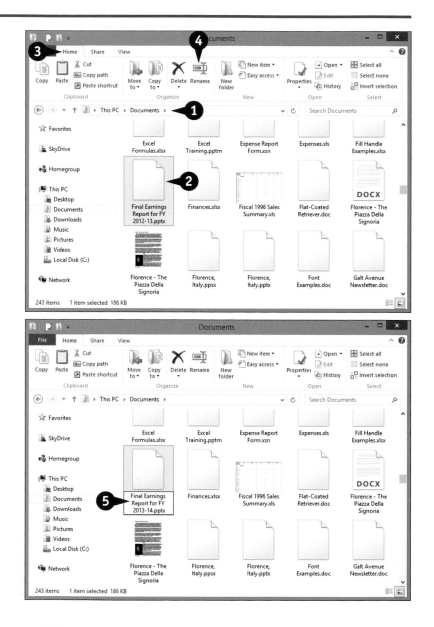

Create a New File

You can quickly create a new file directly within a file folder. This method is faster, and often more convenient, than running a program's New command. In Windows, you can create several different file types, the most important of which are the Bitmap Image (a drawing), Rich Text Document (a WordPad file), Text Document (a Notepad file), and Compressed (Zipped) Folder (which combines multiple files in a single file, as described in the section, "Extract Files from a Compressed Folder"). You can also create a new folder.

Create a New File

1 Open the folder in which you want to create the file.

2 Click the **Home** tab.

3 Click **New item**.

4 Click the type of file you want to create.

Ⓐ If you click **Folder**, Windows creates a new subfolder.

Note: The New item menu on your system may contain more items than you see here because some programs install their own file types.

Ⓑ An icon for the new file appears in the folder.

5 Type the name you want to use for the new file.

6 Press Enter.

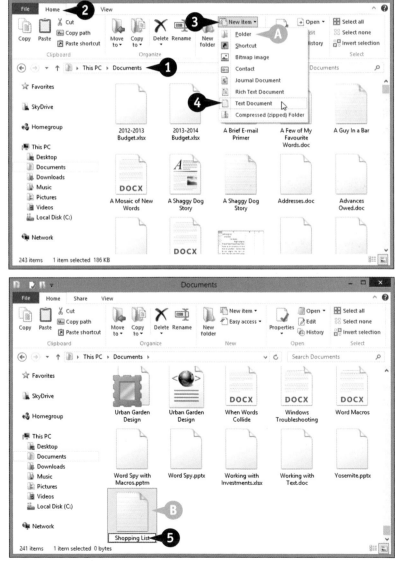

Delete a File

When you have a file that you no longer need, instead of leaving the file to clutter your hard drive, you can delete it. Make sure that you delete only those documents that you have created or that someone else has given to you. Do not delete any of the Windows system files or any files associated with your programs, or your computer may behave erratically or crash.

Delete a File

1 Open the folder that contains the file you want to delete.

2 Click the file you want to delete.

Note: If you need to remove more than one file, select all the files you want to delete.

3 Click the **Home** tab.

4 Click the top half of the **Delete** button.

Note: Another way to select the Delete command is to press `Delete`.

 Windows removes the file from the folder.

Note: Another way to delete a file is to click and drag it to the desktop's Recycle Bin icon.

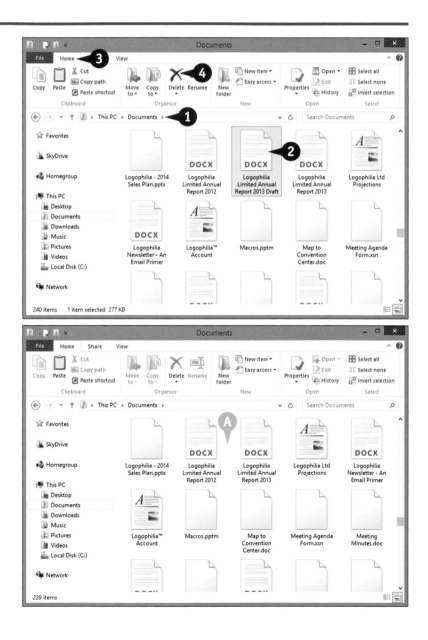

Restore a Deleted File

I f you delete a file in error, Windows enables you to restore the file by placing it back in the folder from which you deleted it. You can restore a deleted file because Windows stores each deleted file in a special folder called the Recycle Bin, where the file stays for a few days or a few weeks, depending on how often you empty the bin or how full the folder becomes.

Restore a Deleted File

1 Double-click the desktop **Recycle Bin** icon.

The Recycle Bin folder appears.

2 Click the file you want to restore.

3 Click the **Manage** tab.

4 Click **Restore the selected items**.

The file disappears from the Recycle Bin and reappears in its original folder.

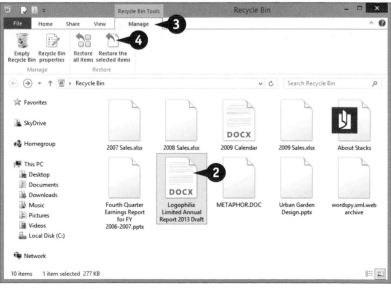

Add a File to Your SkyDrive

If you are using Windows under a Microsoft account, then as part of that account you get a free online storage area called *SkyDrive*. You can use the SkyDrive app to add any of your files to your SkyDrive. This is useful if you are going to be away from your computer but still require access to a file. Because the SkyDrive is accessible anywhere you have web access, you can view and work with your file without using your computer.

Add a File to Your SkyDrive

① On the Start screen, click **SkyDrive**.

The SkyDrive app appears.

② Click the SkyDrive folder in which you want to store a file.

3 Right-click the screen.

The application bar appears.

4 Click **Add items**.

5 Click the location ☑.

6 Click **This PC**.

7 Select the folder that contains the file that you want to upload.

The SkyDrive app displays a list of the files in the selected folder.

8 Click the file that you want to send to your SkyDrive.

9 Click **Copy to SkyDrive**.

The SkyDrive app uploads the file.

TIPS

How do I access my SkyDrive online?
You need to open Internet Explorer and navigate to the SkyDrive site, https://skydrive.live.com. After you are logged in to your SkyDrive, you can use it to create new folders, rename files, delete files, and more.

Can I create new documents using SkyDrive?
Yes. As part of your SkyDrive, Microsoft gives you access to the Office Web Apps, which are scaled-down, online versions of Microsoft applications. To create a document using one of these programs, navigate to your online SkyDrive, click **Create**, and then click **Word document**, **Excel workbook**, **PowerPoint presentation**, **OneNote notebook**, or **Excel survey**.

Extract Files from a Compressed Folder

If someone sends you a file via e-mail, or if you download a file from the Internet, the file often arrives in a *compressed* form, which means the file actually contains one or more files that have been compressed to save space. To use the files on your computer, you need to extract them from the compressed file. Because a compressed file can contain one or more files, it acts like a kind of folder. Therefore, Windows calls such files *compressed folders*, *zipped folders*, or *Zip archives*. You can view these files or extract them from the folder.

Extract Files from a Compressed Folder

View Compressed Folder Files

1 In File Explorer, open the folder containing the compressed folder.

A The compressed folder usually appears as a folder icon with a zipper.

2 Double-click the compressed folder.

B File Explorer displays the contents of the compressed folder.

Note: File Explorer is only displaying the contents of a compressed folder; it has not extracted the files. To extract the files, follow the steps in the next subsection.

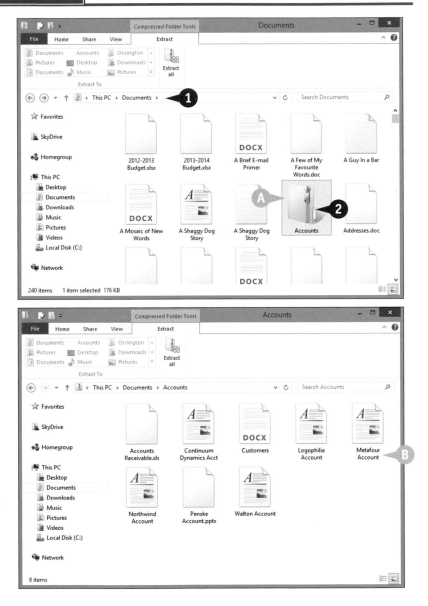

Extract Compressed Folder Files

1 In File Explorer, open the folder containing the compressed folder.

2 Click the compressed folder.

3 Click the **Extract** tab.

4 Click **Extract all**.

The Select a Destination and Extract Files dialog box of the Extract Wizard appears.

5 Type the location of the folder into which you want to extract the files.

C You can also click **Browse** and choose the folder.

6 If you want to open the folder into which you extracted the files, click **Show extracted files when complete** (☐ changes to ✔).

7 Click **Extract**.

Windows extracts the files.

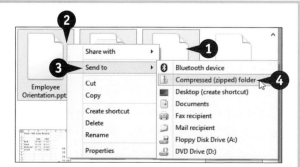

TIP

How can I create a compressed folder?

1 Select the files and folders you want to store in the compressed folder.

2 Right-click any selected item.

3 Click **Send to**.

4 Click **Compressed (zipped) folder**.

The compressed folder appears.

Burn Files to a CD or DVD

If your computer has a recordable CD or DVD drive, and you have a CD or DVD disc that can be used for recording data, you can copy — or *burn* — files and folders to the recordable disc. This enables you to store a large amount of data in a single place for convenient transport and storage. Burning files to a CD or DVD is also an easy and efficient method for backing up a few crucial files. You can also burn files to a CD or DVD to share with another person who does not have an Internet connection.

Burn Files to a CD or DVD

1 Insert a recordable disc into your recordable CD or DVD drive.

The AutoPlay notification appears.

2 Click the notification.

3 Click **Burn files to disc**.

If you have never used the disc for burning files, the Burn a Disc dialog box appears.

4 Type a title for the disc.

5 Click **Like a USB flash drive** (○ changes to ●).

6 Click **Next**.

Windows formats the disc and displays a dialog box to show you the progress.

When the format is complete, the AutoPlay notification appears, but you can ignore it this time.

7 Open the folder containing the files you want to copy to the disc.

8 Select the files.

Ⓐ The status bar shows you the total size of the selection.

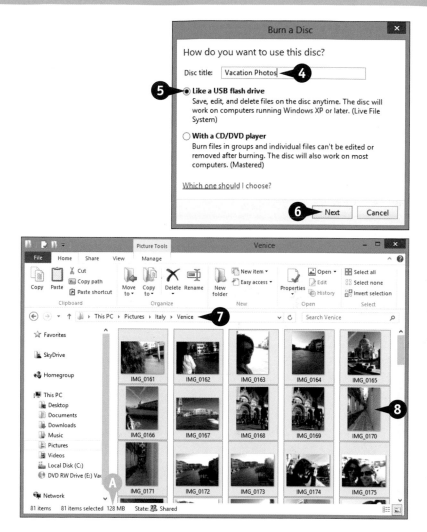

Does it matter what type of recordable CD or DVD I use?

No. Normally, CD-R and DVD-R discs allow you to copy files to the disc only once. After you finalize the disc, it is locked and you cannot copy more files to, or delete files from, the disc. However, Windows uses a system that enables you to copy, recopy, and delete files with any recordable disc.

How much data can I store on a recordable CD?

Most recordable CDs hold about 650MB (megabytes) of information. If a typical word processing document is about 50KB (kilobytes), this means you can store about 13,000 files on a recordable CD. For larger files, such as images, you can store about 650 one-megabyte files on the disc.

continued ▶

Traditionally, CDs and DVDs only allow you to burn files to them once, and you can then no longer burn any more files to the disc. However, Windows supports a different burning mode called Live File System that enables you to burn files to a disc multiple times, similarly to copying files multiple times to a USB flash drive. With the Windows method for burning files to a CD or DVD, you only need to format the disc once. After that, you can burn more files to the disc, delete files from the disc, and more.

Burn Files to a CD or DVD (continued)

9 Click the **Share** tab.

10 Click **Burn to disc**.

Note: If you want to copy everything in the folder to the disc, do not select any file or folder and click **Burn to disc.**

A Windows burns the files to the disc.

B Windows opens the disc and displays the copied files.

11 Repeat steps **8** to **10** to burn more files to the disc.

12 Right-click the disc.

13 Click **Close session**.

Windows closes the disc session to allow the disc to be used on other computers.

⊙ This message appears when the disc is closed.

14 When the Disc Ready message appears, click the disc.

15 Click the **Manage** tab.

16 Click **Eject**.

Windows ejects the disc.

TIP

I want to start over with a CD-RW or DVD-RW disc. Is there an easy way to erase the disc?
Yes. Follow these steps:

1 Open File Explorer.

2 Click **Computer**.

3 Click the disc icon.

4 Click the **Drive** tab.

5 Click **Format**.

The Format dialog box appears.

6 In the Volume Label text box, type a new disc name.

7 Click **Start**.

Windows warns all data will be erased.

CHAPTER 12

Sharing Your Computer

If you share your computer with other people, you can create separate user accounts so that each person works only with his own documents, programs, and Windows settings. This chapter shows you how to create and change user accounts, how to log on and off different accounts, how to share documents between accounts, and how to connect and work with a homegroup.

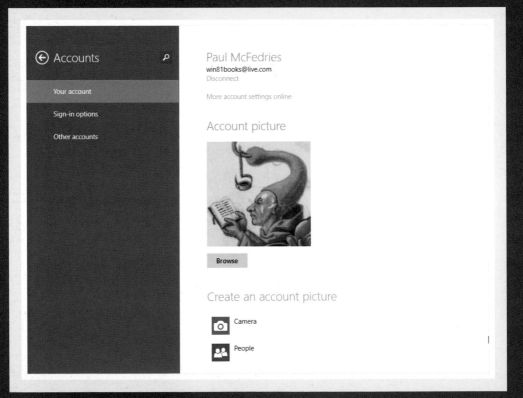

Display User Accounts

To work with user accounts, you need to display the Windows Accounts settings. A *user account* is a collection of Windows folders and settings associated with one person. In this chapter, you learn how to create new user accounts, change a user account's picture, change a user account's password, and delete a user account. To perform any of these tasks, you must first display the Accounts screen of the PC Settings app.

Display User Accounts

1 Move the mouse pointer (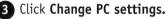) to the top-right corner of the screen.

A The Charms menu appears.

Note: You can also display the Charms menu by pressing ⊞+ⓒ

2 Click **Settings.**

The Start settings pane appears.

3 Click **Change PC settings.**

The PC Settings app appears.

④ Click **Accounts**

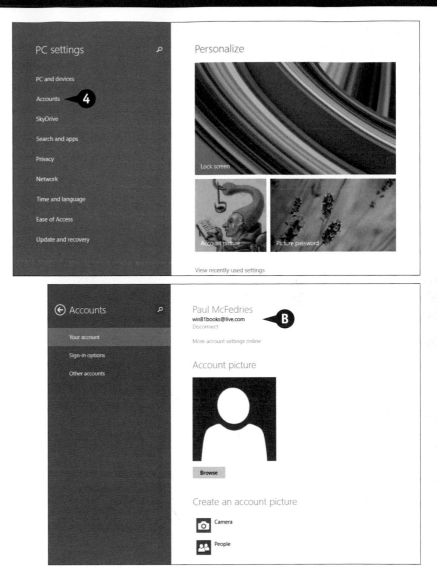

The Accounts screen appears.

Ⓑ Information about your account appears here. Later, after you have switched to another account, information for the current account appears in this spot.

TIP

How do user accounts help me share my computer with other people?
Without user accounts, anyone who uses your computer can view and even change your documents, Windows settings, e-mail accounts and messages, Internet Explorer favorites, and more. With user accounts, users get their own folders (Documents, Pictures, Music, and so on), personalized Windows settings, e-mail accounts, and favorites. In short, users get their own versions of Windows to personalize without interfering with anyone else's. In addition, user accounts enable you to safely share documents and folders with people who use your computer and with people on your network.

Create a User Account

If you want to share your computer with another person, you need to create a user account for that individual. This enables the person to log on to Windows and use the system. The new user account is completely separate from your own account. This means that the other person can change settings, create documents, and perform other Windows tasks without interfering with your settings or data.

You can create a local user account or a Microsoft account. For maximum privacy, you should safeguard each account with a password.

Create a User Account

1 Display the Accounts screen of the PC Settings app.

Note: See "Display User Accounts," earlier in this chapter, to learn how to display the Accounts screen.

2 Click **Other accounts**.

3 Click **Add an account**.

The sign up screen appears.

4 For a local account, click **Sign in without a Microsoft account (not recommended).**

Note: If you want to create a Microsoft account instead, see Chapter 1 for more information.

⑤ Click **Local account**.

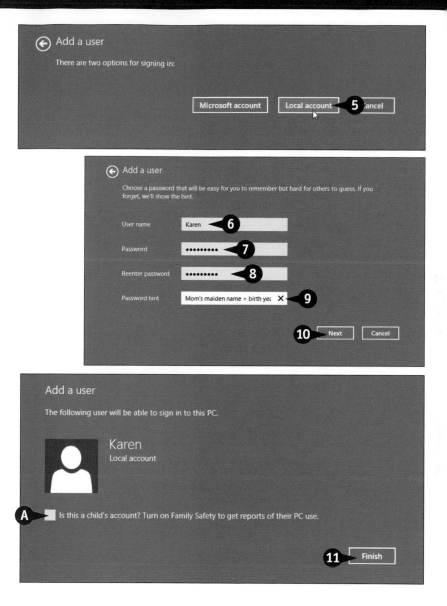

The local account version of the Add a User screen appears.

⑥ Type the name you want to use for the new account.

⑦ Type the password.

Note: The password characters appear as dots for security reasons.

⑧ Type the password again.

⑨ Type a hint that will help you or the user remember the password.

⑩ Click **Next**.

Windows creates the account.

Ⓐ If you are setting up an account for a child, you can click this check box (☐ changes to ☑) to track and control the child's PC usage. See Chapter 13 for details.

⑪ Click **Finish**.

TIP

How do I create a secure password?

Here are some guidelines to follow:

- Do not use an obvious password such as the user's account name or the word "password."

- Make sure the password is at least eight characters long.

- Use at least one character from at least three of the following four sets: lowercase letters, uppercase letters, numbers, and symbols.

Switch Between Accounts

After you have created more than one account on your computer, you can switch between accounts. This is useful when one person is already working in Windows and another person needs to use the computer.

When you switch to a second account, Windows leaves the original user's programs and windows running. This means that after the second person is finished, the original user can sign on again and continue working as before.

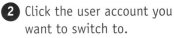

Switch Between Accounts

① On the Start screen, click your user account tile.

② Click the user account you want to switch to.

Windows prompts you for the user account password.

 Type the password.

④ Click Submit (→).

Ⓐ The user's name and picture now appear in the Start screen.

Note: The first time you switch to a new account, Windows takes a few moments to configure the account.

TIP

What happens if I forget my password?
When you set up your password as described in the previous section, Windows asks you to supply a hint to help you remember the password. If you cannot remember your password, follow these steps:

① In the sign-on screen, leave the password text box blank.

② Click **Submit** (→).

Windows tells you the password is incorrect.

③ Click **OK** to return to the sign-on screen.

Windows displays the password hint.

Change Your User Account Picture

You can add visual interest to your user account as well as make it easier to tell one user account from another by adding a picture to the account. When you create a user account, Windows assigns it a default picture, which appears in the user's Start screen tile, the Accounts screen of the PC Settings app, and the sign-on screen. Unfortunately, this default picture is a generic silhouette of a person's head and upper torso, so it is not very interesting or useful. If you have a more suitable picture that you would prefer to use, you can change your picture.

Change Your User Account Picture

1 On the Start screen, click your user account tile.

2 Click **Change account picture**.

The PC Settings app appears with the Your Account screen displayed.

3 Click **Browse**.

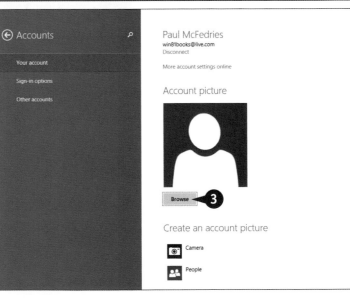

The Account Pictures screen appears.

4 Click **This PC** and then click the folder that contains the picture you want to use.

5 Click the picture you want to use.

6 Click **Choose Image**.

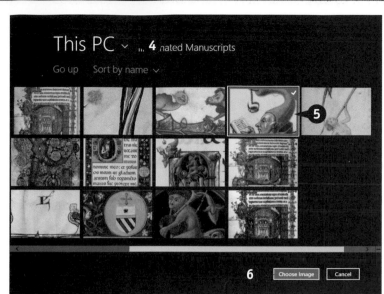

This PC ∨ **4** nated Manuscripts

Go up   Sort by name ∨

5

6   Choose Image   Cancel

A Your account tab appears and displays the new picture.

⊕ Accounts

Your account

Sign-in options

Other accounts

Paul McFedries
win81books@live.com
Disconnect

More account settings online

Account picture

A

Browse

Create an account picture

Camera

People

TIP

How do I use a webcam photo as my user account picture?

Repeat steps **1** and **2**. Click **Camera**. The Camera app appears. Position yourself within the screen. Click the screen to take the picture. The Camera app displays the photo and adds a rectangle that defines the area of the photo it will use for your account picture. Click and drag the rectangle to the position you want. Click and drag the rectangle corners to set the size and shape of the rectangle. Click **OK**.

Change a User's Password

If you set up a user account with no password, or if you find it difficult to remember your password, you can change the password. Assigning a password to each user account is good practice because otherwise someone who sits down at the PC can sign in using an unprotected account. It is also good practice to assign a strong password to each account, so that a malicious user cannot guess the password and gain access to the system. Whether you want to assign a password or create a password that is stronger or easier to remember, you can use Windows to change an existing password.

Change a User's Password

1 If you want to change another user's password, sign in as that user.

2 Display the Accounts screen of the PC Settings app.

Note: See "Display User Accounts," earlier in this chapter, to learn how to display the Accounts screen.

3 Click **Sign-in options**.

4 Under Password, click **Change**.

Note: If the account has no password, click **Add** in the Password section.

If you are using a Microsoft account, Windows prompts you to sign in.

Note: If you are using a local account with a password, skip steps **5** and **6**. If the account has no password, you can also skip step **7**.

5 Type your Microsoft account password.

6 Click **Finish**.

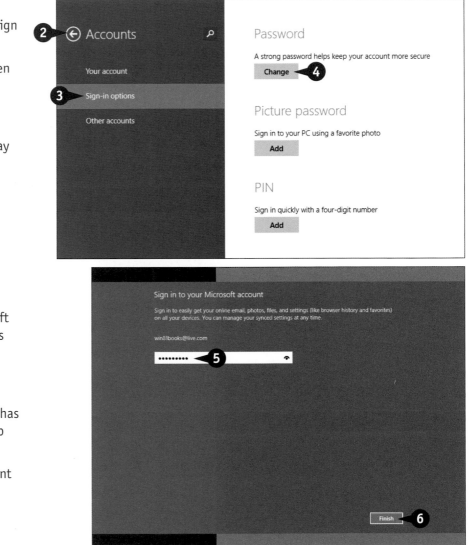

Windows prompts you for your old and new passwords.

7 Type your old password.

8 Type the new password.

9 Type the new password again.

A If you are not sure whether you typed a password correctly, click and hold the ⬛ icon to temporarily display the password.

10 Click **Next**.

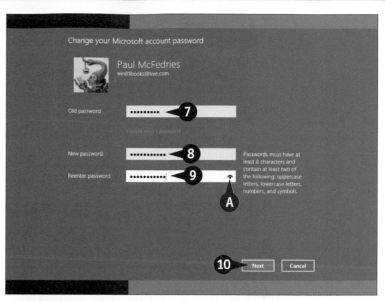

11 Click **Finish**.

Windows updates the user account password.

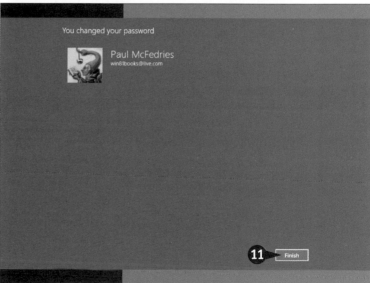

TIP

Are there any other precautions I can take to protect my password?
Yes, besides creating a strong password, you can safeguard your password by following these guidelines:

- Do not tell anyone your password.
- Do not write down your password.

- Make your password easier to remember by using a mnemonic device. For example, you could use the first letters as well as any numbers that appear in the name of a favorite book or movie.

Delete an Account

If you create a user account temporarily, or if you have a user account that is no longer needed or no longer used, you can delete that account. This reduces the number of users that appear in the Users tab of the PC Settings app, as well as the Windows sign-on screen, which can make these screens a bit easier to navigate. Deleting a user account also means that Windows reclaims the disk space that the account uses, which gives you more room to store files in your other accounts.

Delete an Account

1 Sign out of the user account you want to delete.

Note: To sign out of an account, click the user account tile on the Start screen, and then click **Sign out**.

2 Display the Accounts screen of the PC Settings app.

Note: See "Display User Accounts," earlier in this chapter, to learn how to display the Accounts screen.

3 Click **Other accounts**.

The Other Accounts screen appears.

4 Click the user account you want to delete.

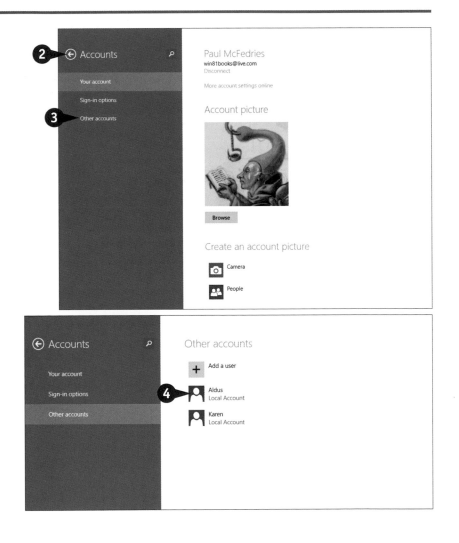

5 Click **Remove**.

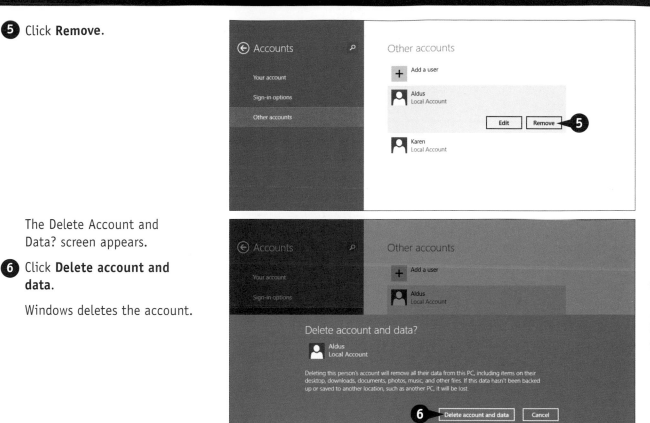

The Delete Account and Data? screen appears.

6 Click **Delete account and data**.

Windows deletes the account.

Why can I not delete my original Windows account?

Windows configures the original user account as the administrator account on the computer, which means it is the only account that is allowed to perform tasks such as creating and deleting user accounts. Windows does not allow you to delete this account because it requires that there always be at least one administrator account on the computer. When you are logged in with another account, you cannot access the Other Accounts screen, so you cannot use it to delete your original Windows account.

Create a Homegroup

You can share documents and media easily with other Windows computers by creating a homegroup on your network. A homegroup simplifies network sharing by making it easy to create a homegroup and share documents with other computers and users who are also connected to that homegroup.

You use one Windows computer to create the homegroup, and then you use the homegroup password to join your other Windows computers. For more information, see the section, "Join a Homegroup," later in this chapter.

Create a Homegroup

1 On the Start screen, press .

2 Click **Change PC settings**.

The PC Settings app appears.

3 Click **Network**.

The Network screen appears.

 4 Click **HomeGroup**.

5 Click **Create**.

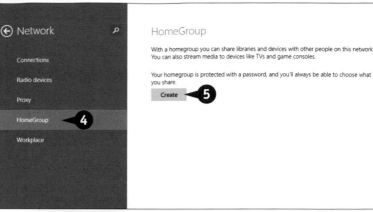

Windows creates the homegroup and displays the HomeGroup screen.

6 Click the switch to **On** for each type of file you want to share with the homegroup.

7 If you want devices on your network to be able to play your shared data, click this switch to **On**.

8 Make a mental note of the homegroup password.

You can now join your other Windows 8.1, Windows 8, or Windows 7 computers to the homegroup, as described in the next section.

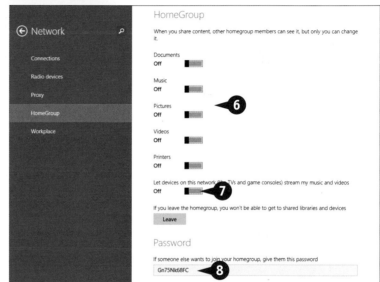

TIPS

I have lost my homegroup password. How do I view it again?

One method is to repeat steps **1** to **4**. Alternatively, press ⊞+Ⓦ to open the Settings search pane, type **homegroup**, and then click **Change homegroup password**. Click the **View or print the homegroup password** link to see your password. To print the password, click **Print this page**.

How can I change the homegroup password?

On the Start screen, press ⊞+Ⓦ to open the Settings search pane, type **homegroup**, and then click **Change homegroup password**. Click the **Change the password** link and then click **Change the password** to generate a new homegroup password. If computers have joined the homegroup, provide them with the new password.

Join a Homegroup

If your network has a homegroup, you can join your Windows computer to that homegroup. This enables you to access shared resources on other homegroup computers, and to share your own resources with the homegroup. This section assumes you or someone else on your home network has already set up a homegroup as described in the "Create a Homegroup" section and that you have the homegroup password.

Join a Homegroup

1 On the Start screen, press
⊞+🔲.

2 Click **Change PC settings**.

The PC Settings app appears.

3 Click **Network.**

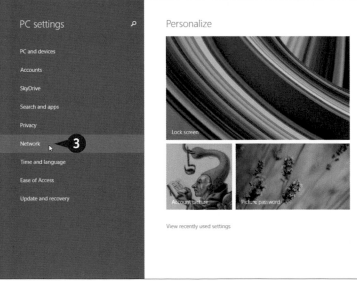

4 Click **HomeGroup**.

Windows prompts you for the homegroup password.

5 Type the homegroup password.

6 Click **Join**.

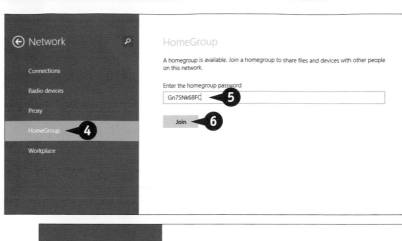

Windows joins the homegroup and displays the Homegroup screen.

7 Click the switch to **On** for each type of file you want to share with the homegroup.

8 If you want devices on your network to be able to play your shared data, click this switch to **On**.

You can now access other homegroup computers and share your files with the homegroup.

TIPS

When I try to join a homegroup, Windows tells me my password is not correct. What am I doing wrong?

First, double-check that you have been given the correct homegroup password and that you are typing that password correctly. Second, understand that homegroup passwords are case-sensitive, so you must enter the uppercase and lowercase letters exactly as they appear in the original homegroup settings. Make sure your keyboard does not have Caps Lock turned on.

Can I leave a homegroup if I no longer need it?

Yes. On the Start screen, press ⊞+🔲 to open the Settings pane, and then click **Change PC Settings**. Click **Network**, click **HomeGroup**, and then click **Leave**. Windows removes your computer from the homegroup.

Share a Document or Folder

You can share documents and folders of your choice with your homegroup, if your network has one. You can also share a document or folder with other users set up on your computer. Sharing a document or folder enables you to work on a file with other people without having to send them a copy of the file. You can set up each document or folder with View or View and Edit permissions. View permission means that users cannot make changes to the document or folder; View and Edit permission means that users can view and make changes to the document or folder.

Share a Document or Folder

Share with the Homegroup

1 On the Start screen, click **Desktop** (not shown).

2 Click **File Explorer** (📁).

3 Open the folder containing the item you want to share.

4 Click the document or folder you want to share.

5 Click the **Share** tab.

6 Click **Homegroup (view)**.

A To allow homegroup users to make changes to the item, click **Homegroup (view and edit)** instead.

Share with a Specific User

1 Open the folder containing the item you want to share.

2 Click the document or folder you want to share.

3 Click the **Share** tab.

4 Click **Specific people**.

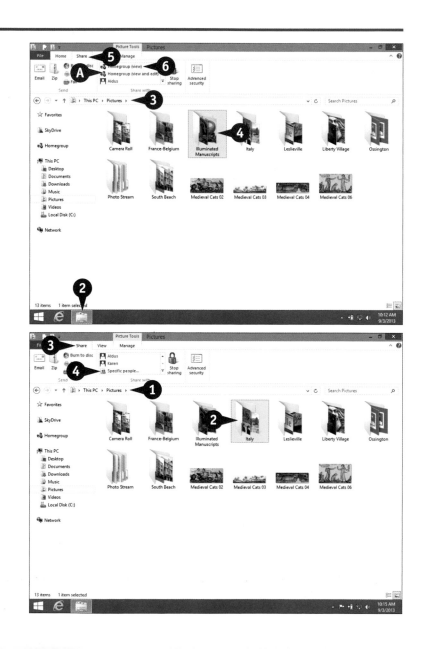

The File Sharing dialog box
appears.

5 Click and then click the
name of the user.

6 Click **Add**.

7 Click and then click the
permission level.

Note: Read permission is the
same as View, and Read/Write is
the same as View and Edit.

8 Click **Share**.

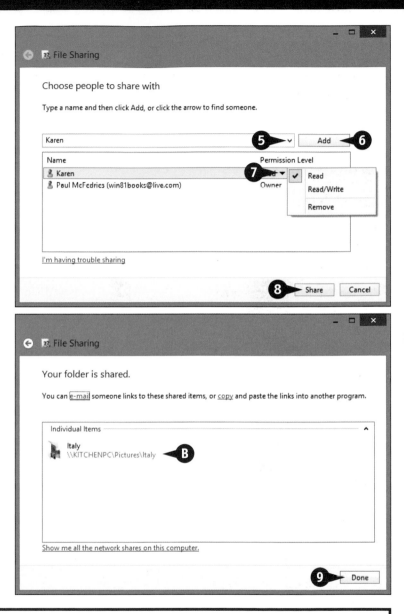

Windows shares the
document or folder.

B Be sure to give the user the
address that appears here.

9 Click **Done**.

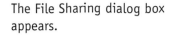

**How do the other users access the shared
document or folder?**

You need to send them the address that appears in
the final File Sharing dialog box. You have two
choices: Click **e-mail** to send the address via e-mail,
or click **copy** to copy the address to memory. You can
then open a program such as WordPad, click **Edit**, and
then click **Paste** to paste the address.

**Can I see all the documents and folders that I
am sharing with other users?**

Yes, you can do this in two ways. In the final File
Sharing dialog box, click **Show me all the
network shares on this computer**. Alternatively,
in any folder window, click **Network** and then
double-click your computer.

View Network Resources

To see what other network users have shared on your homegroup, you can use the Homegroup folder to view the other computers and see their shared resources. To get access to the shared homegroup resources, you must know the homegroup's password and have joined the homegroup. If your network does not have a homegroup, you can use the Network folder instead. A network resource can be a folder, hard drive, CD or DVD drive, removable disk drive, printer, scanner, or other shared device.

View Network Resources

View Homegroup Resources

1 On the Start screen, click **Desktop** (not shown).

2 Click **File Explorer** (📁).

3 Click the **Homegroup** folder.

Ⓐ Windows displays icons for each user who is sharing data in the homegroup.

4 Double-click the user who is sharing the resource you want to access.

Windows displays the resources the user is sharing.

Ⓑ If the user has an account on multiple PCs, you see a section for each PC.

Ⓒ The resources that the user is sharing on the computer appear here.

5 Double-click an icon to access the resource.

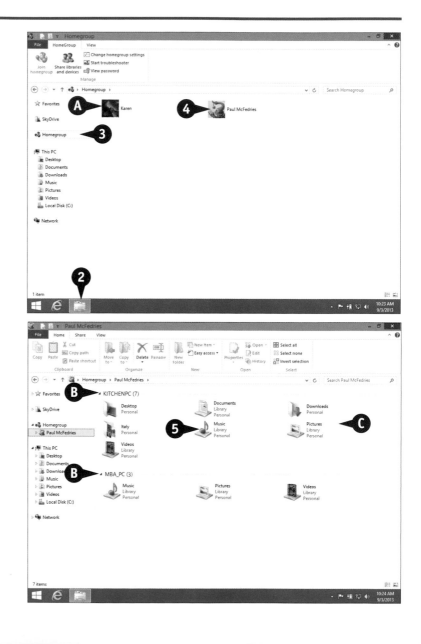

View Network Resources

1. On the Start screen, click **Desktop** (not shown).

2. Click **File Explorer** (📁).

3. Click the **Network** folder.

D Windows displays icons for each computer that is sharing resources.

4. Double-click the computer that is sharing the resource you want to access.

E The resources the computer is sharing appear here.

5. Double-click an icon to access the resource.

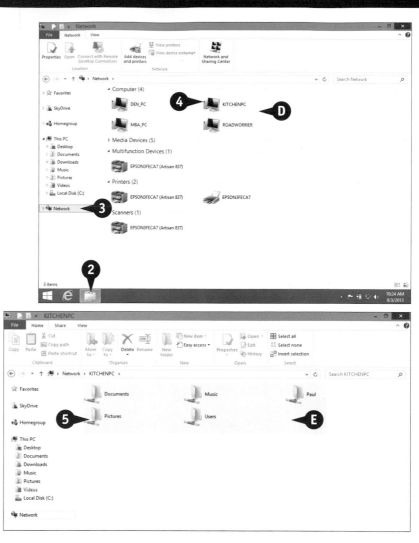

TIPS

How can I fix network problems?

Windows comes with troubleshooting tools for networks. If you are having homegroup trouble, launch File Explorer, click the **Homegroup** folder, click the **Homegroup** tab, and then click **Start troubleshooter.** If you are having network trouble, right-click the network icon in the taskbar's notification area, and then click **Troubleshoot problems.** In both cases, follow whatever repair techniques Windows suggests.

How do I change my computer's network name?

On the Start screen, type **name** and then click **View your PC name** in the search results. Windows opens the PC Info screen of the PC Settings app. Click **Rename**, use the Rename Your PC text box to type the new name, and then click **Save.**

CHAPTER 13

Implementing Security

Threats to your computing-related security and privacy often come from the Internet and from someone simply using your computer while you are not around. To protect yourself and your family, you need to understand these threats and know what you can do to thwart them.

Understanding Windows Security

Before you get to the details of securing your computer, it helps to take a step back and look at the security and privacy tools that Windows makes available. These tools include your Windows user account password, User Account Control, Family Safety, Windows Firewall, Windows Defender, and the private browsing feature in Internet Explorer. Taken all together, these features represent a *defense-in-depth* security strategy that uses multiple layers to keep you and your data safe and private.

User Account Password

Windows security begins with assigning a password to each user account on the computer. This prevents unauthorized users from accessing the system, and it enables you to lock your computer. For more information, see the section, "Lock Your Computer," later in this chapter.

User Account Control

User Account Control asks you to confirm certain actions that could conceivably harm your system. When you are using your main Windows user account, your computer's administrative account, click **Yes** to continue; for all other accounts, you must enter the administrative account's password to continue.

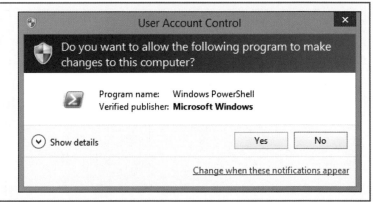

Family Safety

If one or more children use your computer, you can use the Windows Family Safety feature to protect them from inadvertently running certain programs, playing unsuitable games, and using the computer at inappropriate times. For more information, see the section, "Set Up Family Safety," later in this chapter.

Set up Family Safety

Use Family Safety to get reports of your kids' PC activities, choose what they see online, and set time limits, apps restrictions, and more.

To turn on Family Safety, add a new child's account, or change an existing account to a child's account in Accounts.

To turn off Family Safety for an account, change the account type from Child to Standard in Accounts.

Windows Firewall

When your computer is connected to the Internet, it is possible for another person to access your computer and infect it with a virus or cause other damage; as a result, Windows comes with its Windows Firewall feature turned on. This prevents intruders from accessing your computer while you are online.

Windows Defender

Spyware is a software program that installs itself on your computer without your knowledge or consent. This type of program surreptitiously gathers data

Malware Detected
Windows Defender is taking action to clean detected malware

from your computer, steals your passwords, displays advertisements, and hijacks your web browser. To prevent spyware from installing on your computer, Windows includes the Windows Defender program.

InPrivate Web Browsing

The Internet Explorer web browser normally collects data as you navigate from site to site. Most of this data is used to improve your browsing experience, but it can also be used to track

InPrivate is turned on

InPrivate Browsing helps prevent Internet Explorer from storing data about your browsing session. This includes cookies, temporary Internet files, history, and other data.

your online activities. If you plan to visit private or sensitive sites, you can turn on InPrivate Browsing, which tells Internet Explorer not to collect any data during your browsing session.

Reset Your PC

Your computer contains a lot of information about you, including your personal files, your Internet Explorer pinned sites, your e-mail messages, and your Windows settings. If you

Remove everything and reinstall Windows

If you want to recycle your PC or start over completely, you can reset it to its factory settings.

Get started

plan on selling or donating your computer, you can use the Reset Your PC feature to securely remove your data while installing a fresh copy of Windows.

Check the Action Center for Security Problems

In Windows, the Action Center displays messages about the current state of your computer. In particular, the Action Center warns you if your computer has any current security problems. For example, the Action Center tells you if your computer does not have virus protection installed or if the Windows Defender spyware database is out of date. The Action Center will also warn you if your computer is not set up to download updates automatically and if important security features such as User Account Control are turned off.

Check the Action Center for Security Problems

1 Press ⊞+W.

The Settings search pane appears.

2 Type **action**.

Windows displays the "action" search results.

3 Click **Action Center**.

The Action Center window appears.

4 Review the messages in the Security section.

5 Click a message button to resolve the security issue, such as clicking **Turn on now** if Windows Defender is turned off.

6 Click **Security**.

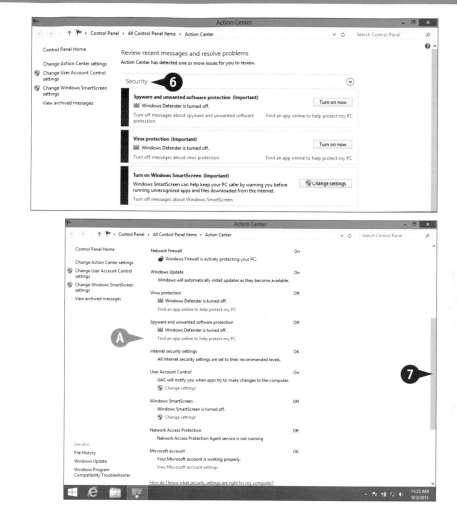

7 Scroll down the Action Center window.

A The Action Center displays a summary of all your system's security settings.

Is there a quicker way to see the Action Center messages?

Yes, if you are working in the Desktop app, you can view the Action Center messages and open the Action Center more quickly by following these steps:

1 Click the **Action Center** icon (🖳) in the taskbar's notification area.

A The current Action Center messages appear here.

2 To launch the Action Center, click **Open Action Center**.

The Action Center appears.

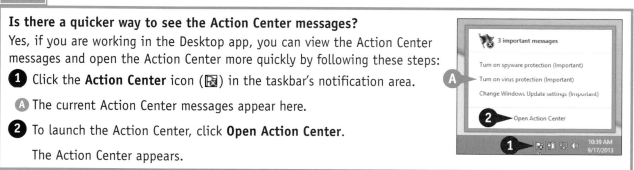

Create a Picture Password

You can make it easier to sign in to your Windows computer by creating a picture password. This is particularly true for a tablet PC. If you find that it is taking you a long time to sign in to Windows using your tablet's touch keyboard, you can switch to a picture password instead. In this case, your password is a series of three gestures — any combination of a click, a straight line, or a circle — that you apply to a photo. Windows displays the photo at startup, and you repeat your gestures, in order, to sign in.

Create a Picture Password

1 Press ⊞+W.

On a tablet, swipe left from the right edge, click **Search**, and then click **Settings**.

The Settings search pane appears.

2 Type **password**.

Windows displays the "password" search results.

3 Click or tap **Set up picture password**.

The PC Settings app appears and displays the Sign-in options screen.

4 Under Picture password, click or tap **Add**.

276

Windows prompts you for your account password.

5 Type your password.

6 Click **OK**.

The Welcome to picture Password screen appears.

7 Click **Choose picture**.

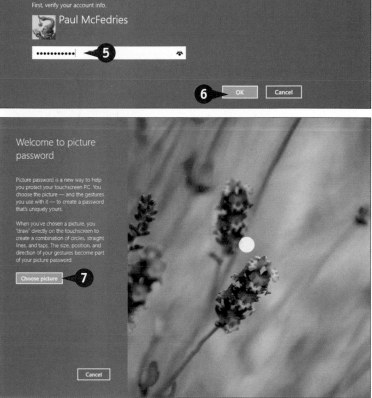

continued ▶

TIPS

Is a picture password safe to use?
Yes. The biggest drawback is that it is possible for a malicious user to view and possibly even record your gestures using a camera. Unlike a regular text password for which the characters appear as dots to prevent someone from seeing them, your gestures have no such protection.

Does the picture password replace my existing text password?
No, your picture password is applied to your user account along with your existing text-based password. It is not difficult to bypass the picture password and sign in using the text password, so it is vital that you still protect your PC with a strong text password.

I n the same way that you should not choose a regular account password that is extremely obvious, such as the word *password* or your username, you should take care to avoid creating an obvious picture password. For example, if you were using a photo showing three faces, an obvious picture password would be a click on each face.

A good picture password not only uses all three available gestures, but also uses them in nonobvious ways. To ensure that you have memorized your picture password, you should sign out of your account a few times and then sign back on using the picture password.

Create a Picture Password (continued)

The Pictures screen appears.

 Click the picture that you want to use.

9 Click **Open**.

The How's this look? screen appears.

10 Drag the picture so that the image is positioned where you prefer.

11 Click **Use this picture**.

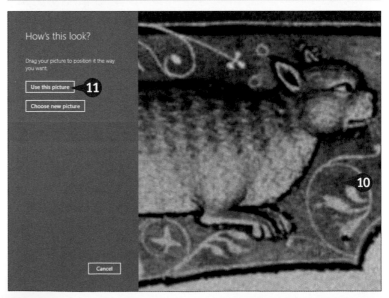

The Set up your Gestures screen appears.

 Use your finger or a stylus to draw three gestures.

13 Repeat the gestures to confirm.

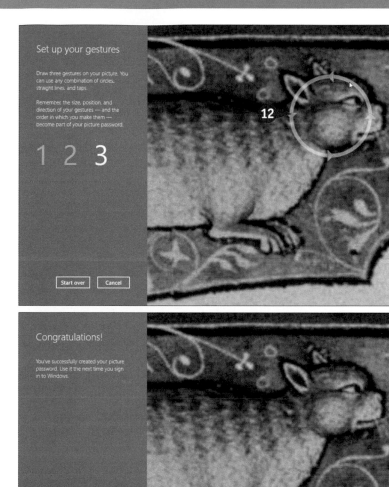

14 Click **Finish**.

The next time that you sign in to Windows, you will be prompted to enter your picture password gestures.

TIPS

What happens if I forget my gestures?
Click **Switch to password** to sign in with your regular password. To get a reminder of your picture password gestures, follow steps **1** to **3** in this section, click **Change**, type your user account password, and click **OK**. In the Change Your Picture Password screen, click **Replay.** Click the picture to see each gesture.

Can I change my picture password?
Yes. Open the Change Your Picture Password screen, choose a new picture, if necessary, and then run through your gestures.

Lock Your Computer

You can enhance your computer's security by locking the device when you leave it unattended. Protecting your account with a password prevents someone from logging on to your account, but what happens when you leave your computer unattended? If you remain logged on to the system, any person who picks up your computer can use it to view and change files.

To prevent this, you can lock your computer. After your computer is locked, anyone who tries to use your computer will first have to enter your password.

Lock Your Computer

Lock Your Computer

1 On the Start screen, click your user account tile.

2 Click **Lock**.

Windows locks your computer and displays the Lock screen.

Unlock Your Computer

1 On the Lock screen, press **Enter** to display the sign-on screen.

A The word "Locked" appears under your username.

2 Click inside the **Password** text box.

3 Type your password.

4 Click **Submit** (→).

Windows unlocks your computer and restores your desktop.

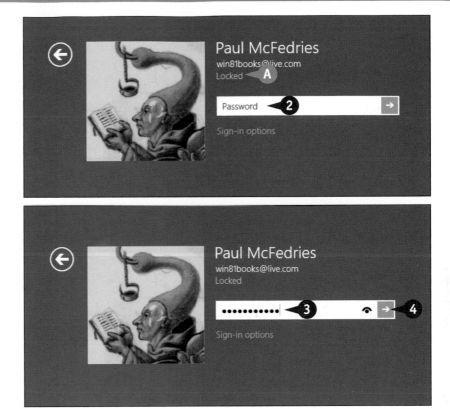

TIP

How can I quickly access the Lock command?
You can press ⊞+L, or configure Windows to automatically lock the computer. To configure Windows, press ⊞+W to open the Settings search pane. Type **lock computer**. Click **Lock the computer when I leave it alone for a period of time**. Click **On resume, display logon screen** (☐ changes to ☑). Use the **Wait** text box to set the number of minutes of idle time after which Windows locks your computer. Click **OK**.

Set Up Family Safety

If your children have computer access, you can protect them from malicious content by setting up parental controls, called the *Family Safety* feature, for activities such as web surfing, playing games, and running programs. Family Safety enables you to set specific limits on how your children perform various activities on the computer. For example, the Windows Web Filter lets you specify allowable websites, restrict sites based on content, and block file downloads. Before you can apply the Family Safety controls, you must set up a Windows user account for each child. See Chapter 12 for more information.

Set Up Family Safety

Activate Family Safety

1 Press ⊞+W.

The Settings search pane appears.

2 Type **family**.

Windows displays the "family" search results.

3 Click **Family Safety**.

The Family Safety window appears.

4 Click the user that you want to work with.

Note: You only see the user list if you have at least one user set up with a Child account. At the Start screen, type **accounts**, click **Add, delete, and manage other user accounts**, click the account, click **Edit**, select **Child** in the Account type list, and then click **OK**.

The User Settings window appears.

 For a Child account, Windows automatically turns on parental controls.

Set Web Restrictions

5 Click **Web filtering**.

The Web Filtering window appears.

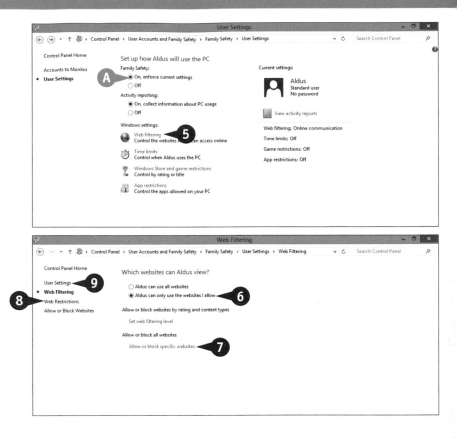

6 Click *User* **can only use the websites I allow** (○ changes to ◉).

7 If you want to control specific sites, click **Allow or block specific websites**, type the site address, and then click **Allow** or **Block**.

8 Click **Web Restrictions** and then click a web-restriction level (○ changes to ◉).

9 Click **User Settings**.

Windows sets the web restrictions, and returns you to the User Settings window.

TIPS

How do I prevent my kids from downloading files?

In the User Settings window, click **Web Filtering** and then click **Web Restrictions** to display the Web Restrictions window. Scroll down to the bottom of the window and click **Block file downloads** (☐ changes to ☑). Click **User Settings**.

Can I choose which game rating system Windows uses?

Yes, Windows supports several game rating systems, including classifications from the Entertainment Software Rating Board (the default system), Computer Entertainment Rating Organization, and Game Rating Board. Return to the Family Safety window, click **Rating Systems**, click the system that you want to use (○ changes to ◉), and then click **Accounts to Monitor**.

continued ▶

Set Up Family Safety (continued)

After you have parental controls activated, you can set up specific restrictions. For example, you can allow and block specific websites, and you can set the web-restriction level to determine the types of sites your children can access.

You can also set up times when children are not allowed to use the computer. The Windows Family Safety feature also enables you to set the maximum game rating that kids can play, allow or block specific games, and allow or block specific programs.

Set Up Family Safety (continued)

Set Computer Time Limits

10 Click **Time limits**.

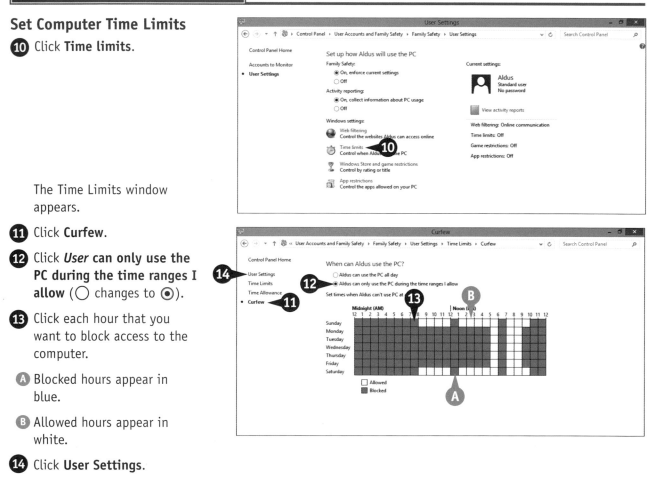

The Time Limits window appears.

11 Click **Curfew**.

12 Click *User* **can only use the PC during the time ranges I allow** (○ changes to ⊙).

13 Click each hour that you want to block access to the computer.

Ⓐ Blocked hours appear in blue.

Ⓑ Allowed hours appear in white.

14 Click **User Settings**.

Windows sets the time limits, and returns you to the User Settings window.

Restrict Game Usage

15 Click **Windows Store and game restrictions**.

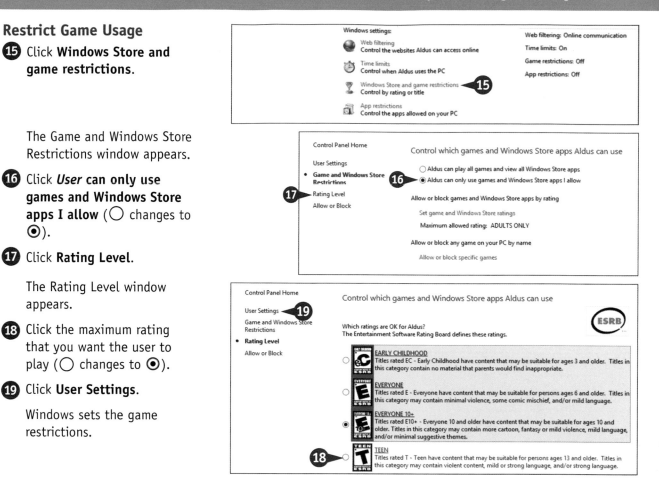

The Game and Windows Store Restrictions window appears.

16 Click *User* **can only use games and Windows Store apps I allow** (○ changes to ◉).

17 Click **Rating Level**.

The Rating Level window appears.

18 Click the maximum rating that you want the user to play (○ changes to ◉).

19 Click **User Settings**.

Windows sets the game restrictions.

TIPS

How do I block a specific game?
In the Game and Windows Store Restrictions window, click **Allow or block specific games**. For the game that you want to block, click the **Always Block** option (○ changes to ◉).

How do I restrict my kids to running certain programs?
In the User Settings window, click **App restrictions**. Click *User* **can only use the apps I allow**, where *User* is the name of the user, and then click the check box beside each program that you want the user to run (☐ changes to ☑).

Browse the Web Privately

If you visit sensitive or private websites, you can tell Internet Explorer not to save any browsing history for those sites. If you regularly visit private websites or websites that contain sensitive or secret data, you can ensure that no one else sees any data for such sites by deleting your browsing history, as described in the Tip. However, if you visit such sites only occasionally, deleting your entire browsing history is overkill. A better solution is to turn on the InPrivate Browsing feature in Internet Explorer before you visit private sites. This tells Internet Explorer to temporarily stop saving any browsing history.

Browse the Web Privately

1 On the Start screen, click **Internet Explorer**.

2 Right-click the screen.

Internet Explorer displays the tab bar.

3 Click **Tab tools** (●).

4 Click **New InPrivate tab**.

A new Internet Explorer tab appears.

Ⓐ The InPrivate indicator appears in the address bar.

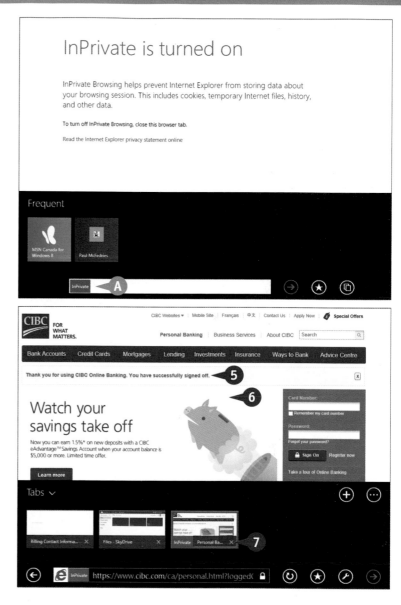

5 Surf to and interact with websites as you normally would, such as the banking site shown here.

6 When you are done, right-click the screen.

7 Click **Close** (🗙) on the InPrivate Browsing tab.

Internet Explorer closes the InPrivate Browsing tab and turns off InPrivate Browsing.

TIP

What is browsing history?
Internet Explorer maintains a list of the sites that you visit, as well as text and passwords that you have typed into forms, the names of files that you have downloaded, and *cookies,* which are small text files that store site preferences and site logon data. Saving this history is dangerous because other people who use your computer can view this information. You eliminate this risk by using a private browsing session. To delete your browsing history, press ⊞+C, click **Settings**, click **Options**, click **Select** in the History section, click **Browsing history** (☐ changes to ☑), and then click **Delete**.

Clear Your Private Information

One of the benefits of the Windows Start screen is that it uses *live tiles* that display constantly updated information. This includes newly received e-mail and instant messages, the current music you are playing, the photo slide show you are playing, and the latest information from the Weather and Finance apps. However, this can be a privacy problem because anyone walking by your computer can see this information with a quick glance. To prevent this, you can temporarily clear all your private information from the Start screen tiles.

Clear Your Private Information

1 Move the mouse pointer (⤵) to the top-right corner of the screen.

The Charms menu appears.

2 Click **Settings**.

The Settings pane appears.

3 Click **Tiles**.

The Tiles Settings pane appears.

 Click **Clear**.

Windows removes all your personal information from the Start screen.

TIPS

Can I prevent an app from ever showing private information in its tile?

Yes, you can turn off the updating permanently for the tile. Right-click the tile and then click **Turn live tile off**.

Should I prevent an app from displaying private information in a notification?

Some notifications can contain private information, so you might want to turn off the notifications for certain apps. Follow steps **1** and **2** in this section to display the Settings pane and click **Change PC settings** to open the PC Settings app. Click **Search & apps**, click **Notifications**, and then beside each app for which you want notifications disabled, click the switch to **Off**.

Reset Your Computer to Preserve Privacy

As you use your computer, you accumulate a large amount of personal data: documents, installed apps, Internet Explorer favorites, e-mail messages, photos, and much more. If you are selling your computer or giving it away, you probably do not want the recipient to have access to all that personal data. To prevent this, you can reset the computer, which deletes all your personal data and reinstalls a fresh copy of Windows.

Reset Your Computer to Preserve Privacy

Note: This section assumes that you have copied your personal files to a backup destination, such as an external hard drive.

 1 Insert your Windows installation media or recovery drive.

Note: To learn how to create a recovery drive, see Chapter 15.

2 At the Start screen, type **recovery**.

The Search pane appears and displays the "recovery" search results.

3 Click **Recovery options**.

The PC Settings app opens.

4 Under Remove everything and reinstall Windows, click **Get started**.

Windows displays an overview of the reset process.

⑤ Click **Next**.

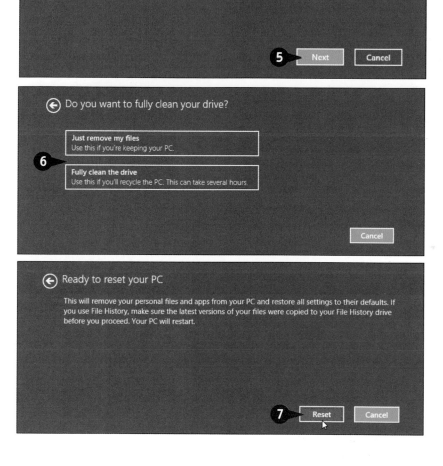

Reset your PC

Here's what will happen:

• All your personal files and apps will be removed.
• Your PC settings will be changed back to their defaults.

⑤ Next   Cancel

Windows asks how you want to remove your personal files.

⑥ Click the removal option that you want.

Do you want to fully clean your drive?

Just remove my files
Use this if you're keeping your PC.

Fully clean the drive
Use this if you'll recycle the PC. This can take several hours.

Cancel

The Ready to Reset Your PC screen appears.

⑦ Click **Reset**.

Windows resets your computer.

Ready to reset your PC

This will remove your personal files and apps from your PC and restore all settings to their defaults. If you use File History, make sure the latest versions of your files were copied to your File History drive before you proceed. Your PC will restart.

⑦ Reset   Cancel

TIP

What is the difference between removing my files and fully cleaning the drive?
The Just Remove My Files option deletes your data in the sense that after Windows is reset, it can no longer work with or see the data. However, the data remains on the computer's hard drive, so a person with special tools can access the data. The Fully Clean the Drive option prevents this by overwriting your information with random data, which can take quite a bit of time but is much more secure.

CHAPTER 14

Getting More from a Tablet PC

Windows comes with many features designed to help you get the most out of your tablet PC. In this chapter, you learn how to use gestures, type with and configure the touch keyboard, add a second monitor, and more.

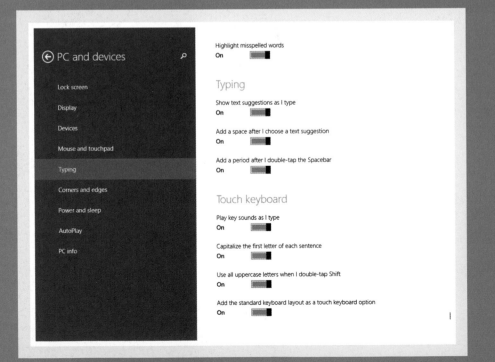

Understanding Gestures

You can get the most out of your Windows tablet by learning the various gestures that you can use to initiate actions, manipulate data, and control the elements on your screen. Traditional computers use the mouse and keyboard to input data and make things happen. A tablet lacks these input devices; instead, you must rely on your fingers because tablets are built to respond to touches on the glass screen surface. Some tablets also come with a small pen-like device called a *stylus,* which you can use instead of your finger for some actions.

Tap

Use your finger to touch the screen and then immediately release it. You use this gesture to initiate an action.

Double-Tap

Tap and release the screen twice, one tap right after the other. You also use this gesture to initiate an action, although mostly with older desktop programs.

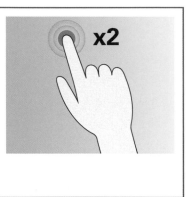

Tap and Hold

Press your finger on the screen for a second or two. This gesture usually displays a menu of options related to whatever screen object you are pressing.

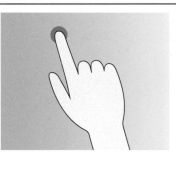

Slide

Place your finger on the screen, move your finger, and then release. You use this gesture either to move an object from one place to another or to scroll the screen in the same direction as your finger.

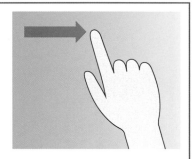

Swipe

Quickly and briefly run your finger along the screen. This gesture is often used to select an object, but there are also specific swipe gestures that display screen elements. For example, you use the swipe gesture to display the Charms menu (for more information, see Chapter 1).

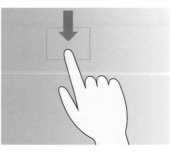

Pinch

Place two fingers apart on the screen and bring them closer together. This gesture zooms out on whatever is displayed on the screen, such as a photo.

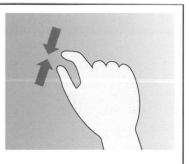

Spread

Place two fingers close together on the screen and move them farther apart. This gesture zooms in on whatever is displayed on the screen, such as a photo.

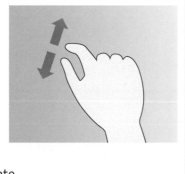

Turn

Place two fingers on the screen and turn them clockwise or counterclockwise. This gesture rotates whatever is displayed on the screen, such as a photo.

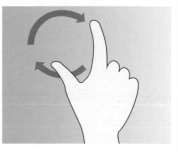

Using Gestures to Control Windows

To use your tablet efficiently and accurately, you need to know how to use gestures to control Windows. Using a tablet is a different experience than using a regular computer, but Windows was built with the tablet in mind, so it is intuitive and easy to learn.

If you have never used a tablet PC before, the main difference is that you use your fingers (or stylus) to run applications, select items, and manipulate screen objects. This might seem awkward at first, but it will come to seem quite natural if you practice the techniques shown here as much as you can.

Using Gestures to Control Windows

Initiate an Action

1 Position your finger or the stylus over the object that you want to work with.

2 Tap the screen.

Depending on the object, Windows either selects the object or performs some operation in response to the tap, such as displaying the desktop.

Swipe the Screen

1 Quickly move your finger or the stylus across the screen in a swipe motion.

Swipe left from the right edge of the tablet to display the Charms menu.

Swipe right from the left edge of the tablet to switch between running applications.

Swipe right or left to navigate the screens. Swipe down on a tile to select it.

A When you select a tile, Windows displays its related commands.

Display the Application Bar

1 Place your finger or stylus at the bottom edge of the screen.

2 Swipe up.

B Windows displays the application bar.

Note: The application bar's contents vary depending on the app you are using.

Move an Item

1 Position your finger or the stylus over the item that you want to move.

2 Tap and hold the item and immediately begin moving your finger or the stylus.

C The object moves along with your finger or the stylus.

3 When the object is repositioned where you want it, lift your finger or the stylus off the screen to complete the move.

TIP

After I tap an app tile, how do I return to the Start screen?
To return to the Start screen, you can

- Display the Charms menu and then tap **Start**.
- Display the list of running apps and then tap the **Start** thumbnail.
- Close the app.

Input Text with the Touch Keyboard

If you are using a tablet or a PC in tablet mode, you do not have a physical keyboard available. To input text, Windows offers the touch keyboard, which is a virtual keyboard that appears on the screen. You input text using this keyboard by tapping the keys. Windows offers several touch keyboard types, and some characters are difficult to find, so you need to know how to use the touch keyboard to get the most out of Windows.

Input Text with the Touch Keyboard

Select a Keyboard

1 In an app, tap the text box area in which you want to insert text.

A Windows displays the touch keyboard.

2 Tap **Keyboard** (⌨).

Windows displays the keyboard options.

B Tap (⌨) for the default keyboard.

C Tap (⌨) for the split keyboard.

D Tap (✍) for the writing pad.

E Tap (🖥) to hide the keyboard.

Input Text

1 Tap the key characters that you want to input and Windows inserts the text.

F To enter an uppercase letter, tap **Shift** (⇧) and then tap the letter.

G To delete the previous character, tap **Backspace** (⌫).

2 To enter numbers and other symbols, tap **&123**.

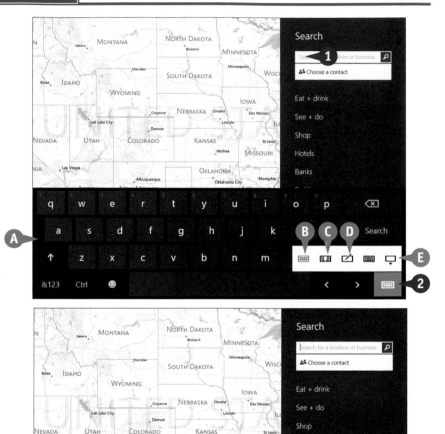

Windows displays the numbers and symbols.

③ Tap **More** (◉) to see more symbols.

④ To see more symbols, tap and hold a key.

Ⓗ Windows displays the extra symbols.

⑤ Slide your finger to the symbol that you want and then release.

Ⓘ Tap **Back** (◉) to return to the previous symbols.

Ⓙ Tap **&123** to return to the letters.

⑥ When you are done, tap (▦) and then tap (🖳) to hide the keyboard.

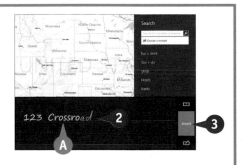

TIP

How do I write text with the stylus?

Follow these steps:

① Follow steps **1** and **2** in the "Select a Keyboard" subsection, and then tap ✎.

② Use the stylus to handwrite the text in the writing pad.

Ⓐ After a few seconds, Windows converts your writing to text.

③ Tap **Insert**.

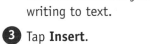

Configure the Touch Keyboard

The touch keyboard offers a number of features that make it easier to use. For example, the touch keyboard automatically adds a period and space when you double-tap the spacebar, and it automatically capitalizes the first letter of each sentence.

However, the touch keyboard also has some features that you might not like — such as the noise it makes each time you tap a key. You can use the PC Settings app to turn on the touch keyboard features that you like and turn off the features that you do not like.

Configure the Touch Keyboard

1 Swipe left from the right edge of the screen.

The Charms menu appears.

2 Tap **Settings**.

The Settings pane appears.

3 Tap **Change PC Settings**.

The PC Settings app appears.

④ Tap **PC and devices**.

⑤ Tap **Typing**.

⑥ Under Touch keyboard, tap each option **On** or **Off**, according to your preferences.

Windows applies your new settings to the touch keyboard.

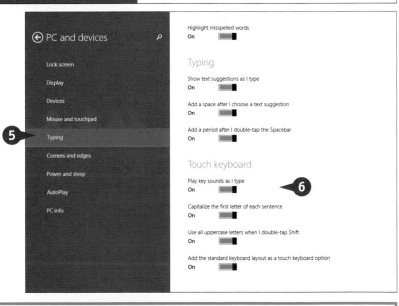

How can I access the standard keyboard layout?
If you tap **On** in step **6**, the next time that you use the keyboard, tap ⌨ and then tap ⌨. This presents all the keys on a normal keyboard.

Configure Your Tablet to Work with a Second Monitor

You can improve your productivity and efficiency by using a second monitor. To work with an external monitor, your tablet must have a video output port, such as VGA, DVI, or HDMI. If you do not have such a port, check with the manufacturer to see if an adapter is available that enables your tablet to connect with an external monitor. After you have connected your tablet and the external monitor, you then need to configure Windows to extend the Start screen to both the tablet screen and the external monitor.

Configure Your Tablet to Work with a Second Monitor

Extend to the External Monitor

1. Connect the second monitor to your tablet.

2. Swipe left from the right edge of the screen.

   The Charms menu appears.

3. Tap **Devices**.

The Devices pane appears.

4. Tap **Project**.

   The Project pane appears.

5 Tap **Extend**.

Windows connects to the second monitor and uses it to display the Desktop app.

Set the Main Display

1 Swipe left from the right edge of the screen and then tap **Search** (not shown).

The Search pane appears.

2 Type **resolution**.

Windows displays the "resolution" search results.

3 Tap **Change the screen resolution**.

The Display screen appears on the desktop.

4 Tap the monitor that you want to set as the main display.

5 Tap the **Make this my main display** check box (☐ changes to ✔).

6 Tap **Apply**.

Windows uses the monitor that you selected as your main display.

TIP

Why does my cursor stop at the right edge of the left screen?
If you find that the cursor stops at the right edge of your left monitor, it means that you need to exchange the icons of the left and right monitors. To do that, tap and drag the left monitor icon to the right of the other monitor icon (or vice versa).

Adjust Screen Brightness

You can extend the battery life of your tablet by turning down the screen brightness. Your tablet screen uses a lot of power, so turning down the brightness also reduces battery drain.

On the other hand, if you have trouble seeing the data on your tablet screen, you can often fix the problem by *increasing* the screen brightness. This is not a problem when your tablet is running on AC power. However, you should not use full screen brightness for very long when your tablet is running on its battery because a bright screen uses a lot of power.

Adjust Screen Brightness

1 Swipe left from the right edge of the screen.

The Charms menu appears.

2 Tap **Settings**.

The Settings pane appears.

3 Tap **Brightness**.

4 Tap and drag the slider to set the screen brightness.

Windows puts the new brightness setting into effect.

Monitor Battery Life

You can use the Power icon in the Desktop taskbar's notification area to monitor your tablet's remaining battery power. When the battery is at maximum charge, the icon shows as all white. As the battery charge falls, the amount of white in the icon also falls. You can also position your stylus cursor over the icon or tap the icon to see a tool tip that shows you the current battery level.

Monitor Battery Life

① On the Start screen, click **Desktop**.

The Desktop app appears.

② In the taskbar, tap the **Power** icon (🔋).

Ⓐ The current battery level appears here.

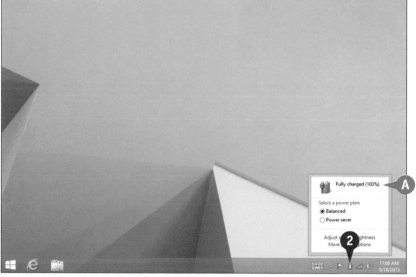

CHAPTER 15

Maintaining Windows

To keep your system running smoothly, maintain top performance, and reduce the risk of computer problems, you need to perform some routine maintenance chores. This chapter shows you how to delete unnecessary files, check for hard drive and other device errors, back up your files, and more.

Check Hard Drive Free Space

To ensure that your PC's hard drive does not become full, you should periodically check how much free space it has left. This is important because if you run out of room on your hard drive, you cannot install more programs or create more documents, and your PC's performance will suffer.

Of particular concern is the hard drive on which Windows is installed, usually drive C. If this hard drive's free space becomes low — say, less than about 20 or 25GB — Windows runs slowly. With normal computer use, you should check your hard drive free space about once a month.

Check Hard Drive Free Space

Note: You can also check the free space on a CD, DVD, memory card, or flash drive. Before you continue, insert the disc, card, or drive.

1 On the Start screen, type **this pc**.

2 Click **This PC**.

The This PC window appears in the Desktop app.

3 Click the **View** tab.

4 Click **Tiles**.

A Information about each drive appears along with the drive icon.

B This value tells you the amount of free space on the drive.

C This value tells you the total amount of space on the drive.

D This bar gives you a visual indication of how much disk space the drive is using.

E Windows is installed on the drive with the Windows logo (⊞).

F The used portion of the bar appears blue when a drive still has sufficient disk space.

G The used portion of the bar turns red when a drive's disk space becomes low.

5 Click **Close** (❌) to close the This PC window.

TIP

What can I do if my hard drive space is becoming low?
You can do three things:

- **Delete Personal Files**. If you have personal files — particularly media files such as images, music, and videos — that you no longer need, delete them.

- **Remove Programs**. If you have programs that you no longer use, uninstall them (see Chapter 2).

- **Run Disk Cleanup**. Use the Disk Cleanup program to delete files that Windows no longer uses. See the section, "Delete Unnecessary Files."

Delete Unnecessary Files

To free up hard drive space on your computer and keep Windows running efficiently, you can use the Disk Cleanup program to delete files that your system no longer needs. Although today's hard drives are quite large, it is still possible to run low on disk space, particularly because today's applications and media files are larger than ever.

Run Disk Cleanup any time that your hard drive free space becomes too low. If hard drive space is not a problem, run Disk Cleanup every two or three months.

Delete Unnecessary Files

1 On the Start screen, type **this pc**.

2 Click **This PC**.

The This PC window appears in the Desktop app.

3 Click the hard drive you want to clean.

4 Click the **Manage** tab.

5 Click **Cleanup**.

After a few moments, the Disk Cleanup dialog box appears.

Ⓐ This area displays the total amount of drive space you can free up.

Ⓑ This area displays the amount of drive space the activated options will free up.

❻ Click the check box (☐ changes to ☑) for each file type that you want to delete.

Ⓒ This area displays a description of the highlighted file type.

❼ Click **OK**.

Disk Cleanup asks you to confirm that you want to delete the file types.

❽ Click **Delete Files**.

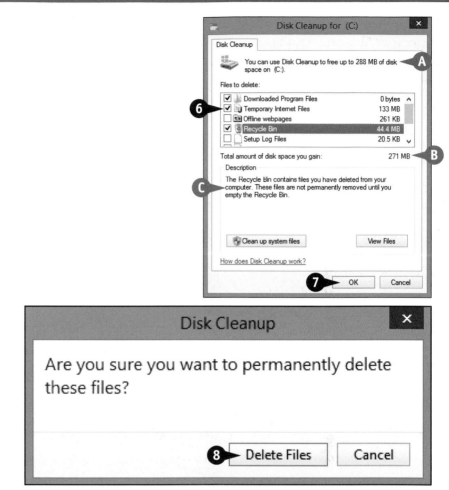

TIP

What types of files does Disk Cleanup delete?
It deletes the following file types:

- **Downloaded Program Files**. These are small web page programs downloaded onto your hard drive.
- **Temporary Internet Files**. These are web page copies stored on your hard drive for faster viewing.
- **Offline Webpages**. These are web page copies stored on your hard drive for offline viewing.

- **Recycle Bin**. These are files that you have deleted since you last emptied your Recycle Bin.
- **Temporary Files**. These are files used by programs to store temporary data.
- **Thumbnails**. These are miniature versions of images and other content used in folder windows.

Refresh Your Computer

If you find that your computer is running slowly or that frequent program glitches are hurting your productivity, you can often solve these problems by resetting your PC's system files. The Refresh Your PC feature reinstalls a fresh copy of Windows. It also saves the documents, images, and other files in your user account, some of your settings, and any Windows apps that you have installed. However, Refresh Your PC does *not* save any other PC settings (which are reverted to their defaults) or any desktop programs that you installed.

Refresh Your Computer

1 Insert your Windows installation media or recovery drive.

Note: To learn how to create a recovery drive, see the section, "Create a Recovery Drive."

2 At the Start screen, type **refresh**.

The Search pane appears.

3 Click **Refresh your PC without affecting your files**.

The PC Settings app runs and selects the Recovery tab.

4 Under Refresh your PC without affecting your files, click **Get started**.

Refresh Your PC explains the process.

5 Click **Next**.

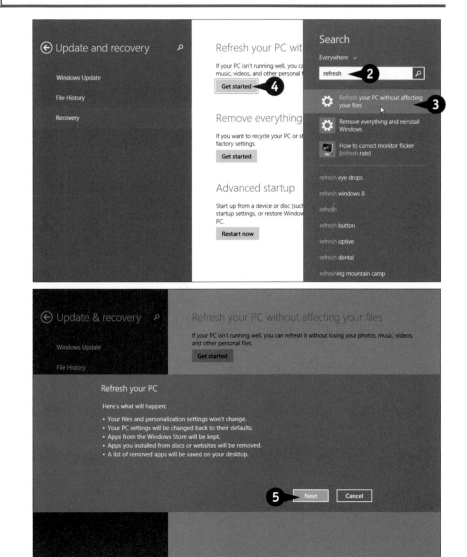

Refresh Your PC displays a list of software you will need to reinstall.

6 Click **Next**.

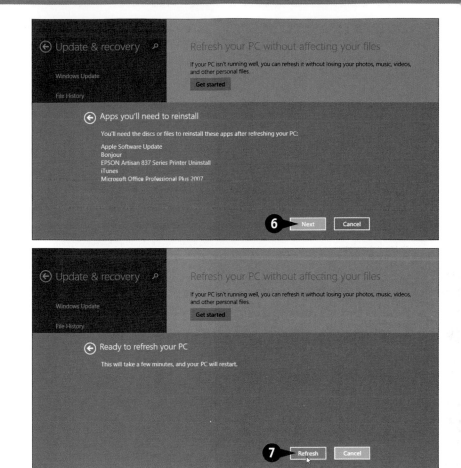

7 Click **Refresh**.

Refresh Your PC reboots the computer and refreshes the system files.

TIP

How do I refresh my computer if I cannot start Windows?

1 Insert the media and then restart your computer.

2 Boot to the media.

Note: How you boot to the media depends on your system. In some cases, you see a message telling you to press a key; in other cases you select the media from a menu.

3 In the Windows Setup dialog box, click **Next**.

4 Click **Repair your computer**.

5 Click **Troubleshoot**.

6 Click **Refresh Your PC**.

7 Click **Windows 8.1**.

8 Click **Next**.

9 Click **Refresh**.

Create a Recovery Drive

You can make it easier to troubleshoot and recover from computer problems by creating a USB recovery drive. If a problem prevents you from booting your computer, then you must boot using some other drive. If you have your Windows installation media, you can boot using that drive. If you do not have the installation media, you can still recover if you have created a recovery drive. This is a USB flash drive that contains the Windows recovery environment, which enables you to refresh or reset your PC, recover a system image, and more.

Create a Recovery Drive

1. Insert the USB flash drive you want to use.

2. Press ⊞+W.

   The Settings search pane appears.

3. Type **recovery**.

4. Click **Create a recovery drive**.

   The User Account Control dialog box appears.

5. Click **Yes**.

Note: If you are using a standard account, enter your PC's administrator credentials to continue.

   The Recovery Drive Wizard appears.

6. Click **Next**.

The Recovery Drive Wizard prompts you to choose the USB flash drive.

7 Click the drive if it is not selected already.

8 Click **Next**.

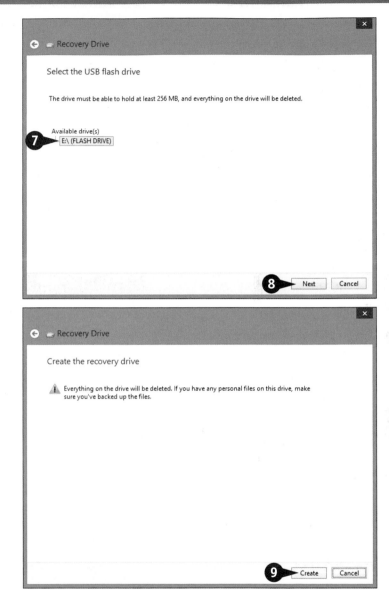

The Recovery Drive Wizard warns you that all the data on the drive will be deleted.

9 Click **Create**.

The wizard formats the drive and copies the recovery tools and data.

10 Click **Finish** (not shown).

TIPS

Can I use any USB flash drive as a recovery drive?

No. The drive must have a capacity of at least 256MB. In addition, Windows erases all data on the drive, so make sure the flash drive does not contain any files you want to keep.

How can I make sure the recovery drive works properly?

You should test the drive by booting your PC to the drive. Insert the recovery drive and then restart your PC. How you boot to the drive depends on your system. Some PCs display a menu of boot devices, and you select the USB drive from that menu. In other cases, you see a message telling you to press a key.

Keep a History of Your Files

There may be times when backing up a file just by making a copy is not good enough. For example, if you make frequent changes to a file, you might want to copy not only the current version, but also the versions from an hour ago, a day ago, a week ago, and so on. In Windows, these previous versions of a file are called its *file history*, and you can save this data for all your documents by activating a feature called File History.

Keep a History of Your Files

Set the File History Drive

1 Connect an external drive to your PC.

Note: The drive should have enough capacity to hold your files, so an external hard drive is probably best.

Note: If you see a notification, click it, click **Configure this drive for backup**, and then skip steps **4** and **5**.

2 At the Start screen, type **history**.

3 Click **File History settings**.

The File History screen appears.

A If Windows detects an external hard drive, it displays the drive here.

Note: If this is the correct drive, you can skip steps **4** and **5**.

4 Click **Select a different drive**.

Note: If Windows does not detect a drive, click **Select a drive**, instead.

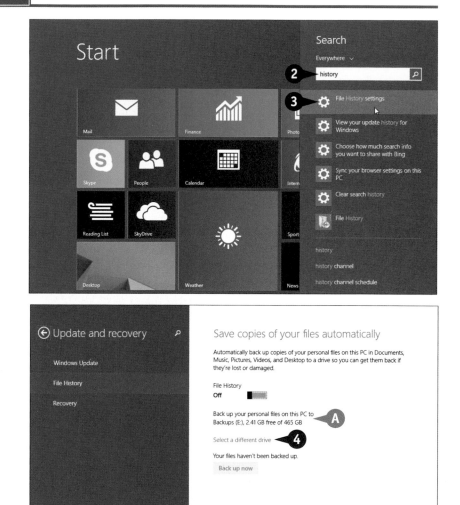

The Select a drive window appears.

5 Click the drive you want to use.

Activate File History

1 Click the File History switch to **On**.

Windows activates File History and begins saving copies of your files to the external drive.

TIP

Is it okay to disconnect the external hard drive temporarily?
Yes. However, if you need to remove the external drive temporarily (for example, if you need to use the port for another device), you should turn off File History before disconnecting the external drive. Follow steps **2** and **3** to open the File History screen and then click the File History switch to **Off**. When you are ready to resume saving your files, follow steps **1** to **3** to reconnect the drive and open the File History screen, and then click the File History switch to **On**.

Restore a File from Your History

If you improperly edit, accidentally delete, or corrupt a file through a system crash, in many cases you can restore a previous version of the file. Why would you want to revert to a previous version of a file? One reason is that you might improperly edit the file by deleting or changing important data. In some cases you may be able to restore that data by going back to a previous version of the file. Another reason is that the file might become corrupted if the program or Windows crashes. You can get a working version of the file back by restoring a previous version.

Restore a File from Your History

1 On the Start screen, press ⊞ + Ⓦ.

The Settings search pane appears.

2 Type **restore**.

3 Click **Restore your files with File History**.

The Home - File History window appears.

4 Double-click the library or folder that contains the file you want to restore.

5 Open the folder that contains the file.

6 Click **Previous Version** (⌐ ‖◀) until you open the version of the folder you want to use.

7 Click the file you want to restore.

8 Click **Restore to Original Location** (◉).

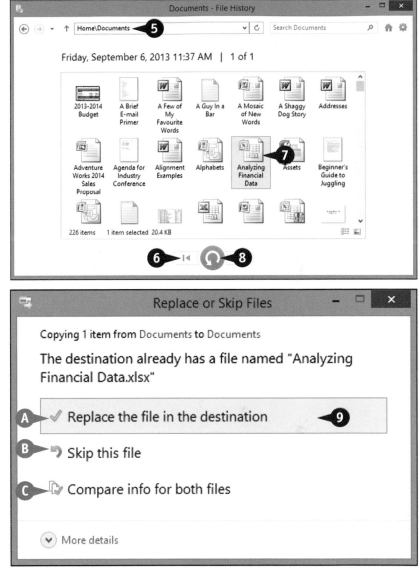

If the original folder has a file with the same name, File History Prompt you.

9 Select an option:

A Click **Replace the file in the destination** to overwrite the existing file.

B Click **Skip this file** to do nothing.

C Click **Compare info for both files** to decide which file you prefer to keep.

Windows restores the previous version.

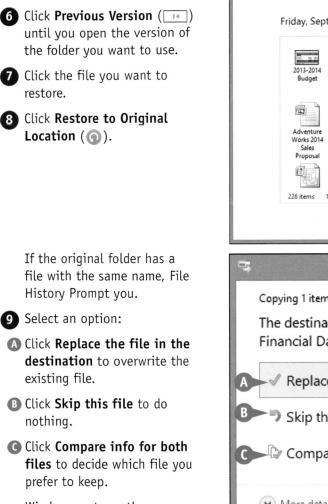

TIPS

Can I restore a folder?
Yes. Follow steps **1** to **6**, click the folder you want to restore, and then click **Restore to Original Location** (◉).

What should I do if I am not sure about replacing an existing file with a previous version?

Click **Choose the file to keep in the destination** in the Replace or Skip Files dialog box. In the File Conflict dialog box, check both versions (☐ changes to ✔), and then click **Continue**. This leaves the existing file as is and restores the previous version with (2) appended to the name.

Check Your Hard Drive for Errors

To keep your system running smoothly, you should periodically check your hard drive for errors and fix any errors that come up. Because hard drive errors can cause files to become corrupted, which may prevent you from running a program or opening a document, you can use the Check Disk program to look for and fix hard drive errors.

Check Your Hard Drive for Errors

1 Press ⊞+E.

File Explorer appears.

2 Click **This PC**.

3 Click the hard drive that you want to check.

4 Click the **Computer** tab.

5 Click **Properties**.

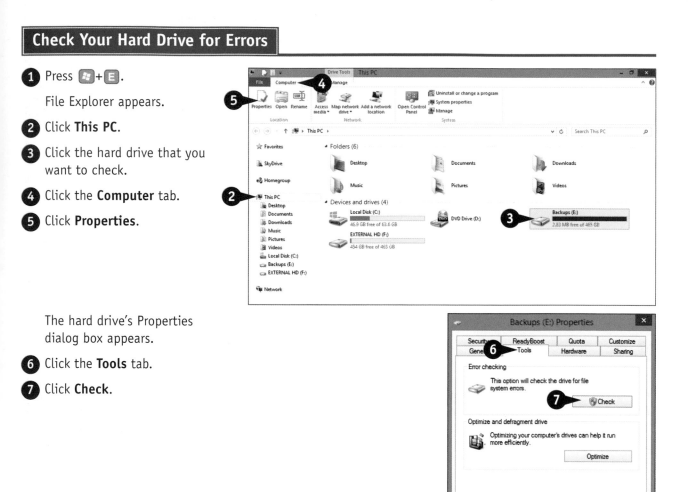

The hard drive's Properties dialog box appears.

6 Click the **Tools** tab.

7 Click **Check**.

Ⓐ If Windows tells you that the drive has no errors, you can click **Cancel** and skip the rest of these steps.

❽ Otherwise, click **Scan drive**.

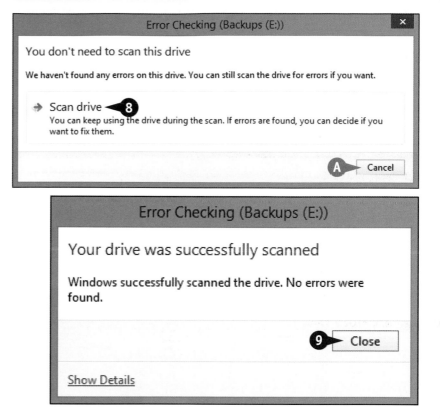

Error Checking (Backups (E:))

You don't need to scan this drive

We haven't found any errors on this drive. You can still scan the drive for errors if you want.

➔ Scan drive ◀❽
You can keep using the drive during the scan. If errors are found, you can decide if you want to fix them.

Ⓐ Cancel

Windows checks the hard drive.

❾ When the check is complete, click **Close**.

Note: If Check Disk finds any errors, follow the instructions the program provides.

Error Checking (Backups (E:))

Your drive was successfully scanned

Windows successfully scanned the drive. No errors were found.

❾ Close

Show Details

TIPS

What is a bad sector?

A *sector* is a small storage location on your hard drive. When Windows saves a file on the drive, it divides the file into pieces and stores each piece in a separate sector. A bad sector is one that, through physical damage or some other cause, can no longer be used to reliably store data.

How often should I check for hard drive errors?

You should perform the basic hard drive check about once a week. Perform the more thorough bad sector check once a month. Note that the bad sector check can take several hours, depending on the size of the drive, so perform this check only when you will not need your computer for a while.

Check Your Devices for Errors

To help ensure that your system is operating smoothly and efficiently, you should periodically check for errors associated with the devices attached to your computer. Device errors usually mean either that you cannot work with a device entirely, or that the device behaves erratically or unexpectedly. You can use the Windows Devices and Printers feature to check your installed devices for errors. You can also use Devices and Printers to troubleshoot your problem devices, and in most cases Windows will be able to fix the problem automatically.

Check Your Devices for Errors

Check for Devices with Errors

1 Press ⊞+W.

The Settings search pane appears.

2 Type **view devices**.

3 Click **View devices and printers**.

The Devices and Printers window appears.

4 Examine the device icons for errors.

A Windows indicates devices with errors using this icon (⚠).

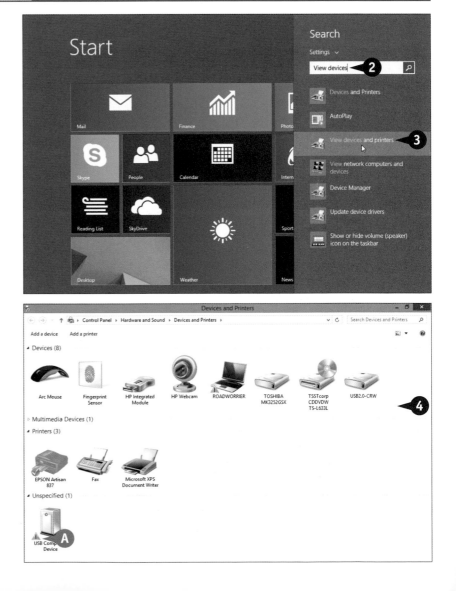

Begin Device Troubleshooting

1 Click a device that has an error.

2 Click **Troubleshoot**.

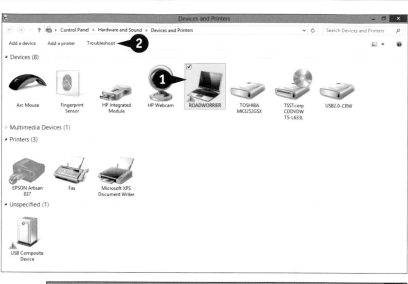

The Devices and Printers troubleshooting wizard appears and displays the first fix.

3 Click **Apply this fix**.

Devices and Printers wizard applies the fix. If this does not solve the problem, Devices and Printers wizard displays the next fix.

B If you are certain this fix is not the solution, click **Skip this fix** instead.

4 Repeat step **3** until the problem is resolved.

TIPS

What is a device driver?
It is a small program that Windows uses to communicate with a device. Many hardware problems are the result of either not having a device driver installed, or having an incorrect driver installed. Most devices come with discs that have the correct device driver, so you should insert that disc when troubleshooting. You can also obtain the latest device driver from the manufacturer's website.

What if Devices and Printers cannot solve the problem?
In this case, you need to either return the device to the manufacturer for repair or replacement, or take it to a local computer shop for fixing.

Defragment Your Hard Drive on a Schedule

Y ou can make Windows, and your programs, run faster, and your documents open more quickly, by defragmenting your hard drive on a regular schedule. File fragmentation means that a file is stored on your hard drive in multiple pieces instead of as a single piece. This slows performance because it means that when Windows tries to open such a file, it must make several stops to collect the various pieces. A lot of fragmented files can slow down even the fastest hard drive. Defragmenting improves performance by bringing all those pieces together, making finding and opening each file faster.

Defragment Your Hard Drive on a Schedule

1 Press ⊞+Ⓦ.

The Settings search pane appears.

2 Type **defrag**.

3 Click **Defragment and optimize your drives**.

The Optimize Drives window appears.

4 Click **Change settings**.

The Optimization Schedule dialog box appears.

5 Click **Run on a schedule (recommended)** (☐ changes to ☑).

6 Click the **Frequency** ☑ and then click the frequency with which you want to defragment (Daily, Weekly, or Monthly).

7 Click **OK**.

A The new schedule appears here.

B If you want to defragment your drives now, click **Optimize**.

8 Click **Close**.

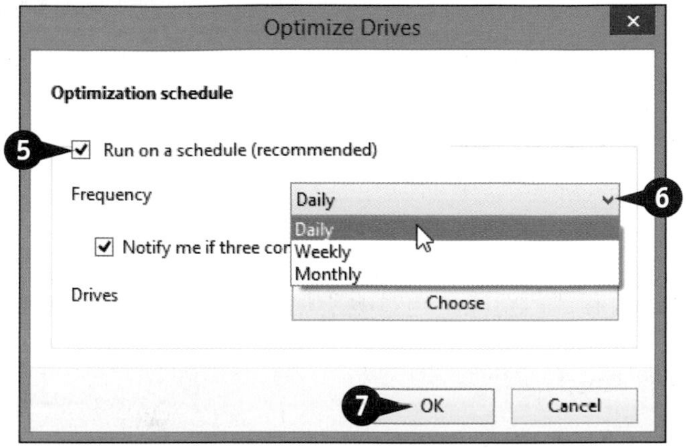

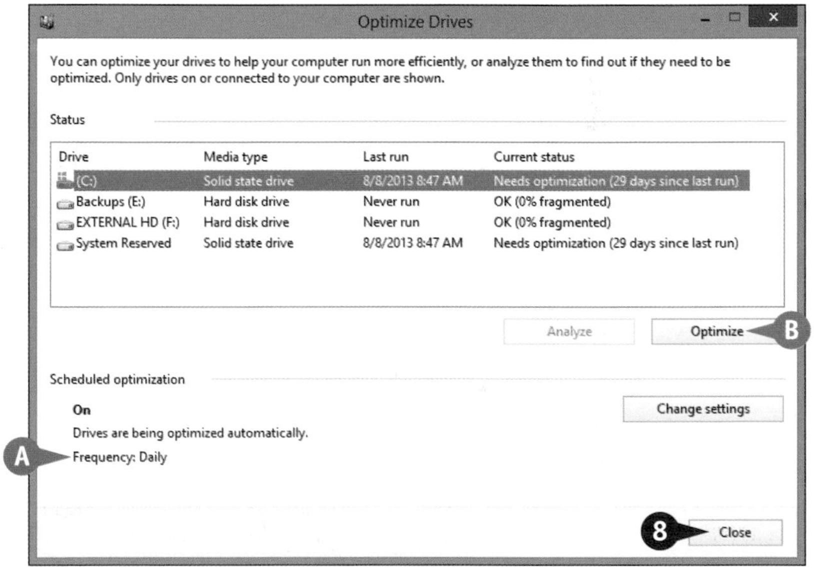

TIPS

How often should I defragment my hard drive?
This depends on how often you use your computer. If you use your computer every day, you should defragment your hard drive weekly. If you use your computer only occasionally, you should defragment your hard drive monthly.

How long does defragmenting my hard drive take?
It depends on the size of the hard drive, the amount of data on it, and the extent of the defragmentation. Budget at least 15 minutes for the defragmenting, and know that it could take more than an hour.

Create a System Restore Point

If your computer crashes or becomes unstable after you install a program or a new device, the System Restore feature in Windows can fix things by restoring the system to its previous state. To ensure this works, you need to set restore points before you install programs and devices on your computer. Windows automatically creates system restore points as follows: every week (called a *system checkpoint*); before installing an update; and before installing certain programs (such as Microsoft Office) and devices. These are useful, but it pays to err on the side of caution and create your own restore points more often.

Create a System Restore Point

1 Press ⊞+Ⓦ.

The Settings search pane appears.

2 Type **restore**.

3 Click **Create a restore point**.

The System Properties dialog box appears.

Ⓐ The System Protection tab is already displayed.

4 Click **Create**.

The Create a Restore Point dialog box appears.

5 Type a description for your restore point.

6 Click **Create**.

System Restore creates the restore point.

System Protection ✕

Create a restore point

Type a description to help you identify the restore point. The current date and time are added automatically.

| Installing old sound card ◄ **5** |

6 ► Create   Cancel

Windows tells you the restore point was created successfully.

7 Click **Close**.

8 Click **OK** to close the System Properties dialog box.

System Properties ✕

Computer Name | Hardware | Advanced | System Protection | Remote

Use system protection to undo unwanted system changes.

System Restore

System Protection

ⓘ The restore point was created successfully.

7 ► Close

Local Disk (C:) (System)   On

Configure restore settings, manage disk space, and delete restore points.   Configure...

Create a restore point right now for the drives that have system protection turned on.   Create...

8 ► OK   Cancel   Apply

TIP

When should I create a restore point?
To be safe, you should create a restore point before you install any software, whether you purchased the program at a store or downloaded it from the Internet. You should also create a restore point before you add any new hardware devices to your system.

Apply a System Restore Point

If your computer becomes unstable or behaves erratically after you install a program or device, you can often fix the problem by applying the restore point you created before making the change. If after you install a program or device you notice problems with your system, the easiest solution is to uninstall the item. If that does not work, then your next step is to revert to an earlier restore point. Windows reverts your computer to the configuration it had when you created the restore point, which should solve the problem.

Apply a System Restore Point

1 Press ⊞+W.

The Settings search pane appears.

2 Type **restore**.

3 Click **Create a restore point**.

4 Click **System Restore**.

The System Restore window appears.

Ⓐ System Restore might show the most likely restore point here. If you do not see a restore point, skip to step **8**.

5 Click **Choose a different restore point** (○ changes to ◉).

6 Click **Next**.

System Restore prompts you
to choose a restore point.

7 Click the restore point you
want to apply.

B If you do not see the restore
point you want, click **Show
more restore points** (☐
changes to ☑).

8 Click **Next**.

The Confirm Your Restore
Point window appears.

9 Click **Finish**.

System Restore asks you to
confirm that you want to
restore your system.

10 Click **Yes**.

System Restore applies the
restore point and then
restarts Windows.

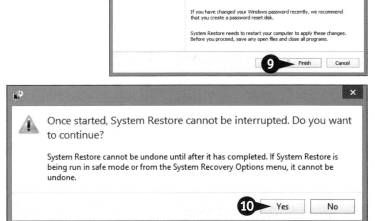

TIPS

Will I lose any of my recent work when I apply a restore point?
No, the restore point reverts only your computer's configuration
back to the earlier time. Any work you performed in the
interim — documents you created, e-mails you received, web page
favorites you saved, and so on — is not affected when you apply
the restore point. However, if you installed any programs after the
restore point, you must reinstall those programs.

**If applying the restore point makes
things worse, can I reverse it?**
Yes. Follow steps **1** to **6** to display
the list of available restore points on
your computer. Click the **Restore
Operation** restore point, and then
follow steps **8** to **10**.

Index

Index